Know and Tell

Also in the CrossCurrents Series

Getting Restless
Rethinking Revision in Writing Instruction

Grading in the Post-Process Classroom
From Theory to Practice

Gypsy Academics and Mother-Teachers
Gender, Contingent Labor, and Writing Instruction

Miss Grundy Doesn't Teach Here Anymore
Popular Culture and the Composition Classroom

Resituating Writing
Constructing and Administering Writing Programs

Textual Orientations
Lesbian and Gay Students and the Making of
Discourse Communities

Writing in an Alien World
Basic Writing and the Struggle for Equality in Higher Education

Know and Tell

A Writing Pedagogy of Disclosure, Genre, and Membership

David Bleich
University of Rochester

CHARLES I. SCHUSTER, SERIES EDITOR

Boynton/Cook Publishers
HEINEMANN
Portsmouth, NH

Boynton/Cook Publishers, Inc.
A subsidiary of Reed Elsevier Inc.
361 Hanover Street
Portsmouth, NH 03801-3912
Offices and agents throughout the world.

We would like to thank those who have given their permission to include material in this book.

"The Vulture" by Franz Kafka from *Franz Kafka: The Complete Stories* by Franz Kafka, edited by Nahum N. Glatzer. Copyright © 1946, 1947, 1948, 1949, 1954, 1958, 1971 by Schocken Books Inc. Reprinted by permission of Schocken Books, distributed by Pantheon Books, a division of Random House, Inc.

Library of Congress Cataloging-in-Publication Data
Bleich, David.
  Know and tell : a writing pedagogy of disclosure, genre, and
membership / David Bleich.
    p.   cm.
  Includes bibliographical references and index.
  ISBN 0-86709-446-X
  1. English language—Rhetoric—Study and teaching. 2. Report
writing—Study and teaching. I. Title.
PE1404.B588 1998
808'.042'071—dc21   98–12307
                                                               CIP

Editors: Peter S. Stillman, Lisa Luedeke
Production: Renée Le Verrier
Cover Design: Jenny Jensen Greenleaf
Manufacturing: Louise Richardson

Printed in the United States of America on acid-free paper.
00 99 98 DA 1 2 3 4 5 6

to Miriam, Judah, and Harold Bleich:
wish you were here

to Lisa and Daniel Bleich:
glad you are here

Contents

Contents

Forethoughts

The Materiality of Language and the Constituencies of Writing Pedagogy

For more than a century, the teaching of writing has been the subject of dispute in postsecondary education. The scholarly literature about this subject is repetitive in its identification of the problems and its proposal for solutions. From generation to generation the problem has not changed: students starting postsecondary education have been judged deficient in the ability to write. Solutions are proposed and tried. Gradually, those who were once judged unable to write finally learned to write in their own subject matters and sometimes beyond. Then they judged that the next generations of students were deficient in the general ability to write.

The struggle over writing pedagogy usually involved the following situation: those who learned to write considered it unappealing to *teach* writing. Many postsecondary faculty members in different subjects acknowledged the need for writing pedagogy by helping their students learn the ways of writing in their own subjects. Many held that writing itself means writing hygiene—technical competence and overall coherence. There was no discipline or subject matter in which the daily practices of writing by either novices or professionals were studied in conjunction with issues of language use and society. Forms of language use in different subject matters, now sometimes understood as "writing across the curriculum," were not part of the academic fields in which most judges of poor writing studied and published research. Most experienced faculty members thought (and think) that writing as a subject matter is neither interesting enough nor deep enough to be understood either by itself or as part of their disciplines. As a result, the de facto solution to the problem of writing pedagogy has been to require junior, apprentice, or peripheral members of the academy to teach it.[1] They are held responsible for poor results spotted by senior and established members.

Many who consider it essential for students to write well in order for their work in many subjects to be judged of high quality insist that a helper class of teachers teach writing according to specifications given by higher-ups. This situation is so extreme that many writing teachers today, perhaps most, have internalized, sometimes without knowing its source, an abstract standard of good writing that urges them to teach as if this standard could then be adapted to all circumstances requiring an articulate voice. The literature of writing pedagogy is filled with routine references to "becoming a good writer" or "improving one's writing," as if writing were analogous to running, where every effort is directed toward identifiable goals such as increasing one's speed or stamina.

This book addresses a problem, therefore, that is common to writing teachers and to most members of the academy. The subject of writing is considered *essential* but *not of interest* to those who consider it essential. Stating the problem in this way makes it accessible to historical and political analysis, which suggests that the substance of the subject has acquired the reduced status of its practitioners.

This book proposes that the subject matter of writing should be reconceived so as to create for it a different identity. The revised view should encourage collaboration between writing teachers and other members of the academy who sense the importance of language use in their own subjects but have not understood how to view their subjects as being borne by language.

The subject of writing and language use is distinctive because one cannot learn it from textbook and exercise approaches alone. To let the knowledge of the subject grow, one must continue to do, not practice, it while studying it. More than other academic subjects, writing and language use require a theoretical understanding integrated with one's ability to do it. Nevertheless, doing a great deal of writing is not enough to qualify someone as a professional in the theory and teaching of writing. Writing and language use form a living subject requiring theory, teaching, and nonhypothetical practice to establish professional credentials. Because of this fact, many who write well in one subject matter are misled into thinking that they write well, period; or more generally, writing well in one academic

---

[1] Susan Miller, *Textual Carnivals: The Politics of Composition* (Carbondale: Southern Illinois University Press, 1991).

subject is assumed to be derived from a talent for good writing. Among academics who pay some attention to students' writing in their own subjects, there is an uncomprehending attitude toward professional teachers of writing, who have come to understand that people have a range of abilities for writing, that writing cannot be taught or learned in toto during one semester or one year, and that one's confidence to write may disappear under many circumstances that call for different forms of writing and language use. Because of the decisive practical and wide-ranging venues for the subject of writing, its teaching is distinctive in a way that has caused trouble in the academy.

The Materiality of Language

A presupposition of this book is that a fundamental part of the history of struggle and only intermittent success in the teaching of writing is that the materiality of language has not been a part of the general understanding of language. *Materiality* as describing language was brought back into discussion (from its pre-Classical appearances in Hebrew tradition) by poststructuralism. It has been taken in different directions by literary and cultural critics but has only rarely been applied to the teaching of writing and language use.[2] Today, it is still a minority perspective. The more accepted perspective may be termed the spirituality of language: the view that there is a meaning that is separate from the word-in-use; a meaning that is separate from the paragraph or the novel or the play itself; a meaning that readers and interpreters articulate in contexts separate from the reading and viewing contexts. In part the classic Western separation of the oral from the literate as discussed by Walter Ong[3] is a manifestation of the spiritualist perspective on language: the oral is of a lower status in society than the written. This value is the main one today in society and in the teaching of writing.

---

[2] A significant contribution in this regard is a study by Christine Iwanicki, "The Materiality of Language: Implications for Pedagogy, Literary Theory, and Literacy" (Ph.D. Diss., Department of English, Indiana University, 1994). Iwanicki brings us up to date on the materiality of language in literary theory; she demonstrates its helpfulness in the analysis of a challenging pedagogical scene of writing.

[3] Walter Ong, *Orality and Literacy: The Technology of the Word* (London: Methuen,1982). I discussed this work at some length in *The Double Perspective* (New York: Oxford University Press,1988; NCTE, 1993). I reiterate this view here: the desire to privilege the written over the oral is based on hierarchical social values that associate literate culture with more privileged groups and oral culture with non-technological groups, women, and children.

The materialist perspective on language, in which the oral and the written were identified with each other as both being material, that is, as writing, was reasserted by Derrida. This view holds that any use of language is material; the differences in how the oral and the written act in society have to do with cultural differences rather than with essential or permanent, built-in differences in the ways of language use.

To assume the materiality of language changes how we think about the teaching of writing and language use. For one thing, we will encourage the exploration of the connections, interactions, and similarities between and of the oral and the written. We will pay serious attention to any uses of language in our classrooms and consider them to be easily transformable into oral or written forms. Several sections of this book engage this issue. These uses are understood in this book as genres or kinds of language. They are uses that sometimes change their superficial forms from oral to written and back again. Sometimes the uses are ritualized and conventionalized, that is, more rigid in their forms, but at other times the genres in which they appear are adaptable. For this reason, thinking with the concept of genre in mind is one of the ways we are presupposing the materiality of language. The genre approach views language as being combined with social and interpersonal configurations and historical circumstances and styles. Genre helps us to see language use as more than simply language, as a phenomenon that helps us understand social life as a lived experience. In most classrooms, the focus remains on the use of language, but these uses are genres whose identities derive from the social identities and group memberships of each class member.

The materiality of language also pertains to the value of disclosure (see Chapter 1), which urges us to recognize that different genres (see Chapter 2) of talk, language use, and writing emerge from all of us at different times and situations, and that these genres are welcome in the writing classroom. The use of the term *writing* in "the writing classroom" and in "writing pedagogy" should be understood in the Derridian sense: the term *writing* refers to all uses of language, even all symbolic processes. The need for disclosure arises because our historical and social placements and memberships (see Chapter 3) are material: they exist and have an effect on all parts of our present experience. To articulate these memberships is what I mean by disclosure. Distinct from expression, confession, and revelation, disclosure is a different value in the teaching of writing. Its practice presents forms and situations with which to search, beyond immediate experience to the individually and collectively remembered, for what has contributed to our present experience.

The concept of lived experience, like the concepts of genre and disclosure, depends on the assumption of the materiality of language, as Linda Brodkey writes:

> While I present lived experience in terms of actions, acts, and actors, such distinctions are admittedly methodological conveniences justified solely in terms of a theoretical commitment to the value of material analysis of language use. I am not trying to *represent* the experience of their writing or my research but to *present* language actions and interactions that can be displayed as acts of language, that is, those uses of language that appear meaningful or significant because they can be analyzed or interpreted as constructing a social reality.[4]

Brodkey stipulates new language with which to approach the language uses of her colleagues, which are also described in her discussion. She is trying to say, from a materialist perspective, that her language is not supposed to represent, not supposed to "present again," the original work but instead to present her own lived experience of these colleagues. There is a discrete jump from the texts of the lived experiences of her colleagues collaborating (about which Brodkey is reporting) and the text of the treatise I am reading. This jump is a change in genre in that Brodkey is highlighting the difference in context between that of the two collaborators and that of the reporting of their work. Her work is—presents—her lived experience of them, not their lived experience. Brodkey's treatise is a mixed genre in that Mary and Bill's work—the citation of their lived experience—has become part of Brodkey's in the text of her book.

The materiality of language gives the concept of the mixed genre (an idea as important for the teaching of writing as materiality, genre, and disclosure; see Chapter 2) a pragmatic identity and plausibility. It makes it easier to understand how the contingencies of social life create new genres by mixing familiar ones in response to new social situations.[5] The teaching of writing has not paid attention to the contingent character of language use and has concentrated on essentialist forms; lately, however, even the process-writing movement has

---

[4] Linda Brodkey, *Academic Writing as Social Practice* (Philadelphia: Temple University Press, 1987), 110. Brodkey refers in this passage to how she is describing the writing behavior of two colleagues whose collaboration she is studying.

[5] For example, a letter published as a newspaper ad becomes "an open letter," a different genre than either a letter or an ad. Or, a *New Yorker* cartoon on a faculty member's door is no longer just a *New Yorker* cartoon, nor a faculty member's notice; it is a new genre: the cartoon on the professor's door.

tended to essentialize the processes themselves. Disclosure prevents essentializing both the products of writing and its processes by keeping us aware of the changing mixtures of the genres of language use. Disclosure introduces the latent and potential contingencies of class members' lived experiences into the texts of discussion, of writing, of collaboration, and of pedagogy. Genre, disclosure, membership, and contingency are part of the perspective represented by the materiality of language.

The Constituencies of Writing Pedagogy

An important consequence in the teaching of writing brought about by assuming the materiality of language is a significant reduction in the level of privacy in writing and a great increase in our awareness of its different collective dimensions. The teaching of writing has, from a pragmatic standpoint, reflected this view, but only provisionally. Eventually, cultural ideology in the West promotes private, individual writing as the way to write. Even when the teaching and practice of writing have taken place collectively, individual writing and language use is still the governing idea. The fact that the teaching of writing is like care or nurturing, however, should teach us that the use of language is also like care and nurturing of interpersonal relationships. Just as the learning of language by infants necessarily takes place in interpersonal situations, so does the learning of writing and language use by older people. School, however, for ideological reasons has denied this fact about learning to write. It has long been accepted by students and teachers that the "microteaching" of writing is desirable. Many postsecondary schools do insure that at least early classes in writing are small, so that there is enough time for teachers to pay continuing attention to the minutiae of students' work. Recently, the recognition of this need for close attention to the writing process has led to the widespread use of peer response groups to accompany the detailed responses of teachers. The more careful, detailed responses to writing people get, the easier it is for them to learn writing and language use. Few now question that personal responses to writing by a variety of readers are fundamental to writing pedagogy.

Writing teachers spend time thinking through different ways of becoming involved in students' work and of getting all class members to become involved in one another's work. Such preparation is complex and time-consuming, but teachers understand that it is necessary in order to teach writing in the most fulfilling ways. However, this style and depth of teacher involvement is not generally considered essential for other subjects, in which teaching generally means lecturing, answering questions, giving examinations, grading essays, and arriving at a final grade. Especially in research universities, the schools with the most influence in our society, the most accomplished faculty members are not involved, for the most part, in hands-on teaching of undergraduates. Because research is considered more important than teaching, the demands for a fully involved teaching style are reduced. But these demands are not reduced for writing teachers in research universities; the lower status of these faculty members is perpetuated by the fact that their subject requires involved teaching on a continual, daily basis. Their subject does not permit them to dilute or distance their teaching presence.[6]

Research universities and others that have first-year writing programs ask their graduate students in English to teach the courses required in the program. The level of preparation varies from nothing, to a few days of preteaching workshop reviews of texts and strategies, to semester-long seminars and follow-up practicum supervision. In schools where there are no graduate students and no faculty who are professionally identified with writing pedagogy, literature faculty members with degrees in English teach writing because of the traditional (usually untrue) belief that if you studied literature, you know how to write anything and how to teach writing. Except for those teachers who have focused on the teaching of writing through professional commitment and identity, most people teaching writing are doing so as a secondary activity.

Over the past twenty years, I have supervised graduate students who were to become specialists in writing pedagogy or specialists in literature or both. My work with them, through their early teaching experiences, their later ones, their dissertations, and their job searches, led me to conceive a conundrum produced by the history of writing pedagogy. This conundrum relates to the various problems I mentioned earlier, but I would like to pose it as follows: Because several constituencies have an interest in the teaching of writing, how shall the subject of writing and language use be conceived to serve all of these constituencies?

I will elaborate on this question by describing how different constituencies have an interest in the teaching of writing. Writing pedagogy is a long process of training, teaching, learning, and follow-up

---

[6] This is a gender issue that is treated as such repeatedly in this book. The gender issue in teaching relates to gender issues in academic styles of work. Readers are referred to the Mothering section in the "More Forethoughts" chapter.

that matters in different ways to different groups of people. This book tries to present the subject of writing and its pedagogy so as to serve these constituencies. Writing, language use, disclosure, genre, and membership—these are the focus of this study, which I hope will contribute to the many ideas and practices now being tried in the current scenes of teaching.

Entry-Level Students

This group of people is changing at such a pace that it is hard to predict which segments of it will appear in our classrooms next year. As has been the case since the general population has sought postsecondary education, first-year students are often "undecided" about what they will finally study and what their work will be. The intentions of entering students change, often more than once. This is partly why a single ideal of standard written English often seems to occupy the thoughts of academics. However, it does not serve first-year students to teach an all-purpose model of writing. A single standard leads to an uncritical approach to greatly differing writing situations, to the false sense that good writing can be adapted to any context, and that such adaptation takes place fluently as soon as one becomes a good writer.

Because of the increasing recognition of difference among individuals and groups of students, writing pedagogy should provide for recognizing the language-use status of each student. What language use styles, forms, and abilities is each bringing to college? This repertoire must be identified, not measured. Because ability is such a diffuse quality, and because so many factors help create different abilities, a writing program would be more prudent to identify particular language orientations of students, especially in relation to their education and cultural backgrounds as well as their vocational plans, than to calculate the quality of a general essay written in a short period of time on a single occasion. The subject of writing must be conceived in such a way that the disposition toward writing and language use brought to school by students can play a role in their thinking when they study the subject more self-consciously. Students' existing abilities must not be reduced to either a deficit or a dialect but must instead be recognized as interesting, complex, and potentially productive sources of writing and language use. Each student's language background and understanding must be considered as a way of contributing to the collective task of finding new ways of handling language. Students should learn to feel confident not just in "their" language, not just in the language use conventions of "their" subject matters, but in their sense of how to use different forms of language in different social, professional, and public situations, oral and written.

In addressing these "shoulds," this book proposes that writing teachers can find sources for students' learning needs in their memberships (see Chapter 3) and that the curriculum should change when these sources are discovered (see Chapter 6). Because of the rapid changes in the undergraduate population and because of the uniqueness of each classroom, I propose that curricula should be more contingent than they are now: teachers and planners should provide built-in ways for curricula to be immediately responsive to the members of classrooms. This change, in turn, requires that cooperative classrooms (see Chapters 5 and 8) become the more usual form in postsecondary schools. The teaching of writing and language use through genre, disclosure, and membership, as well as its continuation through the undergraduate years, is fundamental to students' learning to find work that they love, and work situations that are just and generous.

Graduate Students: Prospective Postsecondary Teachers

For this group the prospect of eventual employment must be taken into account in preparing them to teach writing. The job market is of immediate interest and is an increasingly urgent factor. The commitment to get a doctorate is predicated on the expectation of joining a postsecondary English department. In graduate English programs, students each have different literary and critical interests. Lately, these interests have broadened to include popular culture and its media, beyond the traditional English and American literature curricula. Postsecondary schools have had funding cutbacks that led to the need for a versatile faculty. Because writing courses are so large a percentage of the English undergraduate curriculum, new faculty need significant competence in writing pedagogy within the English curriculum. Prospective faculty members need to show experience, confidence, and intellectual dexterity in ways that help them to participate in writing programs. They need to be willing to teach writing through their scholarly interests, and they need to teach writing in contexts, perhaps, that they have not yet anticipated or experienced. The graduate student constituency needs an English-teaching philosophy that includes a sophisticated, versatile writing pedagogy. Prospective teachers need to know that because their comfort as teachers underlies the motivation to become involved in teaching, they need to think of their own scholarly work as a starting point for their approach to teaching writing and language use.

Faculty Members in Different Disciplines

Although faculty members in departments other than English do not often want to collaborate with writing teachers in order to teach writing, their intuition that writing is important in their subjects needs to be discussed in extended ways. If there is little collaboration among faculty members of different disciplines in the teaching of writing, how can the subject be conceived so as to encourage those in a variety of disciplines to be more amenable to collaboration? The subject of writing needs to be understood in such a way as to be "friendly" to scholars and researchers in a wide variety of disciplines, so that perhaps they can follow their interest in how things are articulated in their own fields. Faculty members' experiences in linked courses of biology, physics, psychology, and writing, for example, suggest that many do consider how things are said in their discipline to be fundamental and certainly of interest to prospective students in those disciplines. This book considers other academic disciplines as having an interest in a conception of writing that speaks not simply to the desire for mechanically clean writing, but also to the language use genres that will present each subject more truthfully and usefully, forms that are responsive to the social roles and responsibilities of different subject matters. The concept of genre helps to include faculty members of diverse disciplines in the teaching of writing without their having to decide explicitly that writing is more or less important than "the substance" of their own disciplines.

As Harriet Malinowitz has suggested, "writing across the disciplines" is not, by itself, a significant departure from traditional approaches to (and ideologies of) writing pedagogy.[7] This practice has compartmentalized the teaching of writing by stipulating the obvious fact that all disciplines write what they know in various ways. To think of language use as falling into genres, however, and to remember that writers have perspectives that should be disclosed, means that the writing in different disciplines also falls into a wide variety of mixed and changing genres, each of which is identified by its memberships in society. To view writing through genre, disclosure, and membership is to call for active, substantive, extended collaborations between writing teachers and teachers of all subjects, collaborations that would break down existing depart-

---

[7] Harriet Malinowitz, "A Feminist Critique of Writing in the Disciplines," in *In Other Words: Feminism and Composition Studies*, ed. Susan C. Jarratt and Lynn Worsham (New York: Modern Language Association, 1997).

mental separations in new ways. This approach would also serve all departments in providing new ways to bring teaching to the forefront of faculty activity and accomplishment.

The University

The interests of a university as a social organization are served by the teaching of writing and language use. The university is one of the public institutions that depend on a sense of accepted language use conventions. It raises money and affects people's lives through mailings, announcements, descriptions of courses and atmosphere, and citations of local history. Writing teachers and students are in position to act as critics, as the "loyal opposition," and as supporters of how business is done. As scientists help support a university through the acquisition of funding, writing programs can influence how different constituencies within the university speak to one another, whether they communicate respectfully, and the extent to which the truth is told and used. Statements are issued by public relations officials; appeals are made by alumni groups; memos are issued by administrators; faculty members' syllabi announce policies and set moods and standards for courses. One responsibility of writing pedagogy is community self-study and self-understanding. When seen in a collective sense, self-examination is an essential social responsibility, and the teaching of writing and language use bears part of this responsibility to bring the community to greater awareness of how it is speaking and writing together.[8]

The Public

Materialist views of writing and language use have taught that many cultural and symbolic forms are social and physical texts. A humanistic education alerts its constituencies to watch for the new genres of writing now in the making, including visual and electronic media. The public should be given the benefit of such broader understanding of writing, especially the chance to see media such as film and e-mail as kinds of writing. Writing pedagogy should teach the public how to recognize new forms as writing and how to be flexible about understanding the thirty-second television spot as a text. In order to educate prospective knowledgeable nonacademic employees, in order for universities to create partnerships with enterprises and

---

[8] In Chapter 4, this responsibility is more pointedly described as involving the reduction of public, collective, conventional lying.

governments, students should be ready to identify the creativity (and possible abuses of) language genres emerging from commercially and politically motivated interests, including journal-borne propaganda. Because language is so potent in public contexts, often inadvertently so, the teaching of language use and writing must make the public aware of the various effects of language use.

This book presents the teaching of writing and language use as addressing the interests of all of the foregoing constituencies. Some may say that this is too much for a single subject to do. But those who teach and learn writing are the largest single professional group in the schools. The subject is one of the main sites of awareness of language use in society. The many who pass through this site stop momentarily to think of how they are choosing their words, their language; they are studying what it feels like and means to say things to this or that person or group; they are stopping to consider how to change these uses and to speak to others about change; they are studying what it means to say "I know" among different groups of people. They are stopping to consider how public uses of language are affecting people's lives and shaping the moods, attitudes, and choices of the powerful. This book treats the subject of writing as if it can and does play these wide-ranging roles. At the same time, it addresses issues that can be acted upon locally by students, teachers, administrators, and others who have something to say and would like to be able to say it with a heartbeat and a backbone.

Chapter One

Academic Teaching, Writing, and Disclosure

Writing Pedagogy in the Context of Academic Teaching

I stayed in school because I wanted to work there, but I have become apprehensive about academic life. I sought higher degrees because I thought the academy was school: a decent, fascinating, and relatively happy place of work. Now, my daily interactions with colleagues at schools where tenure is threatened; with worried, struggling graduate students; and with confused, uncertain undergraduates make the academy not seem like school anymore. Teaching is not valued.[1]

Teaching has subordinate status: most recent reflections on higher education consider the highest category of postsecondary institution to be the research university. The activities of research are understood by members of the academy to be the highest one can do in a university. What could universities become if teaching and research were understood to be of equal status, importance, and consequence? What might teaching become if it were joined with

---

[1] Although this is not news, it is not usually admitted. For a historical view, read Mariolina Salvatori, "Pedagogy and the Academy: 'The Divine Skill of the Born Teacher's Instincts,'" in *Pedagogy in the Age of Politics: Writing and Reading (in) the Academy*, ed. Patricia A. Sullivan and Donna J. Qualley (Urbana, IL: National Council of Teachers of English, 1994), 88–99.

research regularly, and what might research become if it were joined with teaching?[2]

Tenure reviews are conducted in research universities by evaluating an individual's teaching and research records separately. Regardless of what a person may achieve as a teacher, the research record is still considered more important. Tenure is rarely awarded on the basis of teaching alone. Universities that award tenure based on teaching suffer a reduced status: if the faculty achieves only as teachers, the university is itself less valued in society.

The problems of writing pedagogy are closely related to the problems of academic teaching. Suppose research universities declared teaching to be their most important activity. This would mean that writing teachers would rise to the top of the prestige ladder, since they spend the most time teaching. The subject of writing and the practice of teaching are of equally low status in the research university. Both are associated more with care and nurturing than with research, knowledge, and breakthroughs; there is an axiomatic separation between giving attention to students and achieving profitable knowledge. As discussed in this book, writing as a discipline

---

[2] As a result of changes in the political mood of the country and the tenuring of many who learned politics in the 1960s, the academy has become contested ground, and books about it have become important. In the 1980s there were studies like George Keller's *Academic Strategy: The Management Revolution in American Higher Education* (Baltimore: Johns Hopkins University Press, 1983). Universities tried to emulate corporations and their successes, an issue considered in Chapter 7 in the context of grading. Then, there were books like Roger Kimball's *Tenured Radicals: How Politics Has Corrupted Our Higher Education* (New York: Harper and Row, 1990), and Dinesh D'Souza's *Illiberal Education: The Politics of Race and Sex on Campus* (New York: Free Press, 1991), which claimed higher learning was at risk because political advocacy was acknowledged by many faculty members. Recently, there have been reflective, middle-of-the-road sorts of studies acknowledging the need for change but not certain of what it should be. Among these are Jaroslav Pelikan, *The Idea of the University: A Reexamination* (New Haven: Yale University Press, 1992), and Jonathan R. Cole, Elinor Barber, and Stephen R. Graubard, eds., *The Research University in a Time of Discontent* (Baltimore: Johns Hopkins University Press, 1993). In Chapter 6, I discuss briefly Diane Ravitch and Maris A. Vinovskis, eds., *Learning from the Past: What History Teaches Us About School Reform* (Baltimore: Johns Hopkins University Press, 1995). Two individualized studies addressing academic discontent are James Phelan, *Beyond the Tenure Track: Fifteen Months in the Life of an English Professor* (1991) and Richard J. Murphy, Jr., *The Calculus of Intimacy: A Teaching Life* (1993), both published by Ohio State University Press, Columbus, Ohio. In addition to Estela Mara Bensimon and Anna Neumann, *Redesigning Collegiate Leadership: Teams and Teamwork in Higher Education* (Baltimore: Johns Hopkins University Press, 1994), there is the statistical study by Robert T. Blackburn and Janet H. Lawrence, *Faculty at Work: Motivation, Expectation, Satisfaction* (Baltimore: Johns Hopkins University Press, 1995). There has been a range of approaches to the changing situation in higher education.

or a subject matter is a combination of theory, practice, and pedagogy. It is an example of how to unify scholarship and teaching, and it is a discipline regularly available for collaboration with other disciplines. Academic teaching might be understood as a wider context of the teaching of writing. The continuing problems of writing pedagogy over the past century are bound up with the reduced status of teaching in the academy as well as with factors in society that have led to this reduced status.

The most sympathetic attention to this issue[3] does not acknowledge how deep and perhaps how ideological an issue academic teaching is. Generally, universities wish to enhance teaching in their own institutions, but their reasons for this are related to dropping enrollments (private universities) and overcrowding (public ones). The values behind current worries about teaching have not changed from the values that place research universities at the top of the hierarchy of postsecondary schools.

Consider the report by Ernest L. Boyer for the Carnegie Foundation for the Advancement of Teaching. This study is based on a survey of faculty members in five different classes of higher educational institutions, ranging from two-year colleges to research universities. The report recommends a more serious and elaborate attention to teaching in postsecondary education, even as it continues to reaffirm the priority of research and scholarship. While I welcome many of its recommendations, it will be useful to dwell for a few moments on some of its language and presuppositions, which themselves help to create the problems they are trying to solve.

The five kinds of postsecondary schools identified by Boyer are ranked in terms of the degree of emphasis placed on research by the institution. Within each category there are two subcategories, a higher and a lower one according to different criteria (129–130). There are thus nine categories of postsecondary schools in a hierarchical arrangement. The two categories of research universities are differentiated by how much federal support each receives for research. The "doctorate-granting" universities are distinguished by how many degrees they grant in how many disciplines. "Comprehensive Universities and Colleges" (master's degrees only) are distinguished mainly by different sizes of enrollments; liberal arts colleges (bachelor's degrees only) also by enrollment sizes. The

[3] Gerald Graff, *Beyond Culture Wars: How Teaching the Conflicts Can Revitalize American Education* (New York: Norton, 1992); and Ernest L. Boyer, *Scholarship Reconsidered: Priorities of the Professoriate* (Princeton, NJ: Princeton University Press, 1990).

lowest category is "Two-Year Community, Junior, and Technical Colleges." The report does not emphasize directly the status difference in each rank and category, but it is hard to read the report without concluding that it presupposes such differences. While tables give the figures for each category (but not for the subcategories), the statistics are also often cited on an "average" basis: what faculty in all postsecondary school categories believe. There was, in my view, a responsible interpretation of the given data. The categories themselves, furthermore, seem sensible insofar as they describe accurately what kind of postsecondary schools exist in the United States, even to the status of these categories as accepted by the public.

Here then is an immediate consideration: the report utilizes categories whose conditions of rank and status themselves make it seem that teaching is in need of remediation, a need the report is trying to answer. The report's call for a better reward system for teaching begins by urging the conceptualization of teaching as a form of scholarship[4]; but more than to the need to change the category system, the report is addressed to the morality of self-identification in universities. Though the deliberate search for status is rejected, Boyer's recommendations to give a higher priority to teaching bring neither the categories nor their status hierarchy under review.

> It's time to end the suffocating practice in which colleges and universities measure themselves far too frequently by external status rather than by values determined by their own distinctive mission. . . . But let's also candidly acknowledge that the degree to which this push for better education is achieved will be determined, in large measure, by the way scholarship is defined and, ultimately, rewarded. (xiii)

By redefining teaching as one of four kinds of scholarship, the original (highest) importance of research and scholarship is retained, while the sense of teaching as scholarship is meant to raise the status of teaching and to reflect this change by suitable professional rewards. But, will raising the status of teaching have an effect on the presupposed category system? It *can* have such an effect if it is accompanied by a noncompetitive means of identity formation in postsecondary school administrations and communities, an aban-

---

[4] In this first step, the gesture of attention to teaching is withdrawn when the proposal is to make it a form of scholarship: this is a "let them become more like us" gesture that the privileged often make with good intentions but without awareness of social narcissism. In this case, a more appropriate first gesture might be, "Let us consider what we researchers can learn from those whose priority has been teaching."

donment of the "self-measurement by external status." However, the report's ranking of research universities higher, for example, than comprehensive universities suggests a permanent status scale that will continue to encourage competitive upward mobility. In order to end measurement by external status, we need to learn to consider universities as having different functions but not different status. But Boyer's report does not take this step.

As another example, consider one of Boyer's proposals, whose language of the "pursuit of excellence," however generously intended, works against such changes. This language assumes the context of competition and makes it necessary to assess, measure, and reward a principal feature of all forms of scholarship as well as the "new" approach to teaching: "For teaching to be considered equal to research, it must be vigorously assessed, using criteria that we recognized within the academy, not just in a single institution" (37).[5] Even though the report offers important suggestions for broadening the criteria of evaluation in all forms of research and scholarship, it nevertheless retains the sense that no matter how the university functions, the work of its faculty must be subject to some kind of formal external evaluation or surveillance. In the case of teaching, this approach is elaborated with a discussion of "self-assessment, peer assessment, and student assessment," all reasonable and not necessarily harmful components of a collective attention to teaching.

Nevertheless, the values associated with increased attention to teaching are competitive.[6] According to Boyer, "A president at a doctorate university, in commenting on the mission of his institution, put it this way: 'This campus should be a place where both great teachers and great researchers function side by side'" (58). Boyer is emphasizing this president's wish for equality of teaching and research. But the adjective *great* presupposes one of the fantasy

---

[5] In this context we see some of the broader contexts of assessment, which, generally and for writing courses, is considered in Chapters 7 and 8. Boyer is taking a scientific procedure, measurement, from its laboratory context and claiming that it can be applied to verify teaching results. This makes sense only if teaching results are comparable to laboratory results, which are replicable. As suggested in Chapter 6, a distinctive feature of classrooms is their contingent character; contingency in laboratory science is altogether different.

[6] Five years after the Boyer report, the *New York Times* (September 17, 1995) ran an essay, "Power to the Pedagogues," by Christopher Winship and Mark Ratner, which said that existing forms of assessing university teaching are inadequate. However, their "solution" was competition among teachers and competition among schools for teachers. That this should be proposed at all suggests that the ideology that governs teaching has not changed: competition associated with teaching will devalue it as much as competitive grading practices do now.

values on which American society turns. This use of *great* is not very different from its use in "the great state of Texas" heard at political conventions, or the exhortation by those running for office to "keep America great." Greatness remains a part of the mind-set of those wanting to honor teaching in the same ceremonial and even juvenile way that greatness is given as a value to motivate the American population. It remains associated with elitism, with a sense of winning an imaginary worldwide competition for being number one, the value seen at sports events regularly, chanted by large crowds in Western countries.

While Boyer's own language is relatively moderate, here is how he presents one of his most important recommendations about teaching in universities:

> To expect faculty to be good teachers, as well as good researchers, is to set a demanding standard. Still, it is at the research university more than any other, where the two must come together. To bring teaching and research into better balance, we urge the nation's ranking universities to extend special status and salary incentives to those professors who devote most of their time to teaching and are particularly effective in the classroom. Such recognition will signify that the campus regards teaching excellence as a hallmark of professional success. (58)

The conventional sense of this paragraph is that it endorses the joining of teaching and research, which, in part, it does. Nevertheless, consider the following. Should the nation's "ranking universities" be singled out? This statement converts the listing of categories of postsecondary schools into a ranking. Is it their special responsibility to provide leadership? An alternative formulation might read: "The nation's research universities might seek guidance from other postsecondary schools about what they have learned from their long attention to teaching." This would strike a different note and provide support for the dismantling of the system of ranking.

Boyer's phrase "special status and salary incentives" continues the singling out process with its attention to status and its association of status with salary, an association that helps to perpetuate the hierarchical organization of postsecondary schools. In addition, it assumes a special incentive is required for this project, perhaps a form of the profit motive, which maintains the economic pyramid in the rest of society. But suppose, rather, the statement had read, "Those in research universities should find out how many among them have been devoting equal time to teaching and research, how many have integrated them, how these people's professional welfare has progressed, and then invite them to help others achieve these goals." My restatement (with which Boyer might not disagree) strikes less of a behavioral engineering note and bypasses the presumption that status and reward are the only goads to social change because they are what everyone seeks.

Consider the phrase "effective in the classroom." *Effectiveness* is yet another taken-for-granted term used about teaching, resembling a similarly suspicious phrase, "good in bed." (Is it the case that sexual performance is an individual matter, independent of partnership?) In the same sense that sexual performance is only one aspect of maintaining a relationship, effectiveness in the classroom cannot be equated with teaching and is, anyway, a relative value. In many courses, particularly large lecture courses, effectiveness has to do with the ability to hold the attention of large numbers of students, and the quality of teaching is identified with the performance value of the lecturer. While Boyer's phrase is not intrinsically offensive, it does not take into account the ongoing *teaching relationship* among teachers and students, and it seems to call attention to the *performance* of teachers on a class-by-class basis. *Effectiveness* does not legitimately describe human relationships, but rather a successful instrumentality, not necessarily human, as in "effective birth control techniques succeed in preventing pregnancy"; but one would not say "an effective love relationship is one that lasts." Because teaching entails living human relationships, using *effective* to describe it suggests an impoverishment of vocabulary, even in common parlance, when we try to articulate what people want from teaching relationships. Instead of "effective in the classroom," one could say "deeply involved in all forms of teaching." As a substantive experience, involvement matters more in teaching than "effectiveness," which implies that there is a fixed and measurable result of good teaching.

Now consider "teaching excellence as a hallmark of professional success." *Excellence* may be the academic version of *greatness* in more popular venues. Few people question the use of *excellence,* since, in today's anxious academic environment, to question excellence is akin to advocating flag burning. This term, which plays a role in how most of us think, carries with it some of the athletic meaning of achieving at a level better than all others. To excel is to be taken as the best *compared to others.* Again, few question the state of mind that urges everyone to be the best. This value is distant from the value of *doing one's best,* which does not imply comparing oneself to others. The public sense of the term *excellence* implies the tropes and rituals of competition as well as the sense that the quality of one's work is properly understood only when it is measured, a value endorsed by the Boyer report. We can recognize but not measure teaching success; measurement may tell us when we have

achieved the right level of automobile safety, but it will not identify
when good teaching is going on. We do not and ought not strive for
excellence in the sense of outdoing others or even winning a prize.
Rather, we do and ought to strive for reaching our students, for creating an atmosphere of stimulation, excitement, activity, and motivation. We ought to reject the claim that such values can only be
assured by a final system of measurement. If teachers who strive for
something like vitality in teaching situations are distracted by the
anxious feeling that they must excel according to a quantitative measure, it would be hard to take risks in the service of vitality and easy
to find reasons to accommodate to the system. The fundamental fact
that teaching purposes, styles, and needs are changing at every
moment—that they are continuously contingent—will be lost in
teachers' efforts to recreate the "excellence" that has been already
achieved by themselves or others by staying responsive to an ever-
changing population of students. It has become much easier and
more likely to expect vitality than excellence in teaching, especially
because few will seek to measure vitality and involvement, whereas
it is assumed that excellence is something that can be measured and
assessed.

But suppose the term *involvement* were substituted for *assessment:* self-involvement, peer involvement, teacher and mutual
involvement. Wouldn't the resulting terms then necessarily refer to
the substance and daily activity of teaching rather than imply that
the teaching is done first and then "techniques" are used to evaluate
it? Similarly, if the *idea* of involvement more generally took the
place of measurement and assessment, wouldn't the process of evaluation and self-evaluation become an ongoing, internalized aspect
of all teaching?[7] In fact, if one consults the informal conversations
of serious, dedicated teachers on a daily basis, isn't it true that they
share with one another, regardless of what formal evaluation systems exist, what works and what doesn't work? What worked last
year and not this year? What works with this population and not
that? Furthermore, if the idea of involvement is understood in a
more general sense, it applies as well to how research is evaluated.
Research can be understood as being involved with other aspects of
an individual's professional life rather than as an isolated zone of
achievement. Boyer suggests that pursuant to the ideal of "taking
pride in [one's] uniqueness" (xiii), an individual's research could

---

[7] How this might look is considered in Chapter 8.

possibly be viewed as part of other categories of effort, forming for that person a characteristic means of contribution to local or national communities or both:

> When it comes to pulling all the evidence together, we are impressed by the portfolio idea—a procedure that encourages faculty to document their work in a variety of ways. A faculty member could choose the form of scholarship around which a portfolio might be developed. The material used could include many of the varied forms we've described—ranging from publications, to field work documentation, to course descriptions, peer reviews, student evaluations, and even perhaps recordings and videocassetes. (40–41)

This statement could help to point us in a new direction: the direction of unifying the professional program of individual faculty members. But Boyer also invokes the need for "vigorous assessment," and the more remediation and assessment are promoted, the less likely it is that a new direction will be realized.

The Writing Program at Syracuse University has tried to move in this new direction. Among the various examples it cites, Boyer's report mentions this program, which, in December 1989, developed new specific criteria for promotion and tenure in that program. The document in which these criteria are spelled out[8] presents the following issue not raised by Boyer: the specificity of teaching relative to the discipline and subject matter. On the one hand, the wider-ranging criteria for conceptualizing teaching in Boyer's report makes it easier to particularize what teaching is in each subject matter. At the same time, in spite of his endorsement of the portfolio approach, Boyer retains a sense that teaching as an issue may be separated from other university enterprises such as research and service, a common view in almost all universities. On the other hand, the Syracuse Guidelines demonstrate the particular meaning of teaching as it relates to the subject matter of writing and language use. They move toward changing the idea of teaching to one in which the evaluation of teaching is more benign and naturalistic while less controlling and hierarchical than it is now. Here is a general statement of how the Syracuse Writing Program treats teaching:

> We interpret teaching broadly as contributions to the educational enterprise, necessarily but not exclusively with the program and university. Activities under this heading include individual classroom teaching; tutoring and acting as a program writing consultant

---

[8] Louise Wetherbee Phelps et al., "The Writing Program Promotion and Tenure Guidelines," Syracuse University, Syracuse, NY.

(to other writing teachers, classes, students, faculty in other disciplines); co-teaching with others; supervising independent study projects; advising; arranging and supervising internships; serving on graduate examination and thesis, dossier, or dissertation committees; mentoring other teachers; and leading or participating in workshops and co-curricular projects. In addition, teaching includes course and curriculum development work and the design and implementation of professional development for teaching assistants, and professional instructors in writing. Finally, teaching includes an array of nontraditional roles in writing across the curriculum, for example, offering workshops or acting as an advisor to teaching assistants in other disciplines. (4)

If all of these activities are eligible for inclusion in a teaching portfolio, it is clear that evaluation in the sense of measurement is far in the background and perhaps altogether out of the picture. The portfolio technique tries to show that different forms of teaching are connected to one another in a kind of program or style. It assumes that *every* teacher teaches in a variety of styles and contexts in addition to classroom teaching.

Also noteworthy is the integration of the concept of teaching with the subject matter of writing. Composition as a subject in itself should be considered an academic discipline[9] as one of the authors of the Syracuse Guidelines, Louise Phelps, has discussed. This discipline demands various approaches to teaching, such as tutoring and curriculum design, collaborative work, and portfolio evaluation. The Syracuse Guidelines acknowledge that the discipline requires a wide-ranging alertness on the part of all writing teachers to special combinations of literacy theory and teaching practice, a point further elaborated by Phelps in her 1991 essay.[10] From the Boyer report we get the sense too often that teaching practices are similar across subject matters and that these practices do not need to be conceptualized per department, per discipline, per university, per teacher,

---

[9] The face value of this proposal is appealing. But does the study of writing and language use really want to emulate other disciplines? My answer is no, as discussed at length in this book. I think that the difference between this discipline and others is a basis for revising the concept of "discipline." A feature of this basis is the involvement of writing and language use in the detailed thinking of other disciplines. This level of involvement suggests a model of how other disciplines may find connections to one another, leading toward more flexible senses of, for example, the academic department.

[10] Louise Wetherbee Phelps, "Practical Wisdom and the Geography of Knowledge in Composition," *College English* 53 (December 1991): 863–885.

and even per student.[11] On the other hand, the Syracuse Guidelines suggest that just as teaching has a distinctive identity when it comes to the discipline of writing, it also has different identities within that program and for that program, identities that may not fit other universities and other programs. In any event, the shift toward portfolio evaluation does respond to the ideological aspect of evaluation, whether it is applied to student writing or to the teaching of writing. Attention to portfolios shifts the idea of evaluation into a discourse of particularization, to standards of "local knowledge," to needs, values, and purposes of local school and university situations, as well as to the requirements of different disciplines. In part, the Boyer report does advocate this change, but more is involved in such a change than is discussed in the report.

Academic Teaching Through Disclosure and Collaboration

Initiatives in the teaching of writing have changed the subject matter and the sense of what academic teaching can be. One of these initiatives has been disclosure of individual and collective knowledge, feeling, and experience, which have traditionally been out of bounds in postsecondary teaching. Individual students' disclosures of some of the stories in their lives have motivated them to say more and to articulate their thoughts more forcefully. Most teachers expect that at least some level of personal disclosure helps to overcome inhibitions about writing and communicating with others. Many also think that political disclosure is a good way for class members to speak and write with a greater sense of responsibility to society. Many forms of collective membership[12] have become issues in claiming and announcing knowledge. Personal and collective disclosures taking place in schools and universities have changed the contexts of knowledge as well as the knowledge itself. Disclosure is important because it has changed the teaching of writing, changed teaching, and changed how we give and get knowledge.

---

[11] This point is discussed in some detail in Chapter 6, with reference to Edward Pauly's *The Classroom Crucible* (New York: Basic Books, 1990), which treats this issue in regard to preuniversity schools.

[12] A factor treated in more detail with regard to language and literature in Chapter 3.

Teaching through disclosure, which has grown out of self-consciously practiced subjectivist styles of teaching by some faculty members, reminds us that "truth" includes the personal, the emotional, the ideological, and sometimes the irrational in each subject matter. Disclosure counteracts individuals' blind spots and censorings and asks us to take notice of the historically grounded suppressions, denials, and lies that accompany received cultural traditions and received knowledge. In order for academic teaching to contribute to society's striving for just, comprehending, and peaceful social relations, practices of disclosure encourage teaching in many directions and by everyone who enters the classroom.

Teaching through disclosure enlarges research as a foundational academic value. It treats academic institutions as schools that admit that knowledge could be more fully mobilized by local experiences, social priorities, and wider human urgencies. In this effort, disclosure-oriented postsecondary teaching might be responsive to ideals that Boyer and others have expressed.

The subject of writing and language use, through its roles in text production, publication, announcement, and established, conventional disclosure processes, is part of other subjects. Attempts at teaching writing toward the ideals of openness and candor encouraged expressive or free writing and reader response in English classes. These efforts have remained part of the teaching repertoire for many writing teachers, but they have not grown into a comprehensive pedagogy partly because of their exclusive attention to individual expression and personal issues. Writing was viewed as a single, fixed, inner capability, rather than as an ability that varies with each person's ways of being in society.[13] Within individualistic pedagogy, disclosure poses problems; attached to a cooperative pedagogy, however, as further suggested in Chapter 8, there are fewer problems and many advantages. To illustrate this situation, consider the following exchange in the Chronicle of Higher Education.[14]

---

[13] There is some analogy between this designation of a single writing ability and conceiving of IQ as a single factor, as discussed by Stephen Jay Gould in *The Mismeasure of Man* (New York: Norton, 1981). In the same sense that Gould showed the artificiality of that conception, the present study assumes that there is no one thing called writing ability that all people can develop. I discuss in Chapter 2 how the genre idea more accurately describes different people's writing abilities. Many "single factors" are features of educational measurement, and they falsify their objects of measure just as in the case of IQ. This issue is discussed further in Chapter 7.

[14] February 17, 1993.

The first essay was "The Ethics of Requiring Students to Write About Their Personal Lives" by Susan Swartzlander, Diana Pace, and Virginia Lee Stamler, all of Grand Valley State University in Allendale, Michigan. Swartzlander is an English faculty member and the other two authors are psychological counselors. The authors are responding to some students who, fearing the adverse judgment of the teacher if they did not disclose, reported discomfort about revealing such events in their families as sexual and physical abuse, rape, and alcoholism. The authors are concerned that often the English instructor asking for personal disclosure is male and often the students feeling threatened are female. However, their general concern is that the use of personal journals, autobiographical writing, and other genres of self-announcement are often treated too casually, sometimes carelessly, and without anticipation of just how important these writings are to the writers. A similar hesitation is expressed regarding what nonwhite students feel ready to share: if a classroom majority is white or if the teacher is white, shouldn't nonwhite students be permitted to decline an assignment if a safe atmosphere with regard to race has not yet been established? Finally, the authors are especially concerned that personal writing in the classroom "not foster the perception that students must 'deal with' their emotional problems in their writing or that they will succeed in courses if they can write about dramatic personal experiences."[15]

The tone of the original essay was reasonable, and the warnings it presents should be taken seriously by anyone who believes that personal materials have a place in the study of our subject matter. However, two of the letter writers responding to the essay said that the authors were "guilty of questionable ethics themselves" because of their "reverse sexism" (David J. Hibler) and their "misrepresentation [of] the entire academic field of composition" (Mark Wiley). The original essay and the responding letters[16] demonstrate the gender/political sensitivity of disclosure: the men responding to the criticism of disclosure seemed less inclined to negotiate than the women, such as Lucie Arbuthnot, who advocated more expressive writing and accepted the warnings, but made a case for personal writing as being important to "help students discover the joys of writing."

---

[15] *Chronicle of Higher Education*, February 17, 1993, B2. True, but if teaching and therapy were less criticized as helping practices, it would be easier to deal with the personal in class and to claim impersonal or collective knowledge through therapy.

[16] *Chronicle of Higher Education*, March 10, 1993.

About a year later, in the same publication,[17] Daphne Patai's
essay, entitled "Sick and Tired of Scholars' Nouveau Solipsism"
appeared in "Point of View" on the back page. Patai said that self-
reference—in the form of autobiographical materials when discussing cultures and issues distant from oneself—has too often reached
the point of "individual and collective breast-beating, grandstand-
ing, and plain old egocentricity," even in the work of scholars she
admires (such as Ruth Behar and Nancy Miller). Her reminder:
"there still *was* a world out there" (A52), and it is the job of scholars
to study it while the rest of us regulate their acknowledged subjectivity by "agreed-upon procedures that distinguish facts from interpretation, sound arguments from hollow claims, hyperbole from
straight talk." Like the warnings of the previous essay, Patai's argument makes sense: it is not all that easy to know when we as scholars, aiming to account for our roles and the influences on the
subjects we study, are actually inflating our own importance and
misappropriating a scene of inquiry for the purposes of announcing
our own lives and our own politics to our colleagues and to the rest
of the world.

Nevertheless, there are examples in the scholarly literature of
many who have proceeded according to styles of self-disclosure,
examples that may allay the concerns of the contributors to the
Chronicle of Higher Education and others in the academy and that
may help show how personal and collective disclosure can enrich
teaching and scholarship. Two examples appeared in the November
1992 issue of *College English*.[18] Lynn Z. Bloom's account of her professional struggles in the midst of raising children and being responsive to her husband's professional development is meant, in part, to
teach and inform others that their comparable struggles are generic.
Once individual struggles are recognized as collective, a collective
approach to their solution may be sought, thus helping to bring the
solution to more people.

Carole Deletiner's essay "Crossing Lines" offers several of her
classroom experiences as well as some connections between student
and teacher self-disclosures. Working with students who are themselves struggling in their personal lives, Deletiner shows the language she used in her own essay to achieve solidarity with her
students. She offers instances of their own work as well as comments they offered on the kind of class she ran. She reports on the

---

[17] *Chronicle of Higher Education,* February 23, 1994.

[18] Lynn Z. Bloom, "Teaching College English as a Woman," and Carole Deletiner,
"Crossing Lines," both in *College English* 54 (November 1992): 818–25, and 809–17.

suspicion of her colleagues and supervisors as well as on the mis-perception of what was actually taking place in her class when she was visited by superiors. This account portrays how student and teacher self-disclosure appearing under conditions of trust can guide the disenfranchised toward faster recognition by the majority and contribute to the enlightenment of the already privileged regarding their use of language and their implication in this subject.

Deletiner's use of self-disclosure as a scholarly effort at self-inclusion and curriculum change provides a foundation for a variety of collaborative pedagogies. Classroom and research collaboration are also aspects of teaching not explored in the Boyer report, proba-bly because they change the underlying assumptions of academic life, which are individualism, apprentice learning, and academic integrity achieved through isolated research, study, and writing—assumptions that Boyer and others do not think need to be changed. As I discuss in Chapters 3, 4, 5, and 8, collaboration accompanies disclosure, and it needs to be integrated into research, scholarship, and other forms of disciplined inquiry. As practices that are bound together, disclosure and collaboration work toward uniting teaching and research.

However, many who are involved in new efforts at classroom and research collaboration[19] encounter trouble as we become impli-cated in our colleagues' lives and histories. Similarly, many who have used, valued, and tried individual and collective self-disclosure in teaching, learning, and research have also reported that its risks may endanger the classroom, the department, and the workplace at large. For some others, collaboration is either senti-mentalized or a means of not taking the classroom seriously. Even for those who accept and understand its potential to change postsec-ondary teaching, the stronger effects of most collaborative practices are blocked by the institutionally governed machineries of testing and grading: there is no way for the results of collaboration to count. The record shows only the judgments of the teachers and never the collective accomplishments of students. In another sense, most of us

---

[19] The reader is referred to the seventeen new essays in *Writing With: New Directions in Collaborative Teaching*, ed. Sally Reagan, Thomas Fox, and David Bleich (Albany: SUNY Press, 1994), and to the twelve new essays in *Journal of Advanced Composition* 14, (no. 1, 1994), a special issue entitled "Collaboration and Change in the Academy," which I edited. Two of the latter essays, those by Leverenz and by Qualley and Chiseri-Strater, are discussed in Chapter 5 of the present book. The reader is also referred to Chapters 6–10 of my *The Double Perspective* (New York: Oxford University Press, 1988; Urbana: NCTE, 1993), especially the last two chapters, for my earlier discussions of the theory and practice of collaboration.

do not understand what a collective accomplishment looks like in school, or its relation to individual accomplishment, understanding that could be acquired through processes of classroom observation, experience, discussion, and publication. We do not know what collective accomplishment, regularly acknowledged,[20] may mean for the future of both individuals and society: we understand only what individual accomplishment means in our of society.

Disclosure can help to bring the subjective and the collective categories of experience together; it can maintain the necessity of understanding the collective within the subjective, and the subjective within the collective. Movements toward and away from affiliation with others seem more comprehensible in the contexts of disclosure, as the more private meanings of our movements become less strange to others, more marked by others' sense of our own histories and cultures, more identified by our own confidence in the connections we have with others and with the history of our own groups.

"Personal writing" is a common form of expressive writing. However, the latter permits rather than teaches serious, disciplined, habitual, and extended disclosure and its integration into curriculum. (The undisciplined character of "expression" most concerns Swartzlander and her colleagues.)[21] Disclosure and collaboration orients teaching around discovering who is in class with us (see Chapters 3–6). It is assumed that what each person brings to the classroom is potentially part of the curriculum for that course; it is expected that the curriculum will be contingent on what teachers and students think is appropriate and helpful to disclose about themselves and their histories. Whatever a teacher prepares to share with students will likely be revised by the new knowledge of who is joining a course. This revision of pedagogy teaches students that the efforts of describing their own experiences and values have an effect on others and on the collective interests of teachers and schools. Even in demographically homogeneous school districts, the popula-

---

[20] One of the implications of Ludwik Fleck's 1935 treatise, *Genesis and Development of a Scientific Fact* (Chicago: University of Chicago Press, 1979), is that the forms of scientific reporting require an individual claim, even though the fact was not discovered by an individual in isolation. Ruth Hubbard's account of the discovery of DNA, *The Politics of Women's Biology* (New Brunswick: Rutgers University Press, 1990) also suggests a collective accomplishment, yet the discovery was presented as the work of two gifted young men.

[21] As discussed in Chapter 8, expression and other forms of disclosure, like most writing and language uses, are disciplined by the collective contexts of their presentation. They are more likely to seem undisciplined in individualist contexts.

tion changes and the fresh perspectives offered by groups just one year younger than last year's groups can change the curriculum significantly. If course curricula are understood as being contingent on the disclosures of a classroom's membership, the basic models of teaching and learning depart from the transmission models that have served for hundreds of years, even though the practice of transmitting knowledge—telling others what you have learned—is always welcome. This change in pedagogy can move academic assumptions from individualism to combined individual, subjective, intersubjective, and collective perspectives.

Disclosure and collaboration require neither confession nor revelation, which take place in completely private and completely universalist contexts, respectively. To confess and reveal have an implied reference to a religious morality, as if one were confessing sins and revealing secrets. Disclosure refers to telling things in intermediate contexts like groups, subgroups, classrooms, and lecture halls, where estimations need to be made about appropriateness and helpfulness to others as well as oneself. Disclosure in teaching presupposes readiness of a collaborative context, which includes a certain level of trust among peers and authority figures as well as the sense that the disclosed information could be germane to the ongoing work of the class.

To practice disclosure and collaboration is to depend on each member of a classroom bringing in an individual history that should become part of the class' subject matter; these histories become part of the process of presenting opinions, interpretations, and reports. This practice means changing the conventions and therefore the expectations, values, and styles of self-reference. But it also implies that disclosure is not likely to take place in a classroom under compulsory conditions: class members should not feel forced to share information about themselves that they consider damaging or embarrassing. Writing teachers often ask, on the one hand, how a topic "relates to you," and on the other, "what it means, objectively." Including new genres of disclosure in a subject matter means writing about that subject's possible role in one's own life, its meanings to different constituencies, and the relation between the personal and public. Disclosure and collaboration ask each member of a class to announce, sooner or later, the terms of membership in the class (see Chapter 3). Such an announcement could contain a variety of facts, including memberships and interpersonal relationships marking one's family, school, ethnic, gender history, one's vocational and economic reasons for choosing courses, one's clothing, eating, and traveling styles, one's aspirations, fantasies, values, and plans. These announcements should appear regularly and ordinarily, and should continue at a pace comfortable to each individual's level of involvement in the class. Things that people learn about one another from these announcements gradually build up motivations and commitments to learn writing and language use as a part of their social identities. This way of learning grounds the subject in personality and relationships, and facilitates its continuing effects long after school.

Different genres and levels of self-disclosure are what many students seek in school. But usually students are prompted to confine announcements of their histories to ultraprivate social locations and not to expect to disclose this knowledge in school. In smaller classes, where personal relationships could flourish, the disclosure of the exclusively individual experience and history often seems enough. Classrooms are becoming crowded even in privileged schools and universities; students feel numbered and not known by name. Testing and measuring interrupt students' lives in and out of the classroom; the tests seem not to refer to what people experience but rather to whether students can correctly perceive the logic of the examination questions. Under these conditions, disclosure and collaboration as ways of teaching are needed to make schools feel more like places where students are honored by having their histories and cultures recognized in the classroom and in the curriculum. Disclosure identifies people in the classroom. If students are gratified when others remember their names now, it suggests that real, extended, and thorough recognition as part of the study process can be the basis for the motivation that is now in most cases provided only by the hope of becoming employed. Disclosure and collaboration teach students to make their work more a part of their identities, their identities more connected to others, and their vocations more palpably implicated in society and in other people's needs.

Disclosure desentimentalizes group work, teaches how to maintain discipline while working with others; it provides a sense of the meaning of collective achievement as going with, extending, and changing the meaning of individual achievement. For example, early forms of modern group work took place through peer revision groups.[22] If critical comments are given without self-disclosure they may or may not help. But when they are given with and through self-disclosure, they also present the perspective behind the critique and thus there is a greater likelihood that both the use and the limits

---

[22] Kenneth Bruffee, whose most recent work is *Collaborative Learning* (Baltimore: Johns Hopkins Press, 1993), was one of the first to try peer group revision, which now has wider currency: business reports in the *New York Times* often report collaborative practices in corporations.

of the criticisms will be heard and that the criticism will seem more trustworthy and therefore more constructive to the recipient. While the principle of self-announcement requires scholars and thinkers to take note of their "subject position" (places in society), it is common sense, courtesy, and respect for coworkers that prompt such disclosure. It changes the interactive discourse so that the individual accomplishment gains autonomy by virtue of its implication in the perspectives of others; the collective accomplishment is enfranchisement of everyone's need to learn from others by imitation and emulation, and to teach others the same way with the sense of including but yet advancing beyond the individualist style.

Disclosure and collaboration are not methods or techniques. I discuss them in this book as principles, orientations, expectations, and ways of arousing ethical and political alertness to the collective situation in classrooms. I expect that teachers cannot declare disclosure to be in effect in some clear and definite way. Rather, over time, if disclosure and collaboration prove sympathetic to teachers and scholars, they will become more fully a part of the style of discussion in classrooms and scholarly meetings. To some extent this is beginning to take place, as the following brief survey suggests.

Disclosure and Academic Subject Matters

Recently scholarship and criticism have shown more inclination toward self-disclosure in the presentation of their subjects and their understandings.[23] Jane Tompkins' book, *A Life in School*,[24] explores her history and values as they developed in academic life, proposing new styles, forms, conventions, and standards of self-disclosure. Diane Freedman, in *An Alchemy of Genres*,[25] includes a considerable number of references to her personal history as a student, a woman, a child of two cultures, and a professional, as she explores "cross-genre writing by American feminist poet-critics." Freedman also co-edited *The Intimate Critique*,[26] an unusual collection of "autobiographical

---

[23] In a forthcoming essay, I refer to self-disclosure in formal scholarship as "self-inscription" and "self-inclusion." This latter term refers to the process of scholars trying, in a more comprehensive way, to describe how they are implicated in their professional *projects*, rather than only in a particular essay or book.

[24] Jane Tompkins, *A Life in School* (New York: Longmans, 1996).

[25] Diane Freedman, *An Alchemy of Genres: Cross-Genre Writing by American Feminist Poet-Critics* (Charlottesville: University of Virginia Press, 1992).

[26] Diane Freedman, Olivia Frey, and Frances Zauhar, ed., *The Intimate Critique: Autobiographical Literary Criticism* (Durham: Duke University Press, 1993).

literary criticism." Also available is Daniel Rancour-Laferrière's collection *Self-Analysis in Literary Study.*[27] G. Douglas Atkins discusses
the personal turn in critical writing, offering his own support for "a
courageous criticism that records personal encounter, evincing an
author's or a text's power and the reader's powerful, whole response:
a responsive because personal criticism."[28]

Nonliterary disciplines have brought out works whose uses of
self-disclosure change the focus of their subject matters. Patricia
Williams' *An Alchemy of Race and Rights*[29] and *The Rooster's Egg*[30]
mix her personal experiences and participation in historic changes
in society with her local experiences in the law academy. These
books encourage us to review critically what we took for granted as
permanent principles of law. The ability to juxtapose one's experience with taken-for-granted ways of proceeding was not always
respectable. By integrating accounts of personal experience with
analyses of legal issues, Williams is one of several who have con-
ferred authority on experience, who have helped to make the Wife
of Bath's ideal a reality.

In linguistics, Robin Lakoff and Deborah Tannen also have led
the way toward honoring self-disclosure as part of the subject matter. Lakoff is one of the pioneers in academic self-disclosure,
although she is not known mainly for that. Departing from the circle
of transformational linguists, she began using some of its tropes of
sentence citation in new ways that made reference to people's lived
experiences.[31] In subsequent work, Lakoff made reference to her
personal life and experience in therapy. Most recently, she
recounted her roles in the academy and her reasons for taking up
the topics she does, for altering what counts as linguistics by plac-

---

[27] Daniel Rancour-Laferrière, *Self-Analysis in Literary Study* (New York: New York University Press, 1994).

[28] G. Douglas Atkins, *Estranging the Familiar: Toward a Revitalized Critical Writing* (Athens, Georgia: University of Georgia Press, 1992), 97. In addition, in a chapter in a forthcoming book, Olivia Frey and Diane Freedman, eds., *Personal Thoughts: The Autobiographical Nature of Research, Scholarship and Knowledge in the Disciplines* (Duke University Press), I discuss, with respect to the work of Robin Lakoff, Naomi Scheman, Ruth Hubbard, Adrienne Rich, how their historical and social standpoints are necessarily linked to how their subject matters take new shape.

[29] Patricia Williams, *An Alchemy of Race and Rights* (Cambridge: Harvard University Press, 1990).

[30] Patricia Williams, *The Rooster's Egg* (Cambridge: Harvard University Press, 1995).

[31] For instance, "Oh dear, you've put the peanut butter in the refrigerator again," versus "Shit, you've put the peanut butter in the refrigerator again." From Robin Lakoff, *Language and Woman's Place* (New York: Harper and Row, 1975).

ing it in contexts that many might call literary.[32] Her style might well transform linguistics into a subject many more people can view with interest.

Deborah Tannen has also helped to place linguistics into contexts of people's experience. Her disclosures relate her marital experiences and her ethnic identity to her scholarly work. As a result, her earlier work on conversational style and her later work on gender have a context that teaches the public more about the subject and shortens the distance between the academic and public communities. Personal information and backgrounds offered by Lakoff and Tannen also reach the public through classroom study of linguistics. Self-disclosures render the subject more accessible to students, who can more easily perceive the motivation and the social role of the scholarly work because of the authors' ability to ground their more abstract considerations in their own lived experiences.

In philosophy, the recent work of Naomi Scheman is noteworthy.[33] Covering a wide range of topics from affective states to epistemology, Scheman periodically refers to her experiences as a traveling academic, as a daughter, and as a politically conscious adult. By shifting her focus, she also lends a sense of living reality to topics that are often abstract and distant in traditional philosophy courses. She places issues of meaning and knowledge in the context of personal responsibility; affective states in the context of attachment; loneliness in the context of social and ethnic identity. Discussing these issues in contexts that also include personal narratives and subjective reflection, Scheman makes the subject of philosophy more accessible, reducing its reputation of being beyond ordinary life experiences.

Some have changed the look and perhaps the substance of some experimental sciences by including their political and historical standpoints. A notable study along these lines is Ruth Hubbard's *The Politics of Women's Biology,* which she describes as an account of her "journey from observing nature to observing science" (2). She tells how this trip was motivated by her belated comprehension of the injustice done to Rosalind Franklin in the discovery of the DNA molecule. Behind this comprehension is the story that Hubbard was a refugee to the United States from Nazi Germany. Thinking she was free

---

[32] Robin Tolmach Lakoff, *Talking Power* (New York: Basic Books, 1990).

[33] Naomi Scheman, *Engenderings: Constructions of Knowledge, Authority, and Privilege* (New York: Routledge, 1993).

of that domination, she did not expect to find a different version of it in the story of DNA. When she become aware of the poor treatment Franklin had received, biology become a different subject for her.

As an emerging scholarly convention, self-disclosure is a way to identify the theory and practice of autobiographical, autoethnographic, or life writing, which is getting more public and academic attention. This interest is changing academic subjects toward different purposes. It is a genre that clarifies traditionally obscure subjects like linguistics and philosophy, and at the same time makes clearer to readers the scope of authority the author actually has. Such writing teaches how to increase our sense of implication in scholarly knowledge and opinion. In this book, I assume that a sense of self-implication is fundamental to writing and language use as a subject of study. Disclosure, in its broad sense, is a response to the challenge of reconsidering scholarship posed by Ernest Boyer. To reconsider scholarship is to reconsider teaching, to find ways of practicing teaching to contribute to scholarship, and to pursue scholarship for pedagogical ends. There are signs that academic faculties, students, and the public are ready to exercise the discipline, the discretion, the patience, and the mutual respect needed to admit individual and collective self-disclosure to the scenes of teaching. Because this project begins with writing, we discern the signs of change by studying the changing genres of writing. The study of genre, of kinds of writing, is becoming fundamental to the teaching of writing and language use.

Chapter Two

Genre, Writing,
and Language Use

Genre and the Understanding of Language Use

Lately, because of the increasing attention given to different cultures in the teaching of English, there has been more attention to genres of writing and language use. Cultural contexts are considered to be essential aspects of the texts, works, and discourses under study. Texts are located in cultures through their genres—the groups of other texts with which they could be compared or associated. Changes in culture are noticed through changes in genre. The connections between genre and personal identity make it appealing to study collective values in individual texts. Genre changes the subject of writing and language use into a more clearly living, changing zone, one that highlights the materiality of language.

Recently, several texts have introduced the genre idea to the teaching of writing and literacy.[1] They suggest that "thinking through genre" has some of the appeal of the New Criticism: the idea is clear enough for everyone to take up. But it also has some of the appeal of psychoanalysis. In its "new-critical" style, teachers and textbook authors present a variety of exercises that involve

---

[1] Bill Cope and Mary Kalantzis, *The Powers of Literacy: A Genre Approach to Teaching Writing* (Pittsburgh: University of Pittsburgh Press, 1993); Aviva Freedman and Peter Medway, eds., *Learning and Teaching Genre* (Portsmouth, NH: Boynton/ Cook, 1993); and Janet Giltrow, *Academic Writing: Writing and Reading Across the Disciplines* (Orchard Park, NY: Broadview Press, 1995). *Language use* is not a common term in these books.

identifying, distinguishing, and characterizing kinds of writing. These exercises can be related to the more difficult task of recognizing the social constituencies of genres: how does an audience relate to a literary form? This question is pedagogically useful for genres that come from popular culture, increasingly a prominent subject matter in writing courses. Furthermore, as with the New Criticism, the use of the genre idea needs hermeneutic ability: to identify a genre, one interprets a context. Judgments may then be verified or corrected by those of other observers.

The psychoanalytic potential of genre is that it marks what is usually unconscious in verbal and symbolic interaction. In daily life, people are not aware of what language genre is in effect at any moment. Even if one is writing a letter, it takes some doing to understand the particular letter in its generic dimensions. But we are usually not aware that the forms we use routinely—forms we likely have used repeatedly and learned in pragmatic situations—are shared, conventional, and generic. The genre action, so to speak, like unconscious action in the psychoanalytic sense, follows certain orderly procedures and paths that are not on our minds as we say what we have to say.

Our unconsciousness of genre is an important factor in our use of it, and in our attempts to become aware of it in the teaching of writing. Genre provides a clear structure through which students can detect their own orientations in history, society, and politics. The burdens of the teaching of writing conceived of purely as skill—the problems of "generalized writing skills instruction"—are related to the authoritarian and didactic contexts of pedagogy (suggested even by the Boyer report), probably the only context most people know about. Today, this context is being challenged, especially by teachers of writing and the humanities. Sites of challenge, such at those discussed in the section Genres as Lived Experiences, are also sites of increased awareness of genre as well as of language in other senses.

A key task of writing teachers is to find out which genres in the language use repertoires of students show the mixture, for example, of received values and emerging values of society.[2] The teachers' search for these genres is part of their responsibility and their own education. By learning students' genres and language use achievements, teachers inform themselves about the students' educational status. The genre idea is a means of identifying students' knowledge

---

[2] An issue discussed in Chapter 4. This discussion cites the writings of men from different zones of society and shows how the genres of their writing are the sites of their growth and change.

of, and abilities with, language and writing. It is also a means, superior to testing, of understanding students' qualities of mind. One can ask for writing in known genres, and one can ask for writing that will not require a particular genre, for example, tell about your grandparents. The result of such requests is an inquiry by both student and teacher as to what could be some suitable genres for that topic, for this audience.

Just as it is usually a struggle to acknowledge that one had unconscious thoughts or wishes, and just as the therapeutic process is a process of education regarding one's own history as a social figure, disclosing genres is education in this extended sense. The contexts of teaching writing and language use demonstrate that kinds of language and writing make sense as ways to understand changes undergone by students and teachers as well as by communities and societies. In these subjects, the study of genre promotes interaction, and interaction among class members makes it necessary to identify genres.

Writing and language use make us aware of our implication in the lives, values, and interests of others. Yet many hold it to be a subject matter that requires authoritarian and vaguely paranoid psychology. Fantasies of the purity of language and writing have burdened language and society for centuries. The idea of genre helps us to learn more reliably about these burdens and perhaps reduce their claims on the present. To pursue the ideas of genre and disclosure in pedagogical programs, we should understand how ideals of social purity have played a role in such apparently benign practices as "generalized writing skills instruction."

The Ideal of Purity

The ideal of purity—the wish for a "pure" language—helps to perpetuate the false belief that language is, and can be studied as, separate from its living contexts. The history of the teaching of language use and writing in modern times has been guided by the ideal of a pure language. To get a sense of the weight of this ideal, I first give an example from an advertisement, then suggest the scope of the history of this value, followed by a story dramatizing how it appears in academic contexts as a practical value.

A recent ad for a BMW 750iL said that it fulfills the wish of a driver who wants "the purest form of a luxury sedan," and who wants to approach "the purity of the driving experience."[3] The language of

---

[3] Several "glossy" magazines.

this ad is, for the most part, unremarkable for a luxury car in the highest price range. Since it costs the most, it is billed as the best. However, the words *purest* and *purity* stood out as I read the ad. The first usage refers to the car, whereas the second refers to the driving experience. The premise of the ad is that there is a class of drivers who seek purity of some sort, or who want their driving to express their ideals of purity. Cadillacs are "standards," Lincolns are "what a luxury car should be," and Lexuses are "pursuing perfection." The BMW is "pure" luxury and driving experience.

There is no single source for the ideal of purity that this ad assumes. There are Plato's pure ideas, and there is the sinlessness associated with the Virgin Mary's conception, as well as the "purity" of those who have not had sexual relations. In the film *Dr. Strangelove,* the paranoid commanding officer (Jack D. Ripper) of the military wing that sent the nuclear bomber to Russia was obsessed with the "purity of essence" of his bodily fluids. Nazis and other racial supremacists want a "pure race." Except in very narrow contexts, it is not too great a leap to think of these demands for purity as signs of paranoid social psychology. In reality, the ideal of purity of BMWs, ideas, the conception of Mary, those who have not had sexual relations, or races of people is a fantasy used to serve political purposes in society.

In Victor Villanueva's discussion of the English Only movement,[4] a variation of this ideal is examined. People did not say there was something wrong with Spanish or any single other non-English language; rather, supporters of this movement claimed that the privileged language—and, tacitly, the privileged people—would become contaminated. The fact that the privileged languages and peoples are already "contaminated" and "impure," as the result of past entry into the language of many foreign components, is forgotten or ignored. Advocacy of a pure language is a part of advocacy for a pure society, which is the ideal—the fantasy—that is causing trouble. If you assume that language cannot be considered separate from society, you cannot maintain ideals of a pure language and a pure society.

---

[4] Victor Villanueva, *Bootstraps* (Urbana, IL: National Council of Teachers of English, 1994). This discussion refers to the initiatives to declare English, over Spanish and other languages, the official language of the United States. One result of this movement's success would be that schools conducted in Spanish would not be recognized.

Yet the search for a standard or a pure language is one of the defining characteristics of modern postsecondary approaches to language use. In this search, as Miriam Brody has described,[5] the "standard" gender becomes a model. Tacitly, a pure language has a masculine gender, and the belief in the existence of a pure gender of language is similar to the Cartesian belief in a pure gender of thought, described by Scheman[6] and by Bordo.[7] Brody suggests that the ideal of language purity is part of the ideal of "manly writing," whose history she traces back to Quintilian.

The locus of its modern form, Brody says, is George Campbell's eighteenth-century adaptation of the "Royal Society's gendered metaphors of the brutal, erotic engagement between science and the natural world" (54). She suggests that his *Philosophy of Rhetoric* (1776) is a key source for the "modes of discourse" (57) still widely used in secondary and postsecondary writing pedagogy. This work is important in the present consideration because of the clarity with which the paranoid element in the search for purity emerges. Brody characterizes Campbell's work as suppressing dialectical diversity in order to establish only one usage style—that of English gentlemen, or the "freeborn Briton" (57).

> Campbell believed that unfortunately the professional, not the gentleman scholar, brought the bias of his craft to language, flooding it with particular jargons. Campbell imagined all of the dialects of Britain as so many divergent roads. English was the road he called "the king's highway," a highway of "pure" and "true" English. In the same gesture, the various dialects, the Scottish, the Welsh, and the dialects of the regional provinces of English, with their different pronunciations and vocabulary, all "diverse one from another, come under the common denomination of impure.". . . Campbell conglomerated a multitude of human speakers extraordinary in variety and dissimilarity and called their speech impure. (59)

Brody notices that for Campbell language "impurities" were "not differences but errors" whose names "raised the mistake to an offense against society and against revered canons of comportment." Campbell's tone and that of the memo-writer I cite later help

---

[5] Miriam Brody, *Manly Writing: Gender, Rhetoric, and the Rise of Composition* (Carbondale, IL: Southern Illinois University Press, 1993).

[6] Naomi Scheman, "Though This Be Method, Yet There Is Madness in It: Paranoia and Liberal Epistemology," in *Engenderings: Constructions fo Knowledge, Authority, and Privilege* (New York: Routledge, 1993), 75–105.

[7] Susan Bordo, *The Flight to Objectivity: Essays on Cartesianism and Culture* (Albany: State University of New York Press, 1987).

establish which people required, advocated, and succeeded in getting a standard dialect recognized: a small group of academic men, serving values of the (politically, militarily) powerful, used their positions to mold and present language in such a way as to reinforce their social status. This desire to restrict language use through promoting its purity, through suppressing the dialects of nondominant communities and ethnic groups, through advocating an official, or standard, conduit of language is a derogation of language use. This ideal strongly influences contemporary writing and language use pedagogies that pass for competent, desirable education.

Toward the end of her study, Brody reflects that even an expressivist writing teacher like Peter Elbow, seemingly inadvertently, enacts his tacit subscription to the styles and standard of "manly writing," perhaps foretold in the title of one of his books, "Writing with Power."[8] Here is Brody's reading of Elbow:

> He suggested that people do not always use real voice because they are frightened of the power that inhabits them: "There's something scary about being as strong as you are, about wielding the force you actually have." Elbow understood this power as something explosive; finally it was nothing less than the explosion of a gun: "In effect, I'm saying, 'Why don't you shoot that gun you have?'" To learn to write well, one should "practice shooting the gun off in safe places," with people the student knows and trusts as audience (310). Presumably, as he became a more confident marksman, the writer/shooter took his weapon into combat. (186)

While one cannot be sure of the meaning of a single metaphor in isolation, the ease with which gun talk enters this discussion of writing is similar to the ease with which military values enter our customs of schoolwork and pedagogy.[9] It is difficult to feel a benign response to Elbow's metaphor, even though its surface intention is to flatter students into thinking they are as powerful with their pens as others are with their guns. Although the word *power* appears in the book

---

[8] Peter Elbow, *Writing with Power: Techniques for Mastering the Writing Process* (New York: Oxford University Press, 1981). Also see below [p. 30]: The memo-writer demanding that students "master" grammar and spelling.

[9] Discussed in Chapter 7, which refers to Douglas D. Noble's book *The Classroom Arsenal: Military Research, Information Technology, and Public Education* (Bristol, PA: The Falmer Press, Taylor and Francis, Inc., 1991). Noble traces the strong military influence on education back to 1917 when the army first legitimized the IQ test that has continued to confuse teaching and learning to the present.

title, Elbow examines neither the issue of political power nor its role in the contexts of teaching and writing. For Elbow, power is exclusively individual.

Elbow's view of writing and teaching is characteristic of many men's ambivalence about academic work.[10] He describes learning as moving between the "doubting game" and the "believing game," a seesaw of values, given out as being evenhanded but feeling so ambivalent that to resolve his own position, as Brody observes, he becomes nostalgic for traditional power. Proposing a value of "free" writing, providing a wide personal context for writing, Elbow advocates writing for its own sake as if it were a self-evident good, as if the extraction of writing from the person is the goal of writing pedagogy, which then presides over scenes of intense struggles to get that writing out. The value of purity in Elbow's work—writing without teachers, for example—applies to an individual writer's "inner meaning," a separate entity, in Elbow's view, that writing is intended to extract. The different genres and identities that combine in each person are not related to or accounted for by constituencies in society. He stresses the need to find the "true inner voice" whose pedagogical identification would convert an ordinary person into a writer.

Like many writing teachers in the academic tradition, Elbow treats the subject of writing as if it were self-contained, as if there were a writing skill before or beyond genre. Even though there are many "writing across the disciplines" projects, the fact that the subject of writing makes no sense apart from society and lived experience has not been an issue of scholarly consideration. Traditionally, this issue has been understood as one of form and content, with writing teachers teaching form and the rest of the academy content. Most critics, teachers, and researchers have viewed genre as an exclusively formal item. This perspective limits the use of genre as a means of understanding and underestimates the significance of writing. Established writing pedagogies continue to assume that the forms of writing can be taught as if they were separable from their subject matters, from their local scenes of use, from history, and from society.

---

[10] An ambivalence that has deeper roots, suggested by writings of the students discussed in Chapter 4 and by the memo discussed shortly. Elbow's book, *Embracing Contraries: Explorations in Learning and Teaching* (New York: Oxford University Press, 1986) wants to strike a unification theme. But his description of students moving back and forth between doubting and believing "games" (253–300) transmits an ambivalent message.

This is the approach mentioned in the Forethoughts section as
"spiritualist," because of the transcendent status given to meaning
and the use of writing as a tool to get the meaning out. To think
more fundamentally about genre is rather to follow a materialist
assumption, where meaning is inseparable from writing and from
society and other readers. There is a religious overtone to the spiritualist approach, as it is related to the religious project of isolating a
privileged transcendental meaning from all other meanings. This
project is closely related to the value of manly writing whose development is traced in Brody's book and tacitly used by establishmen-
tarian writing pedagogies, which depend on textbook-guided
regimens and other courses of study accepting the single factor of a
generalized writing skill.

These values emerge in other contexts in ways to which we
should be alert. The ideal of linguistic purity appears in schools'
and colleges' demands for grammatical and orthographical perfection in language use, spoken and written. Often in the presence of
English teachers, people make jokes about having to watch their linguistic hygiene, as if the main responsibility of an English teacher
were to ensure grammatical cleanliness. It is unfortunately true that
a large part of the teaching of English has been concerned with
training students to eliminate errors of speech and writing. Many
standardized writing tests work by counting technical errors and
assigning the highest scores to the examination texts with the fewest
errors. Quantitative techniques enforce the search for purity in language use and give that search an air of exaggerated urgency. The
argument is rarely made that errors inhibit comprehension by one's
audience. Rather, errors by the individual language user are
assumed to reflect a lack of competence revealing a deeper deficit in
character, discipline, intelligence, or social class. To demonstrate
this fact, here is a story that suggests the sources of the alleged defi-
cits and, in addition, many of the wider concerns necessarily
attached to local pursuits of purity in language use and writing.

A college dean appointed a temporary "committee on the writing requirement." One member was a distinguished humanist, a
teacher for many years, and the kind of faculty member most universities would be pleased to have among them. This person wrote a
one-page memo entitled "The Basic Writing Requirement: Ratio-
nale, Content, Assessment." Consider first this paragraph about the
inclusion of "sentence-level writing" as a subject in a basic writing
course:

> Grammar, punctuation, spelling. These are the fundamentals in the
> absence of which the outside world may rightly conclude that our
> students are semi-literate. Students must master the parts of

speech, gender and number, grammar basics such as verb moods
and tense, and the analysis of sentence structure. They need relentless drill in tense usage, agreement, the formation of the posses-
sive, the use of active verbs, correct punctuation and
capitalization, and editing: the elimination of contractions, collo-
quialisms, jargon, awkwardness, verbosity, redundancy, and repetition.[11] Words are precision instruments, and before students can
accurately express complex thoughts, they need drill in using
words precisely.[12]

Here are conspicuous usages of *drill* and *relentless drill.* Is it true
that drill is needed to teach students to use words as precision
instruments? Would (for example) a biologist be getting drill in
using a micrometer, or a surgeon getting drill in using a scalpel? Was
it an error in diction for a humanist to use *drill* instead of what was
probably meant: *practice?* Or did the memo writer really mean *drill?*
I think so.

At his all-male prep school the memo writer had drill in
grammar, and that is how he learned it. If I had not myself gone to an
all-male (public) high school, I might not have appreciated the sentiment of this faculty member. But I also know how fully I had assimilated the cultural weight of my school, how reliant I had become on
its psychology, and how long it took for me to recognize its antisocial character. Perhaps it is more than just antisocial; it feels somewhat paranoid:[13] "the outside world may rightly conclude that our
students are semi-literate." In the private academic context of this
memo, it may not seem conspicuous to refer to the "outside world"
in this way. But suppose this memo were given to an all-male faculty
committee on the writing requirement, appointed by the male dean?
Some committee members may already have felt a vague paranoid
opposition between "us" and "the outside world." Many faculty
members consider it ordinary to distinguish between the students at
"our university" and "the outside world." But this usage also suggests that they are worried about themselves (not the students) being
shamed or shown up by "the outside world." Because of its scrutiny,
strong measures should be taken to keep ourselves grammatically
and orthographically clean. In this cause, students must master the
fundamentals of grammatical usage. This expectation suggests the

---

[11] Yes, both redundancy and repetition should be eliminated.

[12] Sometime in the past.

[13] In a sense suggested by Naomi Scheman in "Though This Be Method . . ." Scheman
analyzed how the classical Cartesian division between mind and body depends on a
paranoid perspective: the radical separation of self from everything else, leading to the
feeling that everything else is trying to do away with the self.

compulsory quality given to learning as well as the false ideal that knowledge is power and mastery rather than understanding and affiliation with other people and the world.

The memo implies that writing should be taught by provoking students into the fear of being shamed. Its mood is not far from the mood of the following statement that Naomi Scheman cites from a 1748 German discussion on how to educate children:[14]

> Obedience is so important that all education is actually nothing other than learning how to obey. It is a generally recognized principle that persons of high estate who are destined to rule whole nations must learn the art of governance by way of first learning obedience. . . . [T]he reason for this is that obedience teaches a person to be zealous in observing the law, which is the first quality of the ruler.

This paragraph suggests that the value at work in education is a cycle of shaming, that when the shamed person accedes to power, he continues the tradition of ruling by shaming others.[15] The sentiment of the memo is that to educate others one must *make them the same as the teacher*.[16] Because to many, especially male, teachers, education has come to mean, "making students more like us," dif-

---

[14] I cite this passage from Naomi Scheman, *Engenderings*. Scheman cited it from Alice Miller, *For Your Own Good: Hidden Cruelty in Childrearing and the Roots of Violence* (1980), trans. Hildegarde and Hunter Hannum, (New York: The Noonday Press, 1990), 13. Miller cited it from "J. Sulzer, *Versuch von der Erziehung und Unterweisung der Kinder* (An Essay on the Education and Instruction of Children), 1748, quoted in Rutschky." Rutschky is Katharina Rutschky, *Schwarze Paedagogik* [Black Pedagogy], Berlin, 1977 (Miller, 282).

[15] As is done routinely in fraternities, the military, and other groups organized in male, and sometimes female, hierarchies.

[16] Some recent communitarian discussions of teaching still consider that university faculty are supposed to make it possible for students to join "our" community. While there are good intentions in this thought, especially in the work of Kenneth Bruffee, it tacitly participates in traditional narcissism, as there had been until recently no other respected way to conceptualize the interactions of teachers and students in postsecondary schools. The tacit assumption about how learning works is: you the students will learn from us the teachers. There is a further issue. Some of it was mentioned by Scheman: white men are the "unmarked" case and therefore the standard. To achieve equality, everyone else, including, women, should become white men.

Another matter may also be at work: the more privileged, consciously trying to exercise their responsibility to enhance the lives of the less privileged, see no other choice than to make the students like themselves; it is as if only their privilege defines them. They do not see that privilege is only a part of the difference and that therefore a situation of exchange (between faculty and students) is more desirable than faculty's attempts to "make them like us."

ference (from "us") is not to be treated with respect and as having its own integrity but as a sign of shame. To fail in the narcissistic remake of the young is to undermine the ideal of manliness, a historical tradition outlined by Brody in *Manly Writing*.

At the bottom of the memo is a footnote, which is supposed to be read after the clause "they need drill in using words precisely." The footnote reads,

> The fashionable notion that all "discourses" are equal in the sight of God . . . is moot in this connection. In the world as it now exists, some are more equal than others. What our students desperately need is the rigorous training in standard English that they did not receive in primary and secondary school.

The memo writer feels entitled to claim that some discourses are more equal (that is, absolutely, not relatively, better) than others. This author is saying that standard English is to be preferred to other forms of English because the "outside world" wants "our students" to behave according to some "standard." Who is to blame for this deficit? The "primary and secondary schools." This opinion makes another division between "us" and "them." The teachers of primary and secondary schools have failed to prepare "our students" for what "the world" wants, so that we in the academy must work harder to make these children like us. This memo writer may not believe that, after all, mixtures within discourses and differences between them, not equivalences of genres, are shown by comparisons of languages and dialects. Researchers do not ask if discourses are equal to one another; different discourses, rather, show both sameness and difference. This faculty member does not think about how genres actually work but tries to advocate for a separate, pure genre of standard English. The memo hints of sedition on the part of those who believe that generic difference within and between ought to be central in the study of language use and writing. Students do not "desperately" need much more than respect for who they are and what they already know in order for them to mobilize themselves to make use of a university's resources.

The memo started with "what we want the requirement to do":

> Leadership in bureaucratic-industrial societies requires the ability to think and communicate on paper. We owe it to our students and to our society to train them effectively in that craft. And intellectual discipline is impossible without standards; we therefore need to establish a minimum standard in the use of written English. Once that standard is in place, we should proselytize fiercely . . . by promising to train our students for positions of leadership by fostering their command of written argument.

As "relentless drill" stood out in the previously cited paragraph, "proselytize fiercely" stands out in this one. While the writer uses God and proselytizing metaphorically, their use shows further how the author is permitting a pedagogical proposal, presumably guided by values of generosity and care, to be overtaken by an ideal of linguistic purity as well as by evangelical and military zeal. Is this what Ernest Boyer meant in reconsidering scholarship: a Class I research university "proselytizing fiercely" prospective undergraduates on the grounds that our relentless drill in standard written English will prepare them for "leadership in bureaucratic-industrial societies"?

Leaders have professional speech writers and other writing assistants and do not take the time to write their own texts. Moreover, the memo considers more than writing itself; it implies reference to kinds of teaching other than those that directly inculcate "standards." Western social values have made it easy to lump teaching and the teaching of writing into a service or preparatory category as the memo writer has done with regard to primary and secondary school teachers. During the "service" period—childhood and early adolescence—the service had been improperly performed, so the students came to "us" unprepared, meaning without the standards that will help them become like "us." "We," however, may now do what is needed: train the students according to "our" own standards. At this point, religious metaphors say how we are guided to discern which discourses are more equal in the sight of God; converts may be sought to our religion, which is "leadership in bureaucratic-industrial society."

The memo writer needs an assessment procedure to find out "the extent to which students have 'absorbed' the items listed in paragraph (1)" (the first one cited). However, there is also concern with the degree of success of other nations: "Europeans and Japanese seem to have little difficulty in testing—and ensuring—competence in grammar and exposition." Here perhaps are two possible specifications of the general term *outside world*. We are shamed before the Europeans and Japanese because our students can't write and because we as a nation cannot compete. This is the sense in which this memo refers to more widely held values: the health of our total society is still being measured, even by those with whom we writing teachers may be sympathetic, by our ability to win out over other nations of the world.

I have taken some time with the ideal of purity because I think it a danger to society as well as to teaching and thinking. By itself, the foregoing memo may not pose problems for some; but in the context described by Brody it is socially threatening, intellectually false, and pedagogically harmful. It is important to remember the strength of values now in operation when considering changes in how to approach the study of writing and language use.

The Mixed Genre

A signal of the change in approach to genre is given by the interest in mixed genres—their "impurity" as well as their inherent change-ability. Values of greater social inclusiveness have led to this change in academic thinking, but they have not yet achieved stability or widespread understanding. The literary canon has been loosened and broadened, but genre courses like fiction, poetry, and drama are found in undergraduate catalogs, and they tacitly assume a stable formal status for genres. The historical and social contingencies of genres of language and literature have not been considered central,[17] even though from time to time people reflect on genre as if it were a helpful secondary consideration to other matters. Bakhtin, in "The Problem of Speech Genres,"[18] observes that people have been writing about genre "since antiquity." Yet it is also true that because these writings presuppose a fixed taxonomy, the genre idea has remained inert. Bakhtin, as well as Todorov, Jameson, and Fowler, have contributed to the recent reconsiderations of genre. These works have suggested that we may compare, in a sense somewhat different than the one I used, the genre idea with the Freudian unconscious. This is the sense of genre's staying power: in spite of the frequent criticism it gets, it appears again and again in the language as viable. A similar point might be made about "utopia," which, as an essential category of society is not taken too seriously but as a metaphor retains its historic vitality. There is a growth of the genre idea rather than a genre theory, and a key part of that idea is the "mixed genre."

Language and literature genres are more clearly parts of our experience when understood as signs of feeling and political interest. This approach assigns new reference to known genres and proposes the

---

[17] Ralph Cohen, "The Attack on Genre," Patton Lecture, Indiana University, Bloomington, October 16, 1984. In this lecture, Cohen raises the issue of how and why the concept and facts of genre are discredited among literary theorists. But since then, the idea has had more currency among some critics and teachers and scholars of writing and language use.

[18] M. M. Bakhtin, "The Problem of Speech Genres," *Speech Genres and Other Late Essays*, trans., Vern W. McGre; ed. Caryl Emerson and Michael Holquist (Austin: University of Texas Press, 1986), 60–102.

principle of mixture: all kinds and genres, however clearly they are
named and identified, however clearly they may appear in our daily
experience, are nevertheless combined forms, made up of other
clearly identifiable genres, each of which in turn may be identified in
at least some context. Thus, two principles with regard to the understanding of language genres are the necessary social, political, and
experiential reference of all genres, and the necessary mixture characteristic of any one kind.[19]

In his 1984 lectures and in subsequent publications in genre
theory, Ralph Cohen emphasized the principles of change and mixture. Where Peter Elbow does not make use of the fact that writing
appears in genres, Cohen views Derrida as deliberately ruling out
the necessity of genre. Yet writing cannot be handled or thought
about unless genres of writing are also admitted. His brief formulation is that one does not write "writing"; one writes novels or plays
or poems or letters, and the like.[20] Any piece of writing comes to us
in specific forms that are connected with other works in the same or
similar forms and that use still other forms as subgenres in a variety
of ways. Principal and marginal genres emerge from social purposes
and historical circumstances while they are in the process of changing these purposes and circumstances. In this way, a genre becomes
an identifiable kind or species of language that cannot be understood in and of itself but only as it exists in social and historical situations—its existential locus. Writing appears in a form that is made
up of several other forms that, like the form identifying the writing
now, should be understood as being in the midst of social and historical change. Even though, for example, one could conceivably
think of *Finnegan's Wake* as a dream tract, its present historical

---

[19] In addition to Cohen's Patton Lecture (see note 17, above), I cite material from
informal conversations with him, September 24, 1984, and six weeks or so following.
Other citations from Cohen are from his lecture "The Autobiography of a Critical
Problem," presented at the annual meeting of the Midwest Modern Language
Association, Bloomington, Indiana, November 4, 1984. Cohen's concept of the mixed
genre gives the concept of genre the flexibility and range of practical application not
found in previous genre theories. Other discussions of genre by Cohen are "Afterword:
The Problems of Generic Transformation," in K. and M. S. Brownlee, eds., *Romance:
Generic Transformation from Chretien de Troyes to Cervantes* (Hanover, NH:
University Press of New England, 1985), 265–280; "History and Genre," *New Literary
History* 17 (No. 2, Winter 1986), 203–218; and "Do Postmodern Genres Exist?" in
Marjorie Perloff, ed., *Postmodern Genres* (Norman: University of Oklahoma Press,
1989), 10–27.

[20] It is this fact that is least in evidence in the teaching of writing and language use.

form is the novel, though this way of identifying that book could change into a dream tract or a joke or something else by succeeding generations of readers.

This is a materialist use of the genre idea. Cohen has conceived genre as not separable from works and their living situations in the same sense that meanings are not separable from words and their interpersonal contexts of use. In his 1984 response to Derrida, Cohen emphasizes the latter's theoretical excess. He views Derrida's formulations regarding the variability of meaning and genre as correct, but he implies that genres cannot be canceled or denied as a matter of principle: they are there because they are tied to the identity (or lack thereof) of social groups and larger societies.

Cohen's distinctive contribution is the following: "Genre naming or grouping is inevitably both necessary and loose."[21] Traditional approaches to this feature of genres have been constrained by an unacknowledged need to choose between necessary and loose, and Derrida is traditional in this regard. Either there are boundaries or there aren't; for boundaries to be both necessary and loose challenges the axioms of hierarchy and noncontradiction, and represents a fundamental change in the status of definitions as they are used in theoretical discussions. Rather than the abstraction "writing" (which implies a certain equivalence of all kinds), historical, social, and cultural practices and experiences of living people are the points of reference for understanding genres of language, literature, and other writing. The material differences in practice and experience lead to the necessity, though not to the rigidity, of boundaries. The experiences, practices, their boundaries, and their populations all must be identified in their relation to the written forms with which they are associated.

To pursue this task of accurately identifying categories is "to reject the belief that anonymity stimulates fairness."[22] Genres are necessarily political. Anonymity—the habit of nonrecognition of genres—practices nondisclosure and affirmative self-removal. The tacit social wish that anonymity does or should create fairness has kept mixed genres and politically identified or self-conscious genres in the closet. The wish lies behind the false ideological commonplace that it doesn't matter what your race, gender, economic class, or national origin is. For students, faculty, and others to engage in research to self-identify and self-disclose without fear of adverse judgment, graded or otherwise, is to show how much these and

---

[21] Ralph Cohen, "The Autobiography of a Critical Problem."

[22] Ralph Cohen, "The Autobiography of a Critical Problem."

other categories do matter. Not to give one's name and not to name is unfair because tacitly both the categories and the names are being assumed and applied.

If individual people, texts, genres are recognized through being named, it is also true that the name could be understood differently when different elements in a category are more germane. Depending on the observers, there is a range of possible categorical identities in society. To allow that there are genres is to allow that they are always made up of subkinds or cokinds and that the particular mix of each category varies with culture as well as with the perspectives of local observers. The principle of mixed genres of language is an aspect of the fact that there are no pure kinds, genres, species, or languages because culture is always changing.

Lately, some literary critics, aware of the usefulness of genre for political discussion, have reflected on mixed genres and border crossings. One such critic is Diane Freedman,[23] whose key term is cross-genre. Her instances are mixed, like food with distinct ingredients that work together to make a recognizable dish. In addition to the Bible, a text demonstrating generic diversity, Freedman mentions Tristram Shandy and The Song of Solomon for their collections of literary kinds. She writes,

> Yet we still know what to call these works while we are less sure what to call and how to read the mixed-genre prose of a variety of contemporary feminists. Marginalized women's border-crossing critical amalgams usually depend both more heavily and more obviously than novels on the autobiographical, often making explicit their practical or political as well as literary etiologies and aims. Feminist poet-critics strive to weave the practical and material aspects of their lives into a literary mosaic. (69)

Contemporary genres, even if there is dispute over how to identify them, must nevertheless be genres. The disputes themselves are the processes of their being recognized as genres. If they were not recognized, there would be no reason to negotiate how they are to be identified.[24] Older mixed genres have a received identity, as Freedman observes. However, Freedman's book is a combination of life writing, poetry, and criticism. She assembles other authors who use this mixture, and she uses her book to include herself in that community. The loose boundaries and the crossed borders represent a constituency,

---

[23] Diane P. Freedman, An Alchemy of Genres: Cross-Genre Writing by American Feminist Poet-Critics (Charlottesville: University of Virginia Press, 1992).

[24] Ralph Cohen, "Do Postmodern Genres Exist?" in Postmodern Genres (Norman: University of Oklahoma Press, 1989), 11–27.

American feminist poet-critics, that is partly identified by this combination of older forms: poetry, criticism, and autobiography. The task of scholarship is to try, collectively, to identify new forms in relation to history and society. This task is always changing because there are always new voices and new categories of people rearranging themselves and their interests in society.

An additional point is made by Cohen: the critical essay, which is a frequent site of discussion that helps to identify new genres, is itself a genre in the process of change:

> The critical and theoretical essay—and my essay is another example of this—is a genre that has come to be practiced more frequently in the late modernist and postmodernist periods than at any time previously in English literary history. To recognize it as a kind of writing, as a genre, is to demonstrate some of the functions it has for us. The essay is not merely a part of anthologies; it is a genre of its own and critics have traced its changes from Montaigne to the present.[25]

For a critic to raise the issue of genre is also to acknowledge self-implication in literary, social, and historical processes that are being studied from academic starting points. The self-inclusion through autobiography practiced by Freedman and those writing in veins similar to hers (see Chapter 1) becomes significant because its generic novelty—its use in a new combination—has a historical and collective foundation. In addition to new combinations of individual voices, new collectivities are brought together.

Even though Freedman's identity may be in a status of change of coming out as a "mixed" person,[26] it is already an identity—in the process of change, yet identifiable: "necessary and loose." The same could be said of Patricia Williams, as she appears in *The Alchemy of Race and Rights*;[27] the same idea, alchemy, seemed to have come to these two authors in related causes—the establishment of new constituencies. Furthermore, Williams and Freedman are joined by others who have taken up self-inscription as part of scholarship. By including autobiographical writing these critics try to identify as responsibly as possible their public purposes, constraints, and interests, in order that readers of their (our) work, may be reliably guided.

---

[25] Ralph Cohen, "Do Postmodern Genres Exist?" in *Postmodern Genres* (Norman: University of Oklahoma Press, 1989), 24.

[26] In her book she recounts what it is like to be, like Adrienne Rich, "split at the root," in Freedman's case, having a Catholic mother and a Jewish father.

[27] Patricia Williams, *The Alchemy of Race and Rights* (Cambridge, MA: Harvard University Press, 1990).

Genres as Lived Experiences

The idea of lived experience, increasingly used in ethnographic
work in and out of anthropology, describes the changing character of
genres; it connects formal and ritualized elements of social activity
with subjective, phenomenological experience. A text, literary or
not, becomes a genre by virtue of people "living" it among other
people. Groups of people "live" a text or language by reading, speaking, and recognizing it as having some collective status. It is perhaps
easier to see how language genres live when considering instances
of language in actual use. The fact that genres are living and not formal or fixed makes it easier to grasp them as made up of subgenres
and being in continuous processes of change. Viewing genres as
lived experience rather than abstract categories brings out their usefulness as ways of understanding the relations between language
and culture.

Focusing on the relationship between a subordinate language
dialect and a dominant one shows how to view genre as a form of
lived experience. The presence of Spanish and English in the same
society, as Victor Villanueva discussed in *Bootstraps,* makes it hard
to maintain a rigid division between the two languages; he
belonged to groups that spoke "Spanglish." In my experience, Yiddish grammar, vocabulary, and diction have combined with
English to produce incrementally new versions of the English that I
speak; but these new versions may not be identifiable to those
unfamiliar with Yiddish. In Yiddish, English words get into the
daily speech and "become" Yiddish; for some, these are familiar
phenomena.

The relation of Yiddish to German and (in part) to English (i.e.,
to dominant-culture languages) is similar to the relation of Black
English to English. Yiddish is a transformed, adapted German written in the Hebrew alphabet. It gradually became a standard vernac-
ular, just as Black English is. As language kinds, both Yiddish and
Black English are spoken in relatively well-defined communities in
larger and dominant cultures. Yet the members of both communities participate in the larger cultures and aim, partly, to assimilate
in order to become of status equal to the members of the dominant
culture. Assimilation requires the fluent use of the dominant language dialect. Alongside the process of assimilation is the process
of cultivating and nurturing the historically received communal
identities. Regardless of how strong the need for the benefits of
assimilation, there is another need, varying in degree with each person, in members of the subordinate cultures to retain the forms of
"one's own." A pride in one's distinctiveness develops, and the use

of this native sublanguage, including its manifestation in literature, film, and other symbolic, material forms, becomes gradually richer and more authoritative as a carrier of the culture of its people. In the nineteenth and twentieth centuries, Yiddish developed a rich written literature, poetry, and drama. Similarly, African American culture transformed its oral materials into the written genres of the dominant culture. Only recently is this literature getting public notice.

Black English is a mixed genre of language, in the terms we have been discussing.[28] It is English with a somewhat different grammar, vocabulary, and diction. Also, the ways in which new words appear are different from the ways in White Standard English.[29] In spite of the many elements in Black English that are distinctive, and the many that overlap with White English, in spite of the complexity of the relation between the two dialects, we speakers of English have no trouble identifying either Black or White English. We can detect holistic differences as well as secondary or partial differences. In teaching language use and writing our interest is to sort out the meanings of the various differences and samenesses as they bear on our prospective uses of language for most of our public, adult lives.

To show how awareness of genre as a lived experience provides a practical basis for the teaching of writing and language use, I consider two instances; one I experienced in an urban secondary school in Rochester and one as described by June Jordan from her undergraduate teaching experience. I then consider briefly these scenes of teaching in relation to the use of genre by teachers of writing. Each instance suggests that awareness of genres of language and of how these genres identify social interests helps teachers recognize what they and students bring to classrooms.

The Ninth-Grade Classroom

In the fall of 1990, I was a guest teacher for about six months in a ninth-grade classroom in an urban high school in Rochester, New York. This class' regular teacher was a white woman of approximately

---

[28] The Ebonics furor of 1996–97 was about the teaching of Black English but not about whether it exists. It is noteworthy how the proposal to teach it and standard English as a bilingual enterprise makes so many people doubt the intentions of the teachers with regard to achieving equal status for African American students.

[29] Itself a mixture of German, French, Latin, Greek, and many others.

my age.[30] One of our early subjects was the difference between proper and improper English. We had class discussions and essays on this topic. There was an essay assignment that asked students to discuss what they considered the difference between proper and improper English. Here is Ms. K's contribution:

> I miraculously bit into one of my sister's rock-hard meatballs and crunched noisily. I'd seen my brother try to feed a meatball to the dog who had turned up his nose and started eating the cat's food.
>
> "Tommy pass me the sauce please," my sister asked kicking the meatball that my brother left on the floor. When my mom and dad left the dinner table, my brother rudely said, "I ain't passing you nothing." I passed her the sauce and said, "Ain't ain't a word." "Yes it is," my sister piped up, "I saw it in the dictionary."
>
> "So?" my brother snapped.
>
> "Hey," my mom said peeking her head into the kitchen, "who's saying 'ain't'"?
>
> "Mom is ain't a word?"
>
> "Well it all depends on what you think proper English is."
>
> "Proper English is not talking slang," my sister said clearing the table and rolling her eyes.
>
> "Yo girly stop sweating my talk," my brother said grabbing his glass.
>
> "See mommy that's improper English," my sister said baby-ishly.
>
> My father pushed past my mother and said, "There is no proper or improper English, as long as you talk so that someone can understand you." Everyone glared at my brother.
>
> "Yo," he said loudly, "ain't no proper or improper English."
>
> My sister stuck her tongue out at my brother before saying, "Yo, young blood how's about if you let me whip the sneakers off you in a game of king's checkers."
>
> Everyone laughed.

Two sets of issues suggested by this text are those connected with proper and improper English in the situation presented by Ms. K, and those presented by the fact that this was Ms. K's response to the essay assignment. The scene at the dinner table has five people, the two parents and the three siblings. The use of *ain't* in the text is connected with the difference between Black English and White English understood as a standard. Both are spoken in this family.

---

[30] This is the same classroom described in my essay "Reading as Membership," *ADE Bulletin* (Fall 1992): 6–10, where I discussed the students' responses to two stories by Zora Neale Hurston. Several African American students were disturbed that the language in the Hurston stories seemed to represent "how African Americans speak." See note 32, below.

Ms. K characterizes the sister's complaint as "babyish." Ms. K takes both sides of the argument: "ain't ain't a word," she said. But she portrays her sister and mother as holding an opinion different from her brother and father. The female family members are concerned with propriety; the males with spontaneity. At the end, the sister understands both sides and reconciles with the brother. In addition to sibling rivalry, and adolescents and adults, the family's conversation represents black and white, male and female, rich and poor. At some level, Ms. K is aware of these issues and represents each in a different genre.

Ms. K, a precocious and gifted fourteen-year-old student, speaks and writes perfect White English: "I miraculously bit into one of my sister's rock-hard meatballs and crunched noisily." This keynote of her "essay" is given to the two white teachers of her class. She has credentialed herself in the authoritative dialect. She is also an imaginative writer, and one who has been reading a great deal, so she includes the secondary comedy about the dog and the meatball on the floor. In making these moves, and in presenting a story with a dramatic dialogue embedded in it, she declines the discursive-essay assignment that other students wrote. While respectful of school, teachers, and White English, Ms. K substituted one kind of language—the fictionalized narrative dialogue that addresses the assignment metaphorically—for another, the reflective commentary, which would have been a more referential genre.

Classmates of Ms. K had other observations about proper and improper English. Two male students said that proper English is what the rich speak or what those who went to college speak. Another female student wrote "when the women used to wear those big dresses they talk very proper they say things like 1. yes Madam, 2. yes Sir, 3. no Madam, 4. no Sir." For the two boys, the economic-class identification preceded the identification of the language: to them, economic and social classes determine the propriety of the language. The girls, while indirectly identifying the determining class—the women in "big dresses"—further identify obedient language as being the sign of propriety.

These samples suggest that the students had a good basis for learning to distinguish different kinds of language and what each kind means. Both accomplished students and less accomplished ones are aware of who speaks what language, and of the quality and character of those different kinds. Like most ninth-grade students, these lack the experience and discipline to think through their knowledge at some length. However, they understand that each dialect is a genre in the sense of its appropriateness being determined by social values held by the speakers in those specific situations.

The curriculum, however, does not ask them to do this thinking. It asks them to master White Standard English, a necessary task, most teachers (white and black) agree, but not a task that responds to the strongest of these students' motivations. In most classes, "Yo girly stop sweating my talk" is confined to the peripheral conversations of students. In many classes, particularly crowded ones, there is no space to stop and think about the fact that Ms. K, like other African American students, habitually shifts among (at least) two dialects each marked by race and class and often by gender. There is no time to think that all students speak different kinds of language as they move between different classes and communities. In the university there is no time to think that even the most homogeneous group of students enters college with a comparable array of language use genres, each living in its own context, each governed by social and political conventions that are taken for granted and not considered eligible to participate in the teaching of writing.

June Jordan's Classroom

June Jordan's essay "Nobody Mean More to Me Than You and the Future Life of Willie Jordan"[31] explores the foregoing issues as they appeared in one of her undergraduate classrooms. Itself an instance of a mixed genre, her essay may be read as an account of teaching the principle of mixed genres in language use and writing, showing how language is inextricable from the situations of its use. The main event of the essay is the report of a decision by a class of undergraduates to take public action by using the genre written Black English. Although one cannot identify an origin for this genre, it is relatively new and rare. Black English has been mostly oral. However, assimilation and integration into white society produced more and more instances of that orality being recorded by writers and researchers, so that in written form the new genre is not quite the same as oral Black English.[32] As Jordan describes it, her class passed through, in a dramatic way, this change in genre.

---

[31] June Jordan, "Nobody Mean More to Me Than You and the Future Life of Willie Jordan," in *On Call: Political Essays* (Boston: South End Press, 1985), 123–139. Thanks to Marianne Milton for calling my attention to this essay.

[32] As another student's family implied, in the discussion of the response by members of the same class as Ms. K's to the Hurston stories in my essay "Reading as Membership." This is the phenomenon of black students rejecting Black English when they see it in print: because it seems to be a different genre, it also seems to be in some sense not theirs.

Jordan's mixture of genres gives her essay a wider-than-ordinary scope. The first four paragraphs in conventional academic essayese provide a background of not-so-well-known facts that go with the "story" (so named by Jordan) that she is recounting. These facts have to do with the worldwide spread of English, a second language in thirty-three countries and a native language for more than three hundred thirty million people. The living language must be affected by each of the cultures in which it appears, and such effects are continuously felt as residents of these countries move back and forth to other countries. In the United States, Jordan considers, in spite of the thirty million African American speakers of English, "white standards of English persist, supreme and unquestioned" (124). This is in contrast to India, "where at least fourteen languages co-exist as legitimate Indian languages, and in contrast to Nicaragua, where all citizens are legally entitled to formal school instruction in their regional or tribal languages" (124). Thus, the "internal" control of English in the United States creates a tension between its "standard" language practitioners and others who speak English, perpetuating a basis of social inequality indefinitely. This is clearly the case in the relation of White to Black English.

In the main part of the essay, the story with other genres contributing, Jordan's class at SUNY Stony Brook of mostly black and five or six white students learns about the integrity and status of Black English: they moved from considering it a substandard or secondary dialect to seeing it as an important medium indigenous to the culture into which the black students were born and in which they now live and expect to perpetuate. Like the ninth-grade students in Ms. K's class, the undergraduates could not accept the written version of language they themselves speak, as given in Alice Walker's *The Color Purple*:

You better not never tell nobody but God. It'd kill your mammy.

Dear God,

I am fourteen years old. I have always been a good girl. Maybe you can give me a sign letting me know what is happening to me.

Last spring after Little Lucious come I hear them fussing. He was pulling on her arm. She say it too soon, Fonso. I ain't well. Finally he leave her alone. A week go by, he pulling on her arm again. She say, Naw, I ain't gonna. Can't you see I'm already half dead, an all of the children. (125)

Of this passage the students said, in Black English, "'Why she have them talk so funny. It don't sound right. . . . It don't look right neither'" (125).

Such moments happened in my ninth-grade class, and probably also happen in other classes that study writers who recorded the oral vernaculars. They are moments of change in language, where one kind becomes another. The writing of Black English enlarges its locus in community conversation toward a school context that can facilitate the community's self-conscious participation in the mainstream or dominant culture. Both cultures then change in ways that Standard English advocates cannot affect, except by authoritarian fiat, which in language matters has little chance of working. There is no choice but to recognize Hurston and Walker, and their special representations of Black English, as part of the language and literature curriculum, and there is no choice but to recognize what happened to Jordan's students.

Jordan wanted to teach black students about the value of their history and language. Her technique was to translate the Walker passage into White English:

> *Absolutely, one should never confide in anybody besides God. Your secrets could prove devastating to your mother.*
>
> Dear God,
>
> I am fourteen years old. I have always been good. But now, could you help me to understand what is happening to me?
>
>   Last spring, after my little brother, Lucius, was born, I heard my parents fighting. My father kept pulling at my mother's arm, But she told him, "It's too soon for sex, Alfonso. I am still not feeling well." Finally, my father left her alone. A week went by, and then he began bothering my mother, again: Pulling her arm. She told him, "No, I won't! Can't you see I'm already exhausted from all of these children?"

Says Jordan, "Our favorite line was 'It's too soon for sex, Alphonso'" (126). She tells how once the hilariousness of this translation was absorbed, once the students realized the authenticity of their own language as compared to the translation, the curriculum changed, and the task was to teach and learn Black English.[33]

Another shift of genre in Jordan's essay is to a biographical/autobiographical rendition of how June Jordan met and related to Willie Jordan. There is a characterization of the relationship between teacher and student: "He looked like a wrestler. . . . His extreme fit-

---

[33] One of Eddie Murphy's achievements in comedy is his unerring reproduction of some of the more pompous and ridiculous tropes of oral White English. Understanding its comedy could disclose more affirmative aspects of both the black and white cultures in the United States.

ness, the muscular density of his presence underscored the riveted, gentle attention that he gave to anything anyone said" (126). This was a course in contemporary women's poetry, and June Jordan is thinking about how unusual it was for him and other black men to be taking this course. Willie Jordan took the poetry course while the Black English course June Jordan had planned was getting approval. While June Jordan taught the Black English course, Willie was taking an independent study with her on South Africa and had kept his conference appointments regularly. However, he suddenly stopped showing up because his older brother Reggie was killed by the police. This experience became a topic in June Jordan's Black English course.

With the recounting of this situation, June Jordan's essay again changes its genre. For several pages, Jordan lists and describes principles, rules, and qualities of Black English so that her class, as well as those who read her essay, can understand the rules and get a sense of the living feel of the language, its heartbeat and backbone.

A distinctive feature of Black English, according to Jordan, is its representation of "the fact of the human being who is here and now, the truth of the person who is speaking or listening" (129). In a sense, Black English seizes the present moment by using present tenses to describe things that already happened and that will happen. Neither the present nor the speaker can be taken out of the language. One result of this feature is that there is no passive construction in Black English. Another is its eschewing of abstract generalization in favor of metaphorical expression. The measure of linguistic efficacy (not of correctness) is whether it sounds as if someone can or did say it. Pursuant to this thought is the relative unimportance of spelling and the relative importance of syntax—the arrangement of things to be said. A key role of syntax is to create clarity:

> If your idea, your sentence, assumes the presence of at least two living and active people, you will make it understandable because the motivation behind every sentence is the wish to say something real to somebody real. (129)

This principle of Black English is a statement that assumes the mixture of speech and writing. June Jordan suggests that writing could be conceived of as "saying that assumes living people." One can assume in different ways—a hypothetical way, for example, and a presuppositional way. Jordan undoubtedly means the latter; the former describes how writing teachers ask students to assume (hypothesize) a certain audience. In this way the assumption is impersonal. The students are sometimes asked to assume they are writing for people they are not likely to meet, as in an assignment like "persuade a court about the death penalty." If you assume by stipulating actual living people, however, it will be easier to write/speak from and through experience and to avoid guessing at hypothetical language uses. For Jordan, assuming living people is either writing to extend the relationship with people one already knows, or writing toward people with whom one has some "business." Such invocation of present relationships and experience seems to be Jordan's meaning of the real. Jordan's vision of a unified language has very little that is fictional in the usual sense. This is a materialist conception of language: everything is in one category: *the told,* and there is no abstract distinction between the truth and the lie; there is the practical distinction relative to the trust levels in real relationships. While in White English usage, fiction is often considered to be a lie, it would not be so in Black English usage: rather, a way to express an intermediary sense of whether something is true or not would be to say, "I don't know but I've been told." In Black English, there is less of a demand that the truth be given in a literal sense; the active concept of truth has to do with the reliability of interpersonal relationships, with the integrity of society, with the possibility of attaining the promise of one's community and society. Literal truth is part of Black English, but it has a role different from literal truth in White English.

Unable to get an explanation from the police or anyone else regarding Reggie's murder (the story Willie Jordan told June Jordan to explain his absence from his independent study conferences), the students in the Black English class considered how they should respond. The story he told was that "Brooklyn police had murdered his unarmed, twenty-five year old brother, Reggie Jordan. . . . Police ran his family around and around, . . . And Reggie was really dead. And Willie wanted to fight, but he felt helpless" (134). The question for the Black English class was not what to say but what to do. But the only available form of doing was saying. There were several people to speak to, but it was finally agreed that the police needed most to be addressed, rather than the press or the mayor, and so on. The class discussed whether, as a group, to open their statement in Black or Standard English. On the discussion that followed, June Jordan commented:

> I have seldom been privy to a discussion with so much heart at the dead heat of it. I will never forget the eloquence, the sudden haltings of speech, the fierce struggle against tears, the furious throwaway, and useless explosions that this question elicited. . . .
>
> How best to serve the memory of Reggie Jordan? Should we use the language of the killers—Standard English—in order to make our ideas acceptable to those controlling the killers? But wouldn't what we had to say be rejected, summarily, if we said it in our own language, the language of the victim, Reggie Jordan?

But if we sought to express ourselves by abandoning our language would that mean our suicide on top of Reggie's murder? But if we expressed ourselves in our own language wouldn't that be suicidal to the wish to communicate with those who, evidently, did not give a damn about us/Reggie/police violence in the Black community? (135)

This is a real, i.e., true (!), story, so to analyze it for genres may seem not to be participating in its emotional urgency. But analysis should not be assumed to preclude passion; it can take up, transform, and enlarge the issues, facts, or events that were the occasion of this class' outcries. Analysis helps to show that when any writing or language use achieves this degree of commitment, conviction, feeling, and energy, it contributes to the needs and purposes, political and otherwise, of the speakers/writers to understand kinds, registers, styles, and genres of language as choices of social participation. To choose to act, speak, or write in a genre is to make a social choice that matters.

The first paragraph in the previous citation is Jordan's report characterizing the discussion in terms of *its* genres—eloquence and haltings, struggles and throwaways. How conversational these forms of language seem to be; yet they are important because the variation was unique in Jordan's experience: a mobilization of the widest range of thought and feeling with so much "heart at the dead heat of it," a demonstration that language is created by passionate purpose. The second paragraph, in its interrogative forms, presents the mutual challenges each person posed to others: they are different forms, different versions, different aspects, different ingredients of "that one question." An interrogative must always emerge from an interpersonal situation of speech and mutual engagement. One way to put that one question is, What communication will amount to the best action? What things said/written will take the class' passion and pass it through to those who least want to recognize it? What speech will be an act? How can a linguistic articulation be presented so that it cannot be reduced to mere words? The answer is the following paragraph from the letter the class wrote:

... YOU COPS!

WE THE BROTHER AND SISTER OF WILLIE JORDAN, A FELLOW STONY BROOK STUDENT WHO THE BROTHER OF THE DEAD REGGIE JORDAN. REGGIE, LIKE MANY BROTHER AND SISTER, HE A VICTIM OF BRUTAL RACIST POLICE, OCTOBER 25, 1984. US APPALL, FED UP, BECAUSE THAT ANOTHER SENSELESS DEATH WHAT OCCUR IN OUR COMMUNITY. THIS WHAT WE FEEL, THIS, FROM OUR HEART, FOR WE AIN'T STAYIN' SILENT NO MORE. (136)

June Jordan reported that while the Black English underscored the feelings of solidarity in the class, the protest was in fact not heard, even by a black officer who spoke to the class, informing them of the feeling among police of all colors that if you don't overreact, you are underreacting and risking death yourself. Supervening the struggles of race is the ethic of lethal force. Male violence is not singled out by June Jordan, but it comes through as a factor in her description of the total situation. She cites Willie Jordan's final essay in the independent study, which related, in Standard English, the situation of police violence in South Africa to the police violence that killed his brother. Willie wrote, "to a large degree, justice may only exist as rhetoric. . . . Something has to be done about the way in which this world is set up" (138–139). This is the unwelcome outcome of June Jordan's reflection: no matter which English is used, justice boils down only to rhetoric, and police violence is what seems to determine how "this world is set up." Part of the Jordans' thoughts could be that the supervention of violence perpetuates the separation of language from action, deauthorizes language, and converts even its best instances to mere words. While the struggle for identity among June Jordan's students brings out the pragmatic relevances of the mixtures of the oral and the written, Black and White English, this struggle also stands alone in public, defeated by armed men in groups from two to two million.

In her book *The Violence of Literacy*,[34] J. Elspeth Stuckey cites June Jordan's continuing question, "What to Do? What to Do?" (122). Graduate students starting their training to be teachers of writing become impatient on reading Stuckey's book only to come to the end and find the question posed regarding "what to do?" According to the students, the book was supposed to answer the question, not ask it. However, in the context of the struggle Jordan presented in her essay, Stuckey's answer is a good one, even if it will take time for the apprentice teachers to learn it. Stuckey observes,

> Students of nonstandard languages in the United States do not fail because of a language failure; they fail because they live in a society that lies about language. We in English in an information economy in a country that calls itself free make the lie palpable. (122)

The lie about language is what Willie Jordan concluded: language is presented as if it were part of social relations and it rarely is at the moments when it is most needed; it was mere rhetoric, as Willie Jordan observed. Whatever language people learn, it is kept separate

---

[34] J. Elspeth Stuckey, *The Violence of Literacy* (Portsmouth, NH: Boynton/Cook, 1991).

from society by specific values and practices of mainstream society. The immediate palpability of the language, its materiality, which June Jordan suggests characterizes Black English, is not important in the public communities of Standard English. However, regardless of what languages are spoken, the use of language is usually overruled by force and violence.

Genre and Writing Pedagogy

An interesting but provocative discussion of how to integrate the genre idea into writing pedagogy appears in Michael B. Prince's 1989 essay "Literacy and Genre: Towards a Pedagogy of Mediation."[35] He proposes a sequence of assignments for an introductory writing course that moves from the study and use of conversational genres such as letter writing and dialogue, toward decreasingly conversational forms such as summary and argument. Prince values the use of genre as fundamental for the teaching of writing, but he presupposes that the "essayist literacy" advocated in postsecondary writing programs, including writing across the curriculum, is and will remain the standard: "Missing from Elbow's celebration of freewriting is an indication of how students are to move from lyrical self-expression to success writing in school" (745). Prince's sample syllabus is aimed, therefore, to disrupt the

> inherited understanding of "the essay" in order to promote a more meaningful relation to essayist literacy. By the time most students enter college, the command to write an essay evokes a complex interlocking system of directives. These include the requirements to frame a deductive thesis, to expunge the first person pronoun, to begin each paragraph with a topic statement, to generalize specifics and to specify generalities, and so on. Such directives convey strong messages about what kinds of knowledge count and where one may look to find such knowledge. This system extends its influence over writing within all the variations of the essay mode (analysis, comparison-contrast, even narration and description). (744)

The teaching strategy proposed by Prince aims to reach the foregoing point through the self-conscious "disruptive" use of genre in the writing projects of his courses. Will such disruptions have a desirable effect?

---

[35] Michael B. Prince, "Literacy and Genre: Towards a Pedagogy of Mediation," *College English* 51 (November 1989): 730–749.

I don't think so, even though the different assignments, such as "letter of biographical introduction to a classmate," are pedagogically interesting and likely to motivate writing. The problem posed by Prince's syllabus is that essayist literacy is its purpose. The generic variations in that syllabus seem like practice runs for "real" writing, the directives for which students already have learned in high school, as Prince observes. He advocates a "change in generic context and in particular a shift toward genres that inscribe a sense of writing as direct communication" (745). But he thinks that this ideal can be enacted "even if our eventual goal is to have students write the kinds of decontextualized, analytical essays required within most colleges" (745).

This standard of writing is connected to the hierarchical values now increasing their influence in universities, values that were in recession when expressive writing was introduced. To continue teaching students to create decontextualized analytical essays is a political statement about teaching as well as an approach to writing that is only marginally suitable for the population mixtures now in postsecondary schools. Similarly, teaching through genre is a political as well as a pedagogical change, as is teaching language use as the cosubject of writing. Keeping the decontextualized essay as a goal communicates an ideology of language use that many are repudiating. As Prince observes, to convey "strong messages" about "what counts as knowledge" is political as well as epistemological. If we believe that the search for knowledge is embedded in its social, political, and cultural environments, for students to believe that the decontextualized essay is privileged helps to revoke the understanding of genre gained in other parts of the writing syllabus described by Prince.

Teaching genre and disclosure responds to the needs of changing populations in postsecondary classrooms. One of the achievements of the alertness to genre is that it is easier to integrate intellectual and imaginative (academic?) interests with the immediate social needs of language users and writers. In addition, it is essential to disclose and to identify individuals and their affiliations in order to find the most helpful styles of teaching and learning. Consequently, a third factor in the combination of values explored in this book is the membership of classes that are teaching and learning language use and writing.

Chapter Three

Language Use as Membership

Language Use as Membership

People's literacies and language uses reflect their different sets of memberships in society. How and what one reads and writes are governed by interpersonal and collective conditions. Although this fact has been recognized by theorists and researchers,[1] pedagogical mores and social structures have overridden this recognition consistently because school planners, administrators, and many teachers have followed the pattern of teaching a subject by isolating it from other subjects and from society. In school, literacy and language use have been detached from the sense of membership they create in each person, in each group.

Scholars have considered literacy a self-evident good only on the basis of their having separated it from its living contexts. Its independent goodness having been established as an accepted value, the teaching of literacy then tries to separate reading from writing, language from language use; it tries to hide the materiality of language, its inseparability in experience from the scenes of its

---

[1] In the research on language use, this thought goes back to the 1930s, to L. S. Vygotsky and G. H. Mead, as I discuss in *The Double Perspective* (New York: Oxford University Press, 1988; NCTE, 1993). Their view, today, still not in the mainstream, is that children's exposure to the collectivity of language use leads them to internalize its social and dialogic shapes. This means that individual language use on any occasion is a manifestation of an internalized combination of social contexts.

use. The distinction between language and language use[2] participates in separations of theory and practice, of ideas and application,
to the disadvantage of practice and application, use and experience—the material contexts. Academic tradition has separated
thought from practice and has kept the former in a higher status;
this tradition has also kept the question of the social memberships
of students and teachers away from the study of language use and
writing, from the study of how people speak, hear, read, and write,
from the experiences of language use.

In college, cultivating first-language capability is separate from
studying other subject matters. Writing courses supply the necessary but arbitrary contexts: any subject "of interest" to the teachers
(and often, supervisors) accompanied by hypothetical readers. The
teaching of literature involves the study of history and society, but
not usually the social memberships of "these readers in this class."
Reading through one's membership involves several factors: the rec-
ommender, the work, the subject as historically portrayed, and the
language—as written and as read/heard—which are combined into
something that can be experienced, something pertaining to the
reader's life situation at the time of reading. This experience can
then in new ways rejoin the reader to family, to loved ones, to culture, to language, and to other parts of oneself, to values commonly
held. Reading a work at a given time enacts one's membership in
several communities beyond the immediate. Through a similar process, writing gains us access to language so as to enact membership
in our communities.[3]

Beyond saying or writing things, language use means speaking
up, speaking out, identifying in public what others are passing over
(or perhaps concealing), awakening oneself and others to new, even
if incrementally so, social situations. The fact that uses of language
enact and change memberships is increasingly visible in public and
academic forums. On the one hand, reading from within a society,
from the position of citizen, is assumed in school; but on the other

---

[2] This is the same distinction on which Noam Chomsky bases his views of language:
his own work is addressed to "competence" (language); "performance" (language use)
is "mysterious" and not susceptible of scientific study, in his view. Chomsky's view of
language depends on the separateness of the spirit and the letter—the Cartesian
perspective.

[3] With this in mind, see the discussion of Mr. B in Chapter 4. He related the
heterosexuality of *Star Trek* to the heterosexuality of his membership in the male high
school community; his new sense of euphemism rearticulated his gender
memberships. Writing was an act of self-affiliation enabled by the present classroom
context, of recognizing his memberships, and in part of changing them.

hand, each person's citizenship is differently configured from a social standpoint. Those who feel, or are, excluded often pretend membership. Their literacies have a different character. Yet most people are partly in and partly out of any social or school groups in which they find themselves. Most people need to pretend to some extent in order to seem to belong. To understand that one reads and writes through and for membership is to transform language use from a highly individualized activity of self-regulation and self-enhancement to one less clear in method but more familiar in purpose: finding interests in common with readers, authors, and cultures different from ourselves, and identifying the membership, as well as the individual identity, of all. To study language use and literacy in this way is to reduce the need for pretending, and to increase the effort at identifying oneself in multiple senses. These multiple memberships and individual identities are connected to how we already speak and write and what we read: our language and reading genres reflect our interpersonal genres—that is, our relationships and group identities. Attention to language use and memberships lets us feel the public effects of what we may have once thought was a subject confined to school.

Study of different groups of literary respondents shows that even in seemingly homogeneous groups of readers the differences of perception, emphasis, and value among individual readers are so various as to defeat any attempt to predict similar responses. Each class, each group, each collection of readers must, through some degree of self-disclosure, go through the process of finding differences of individual memberships, as well as the common memberships of many, most, and all.

To think of language use as membership markers implies that each person participates in the other, the outgroup, the not-me and the not-us.[4] Disclosure activities teach us about our total configuration of allegiances and help us to discover those of which we were not aware. In classrooms, studying language use means entertaining new memberships. Sometimes literary responses enlarge our perceptions of whose literature a particular work could be. We try to find out how the language of any work of literature can become our

---

[4] When we consider ourselves members, there is always a "them" who are non-members, often considered strange, bad, or inferior. In some situations, nonmembers are considered to be contaminants, a situation that obtained in the search for a pure language standard (see Chapter 2). Majority and minority members often consider each other "them."

own. The study of language and literature contributes to our becoming members of other communities and cultures, and teaches us to invite others to join our own.

In this book, instances of students' writing disclose their memberships. In this chapter, we start with a literary context to offer a different take on the idea of writing. My own and other readers' literary responses are considered as examples of how others and others' language is overtaken in the process of recognizing memberships. The new readings are themselves new writings, blends of reading and writing described by the term *language uses*. But they are active and material in any case, rather than passive and conceptual: in reading or in writing, in overtaking other language, we change our memberships.

Writing as Teaching Membership

Toni Morrison suggests what "seeing as a writer" may mean for students and for the teaching of language use and writing. This idea counters the division between reading and writing, literature and composition, taken for granted in schools. By seeing as a writer, one thinks more comprehensively, Morrison suggests.[5] Perhaps it is consistent with her desire to read "seeing as a writer" as "the perspective of one who uses language conscious of its public roles." Furthermore, she describes a moment of self-recognition: while discovering thinking-as-a-writer, she is also recognizing thinking-as-oneself. Being a writer is the identity through which she reaches us, the public. Morrison reports recognizing that she may use the identity through which she came into the public arena for a new purpose: criticism, in this case, converting a narrowly conceived canon into a group of works whose meaning is available to all members of society. Toni Morrison's literary criticism is a way of reading, of thinking of writing. It describes how a "writerly perspective" teaches a prospective writer to think from one's own memberships and to identify accurately memberships that are not one's own. Although Morrison discusses how this has worked for her by studying established writers, a similar principle applies to students, whose work should be read just as seriously and carefully. The writ-

---

[5] Notice the difference between this formulation and the ideal of "using writing," presented as a guiding principle by Peter Elbow and others.

erly perspective provides teachers with a basis for viewing students' writings as public or collectively applicable thoughts, leading to a clearer sense of students' memberships and perspectives.

In her book *Playing in the Dark*,[6] Morrison tells how she shifted from thinking as a reader to thinking as a writer.

> As a writer reading, I came to realize the obvious: the subject of the dream is the dreamer. The fabrication of an Africanist persona is reflexive; an extraordinary meditation on the self. . . . It requires hard work not to see this. . . .
>
> I began to rely on my knowledge of how books get written, how language arrives; my sense of how and why writers abandon or take on certain aspects of their project. I began to rely on my understanding of what the linguistic struggle requires of writers and what they make of the surprise that is the inevitable concomitant of the act of creation. What became transparent were the self-evident ways that Americans choose to talk about themselves through and within a sometimes allegorical, sometimes metaphorical, but always choked representation of the Africanist presence. (17)

Morrison says that writings are the projections of the writers,[7] and that literature (regardless of authorship) represents how a people thinks about itself. By assuming a public scene of reading, Morrison also changes the traditional Freudian meaning of *dream.* In his 1908 essay, Freud considered the "narcissistic" elements of fantasy to be "disguised" so as to make the fantasy socially acceptable. This sense of the translation of private fantasy into public story retains the dichotomy of the private individual donating his/her passions to an other (society) and thus having to conceal something about the fantasy. Morrison's change suggests that the public document is also the dream, disguised not by the dreamer but by the culture in the process of reading it. A writerly perspective gives more credit to the literature by expecting that it necessarily refers to the society that produces and reads it.[8]

---

[6] Toni Morrison, *Playing in the Dark* (New York: Random House, 1992).

[7] The projection view can be found in Freud's "The Relation of the Poet to Day-Dreaming," in *Freud, Character and Culture,* ed. Philip Rieff (New York: Collier Books, 1963), 34–43; the collectivist view is generally given by myth or motif critics, who demonstrate that literature shares its elements with other works and other societies. However, collectivists do not take into account processes of change, distinguishing their view from the ones discussed here and in Chapter 2.

[8] Chapter 4 considers how this works with regard to male students' writing. I explore how to disclose genres and memberships that are cordoned off, so to speak, by traditional views of literacy.

An example of this view is Morrison's discussion of *Moby Dick*:[9]

> A complex, heaving, disorderly, profound text is *Moby Dick*, and
> among its several meanings it seems to me this "unspeakable" one
> has remained the "hidden course," the "truth in the Face of False-
> hood." To this day no novelist has so wrestled with its subject. (18)

The "truth in the Face of Falsehood" is the theme of the "whiteness of the whale." With regard to the "Whiteness" chapter, Morrison
cites Melville's private struggle "to explain myself here . . . explain
myself I must, else all these chapters might be naught." The whiteness, Melville continues in Morrison's citation, carries the "pro-
foundest idealized significance." From this Morrison infers,

> Melville is not exploring white *people* but whiteness idealized.
> Then, after informing the reader of his "hope to light upon some
> chance clue to conduct us to the hidden course we seek," he tries
> to nail it. To provide the key to the "hidden course." His struggle to
> do so is gigantic. He cannot. Nor can we. (17)

Morrison insists that Melville's desperate isolated passion is not
merely due to abolitionist feelings or opposition to capitalist failures of humanity. The passion of his literature is due, rather, to his
"hidden" questioning of

> the very notions of white progress, the very idea of racial superior-
> ity, of whiteness as a privileged place in the evolutionary ladder of
> humankind, and to meditate on the fraudulent, self-destroying phi-
> losophy of that superiority . . . (18)

This level of questioning, Morrison observes, "was dangerous, solitary, radical work. Especially then. Especially now." Morrison
accounts for the machinery of *suppressing* the assumptions of racial
superiority. She reasons that we must be able to find in Melville's
literature the level of feeling that corresponds to the suppression of
the ultimate shame—the inner but collectively shared belief in the
superiority of white people. This level of inner depravity in individuals and in the society is then symbolized by the bizarre whiteness
of the whale, while the battle against it is located in the one figure,
Ahab, whose personality is at least obsessed but also may be border-
ing on the psychotic. He tries to find justice by stabbing from "hell's
heart" at this whiteness that reduced his body (took his leg) and
overtook his mind. Morrison suggests that the strange character of

---

[9] Toni Morrison, "Unspeakable Things Unspoken: The Afro-American Presence in
American Literature, *Michigan Quarterly Review* 28 (Winter 1989): 1–33.

this novel corresponds to the strange but deeply hidden collective beliefs in the racial superiority of white people and the inability to exorcise these beliefs.

In view of Melville's story of "Benito Cereno," in which the American Captain, to the very end, does not see the corrupting power of slavery, its effects on the slaveholder, it is hard not to entertain Morrison's view of Melville. As he does in *Moby Dick*, Melville isolates American society on a ship, "foreign" in this case, and then shows its depravity. The actual American (Captain Delano) sees only the need to correct the power inversion and has no sense of the social and human devastation wrought by the slavery as an institution. In any event, Morrison's approach to Melville by seeing through the writer's perspective is another way for readers to discover their various memberships that were not before visible to them.

In her essay "Friday on the Potomac,"[10] Morrison reads Daniel Defoe's *Robinson Crusoe* with a similar purpose of identifying its unconscious social vision. She uses the work to find the right way to describe Clarence Thomas' public stance during his confirmation hearings and the struggle he must have gone through to take this stance. Morrison suggests that Thomas fits into the white man's narrative. She says that Thomas, like Friday, turns in his own language for the language of the master. It looks at first as if there was, for Thomas, no choice: the only way toward prosperity, the choice he took instead of vengeance, was by volunteering to become a servant again, and to place the foot of the master on his head; prosperity was a better choice than vengeance. Morrison says that this is what Thomas thought he did. She says he actually gave up his own language and, by implication, his membership in his own people because this was necessary, given the false choice of prosperity versus vengeance he set up for himself:

> One is obliged to cooperate in the misuse of figurative language, in the reinforcement of cliché, the erasure of difference, the jargon of justice, the evasion of logic, the denial of history, the crowning of patriarchy, the inscription of hegemony; to be complicit in the vandalizing, sentimentalizing and trivialization of the torture black people have suffered. Such rhetorical strategies become necessary because, without one's own idiom, there is no other language to speak.

---

[10] Toni Morrison, "Introduction: Friday on the Potomac," in *Race-ing Justice, Engendering Power: Essays on Anita Hill, Clarence Thomas, and the Construction of Social Reality* (New York: Pantheon Books, 1992), vii–xxx.

Both Friday and Clarence Thomas accompany their rescuers into the world of power and salvation. But the problem of rescue still exists: both men, black but unrecognizable at home or away, are condemned first to mimic, then to internalize and adore, but never to utter one single sentence understood to be beneficial to their original culture, whether the people of their culture are those who wanted to hurt them or those who loved them to death. (xxviii–xxix)

Earlier in her discussion, Morrison characterized this "problem of rescue" faced by Friday and by Thomas: "If the rescuer saves your life by taking you away from the dangers, the complications, the confusion of home, he may very well expect the debt to be paid in full . . . full payment, forever. Because the rescuer wants to hear his name, not mimicked but adored" (xxv–xxvi). At this point in the reading, Morrison does not need to say that Thomas wanted to be "rescued" from home. Instead, Defoe's Enlightenment imperialist's novel speaks. Morrison calls the book a success story, because the white man successfully converted the black man to his culture and his religion while still preserving the difference between white and black required by the white man. This, Morrison says strongly, is a difference in *language*, which in both Friday's and Thomas' situations, has become a site of violence—"jargon, evasion, denial," and so on. Morrison's emphasis on language brings us up to date. The recursive historical dereliction of language carried slavery forward, and this dereliction accounts for slavery's power to remain in human society.

Through the reading of the canonical narrative, Morrison reidentifies and revalues this familiar work, this mainstay of the curriculum. She has not censored or criticized Defoe's narrative but has added to it—the story of Clarence Thomas. This new story is as much a part of the literary curriculum as *Robinson Crusoe* is part of the history curriculum. As Morrison did with Melville and the several writers in *Playing in the Dark*, her readings enlarge literary details and ironies; she urges us to see and read beyond organic textual coherence and toward the human, social, political, or cultural contexts. Morrison teaches the principle of reading literature as culturally heterogeneous, as comprehensive in its perception of its own society and in its potential application to our societies.[11]

---

[11] As discussed in Chapter 2, any genre should be understood as being mixed or heterogeneous. To look for correspondences between genres and social situations is to discover more about how language use participates in collective memberships.

Morrison's writerly readings change the meanings of literature and the curriculum. She requires us to orient our perception of individual works, of authors' total *oeuvres,* and of a culture's collected works toward shared dreams and fantasies, toward public, historical reference. Her criticism, like her novels, is meant not for canonization or for a reading list curriculum, but for active use, for overtaking common language and using it for new common purposes, converting received language, if appropriate, to the language of others and inserting it into the cultures of others.

How shall we consider, furthermore, the readings Morrison announced in *Playing in the Dark?* Why did Morrison, long since an established writer, only recently write about reading *canonical* American literature? What might have delayed her announcements that she should *read as a writer?* One answer might be this: Our style of education, with its emphasis on literate psychology and culture, relies on the separation of reading and writing, teaches them separately, and in the academy, has established different professional institutions to study reading and writing. Perhaps the subject of language and literature (English, Comparative, and so on) is meant to unify reading and writing, but there is a split, even within the profession of English between teachers and scholars of "literature" and teachers and scholars of "writing." There is even a third group, off by themselves often enough, called "creative writers." Toni Morrison, educated in America, was subject to this same fragmentation of attention. Now, as she functions in the public light, she announces her sense of something we have intuited from the beginning of our lives: the indivisibility of language and its inseparability from the rest of our lives: reading, writing, speaking, and hearing add up to the indivisibility of orality and literacy.[12] Because of this indivisibility, we achieve membership, albeit slowly and carefully as in any human relationship, in other communities, societies, and cultures. Gradually, our different zones of language use become one, attach to one another in different ways, and as we speak one another's languages, we become members of one another's societies. Morrison's use of her writerly perspective, in addition to proposing new ways of teaching writing and thinking, teaches us to bring together a collective of different memberships poised to interact more productively than we have been able to do thus far.

---

[12] As suggested in the Forethoughts section, this thought is another articulation of the perspective of the materiality of language—the belief that meaning and words are not independently comprehensible.

Getting New Language:
Reading as Teaching (New) Membership

A Recent Reading Experience of Membership

In my graduate school experience (about 1962) the work of Franz Kafka, a German-speaking/writing Czech Jew, was taught by Leon Edel, a North American Jewish scholar. He viewed Kafka in terms that derived from his study of French, British, and American Christian writers—Marcel Proust, Dorothy Richardson, James Joyce, Virginia Woolf, and Henry James.[13] To Edel, Kafka was one of several subjective novelists who presented their protagonists from within, so to speak: either the first person narrator or the stream-of-consciousness narration introduced a dimension of nonreferentiality that contrasted with the declarative simplicities of the nineteenth-century "omniscient" narrator. Edel assigned "A Country Doctor" and asked students to write essays that infer what sort of person the narrator is. "Deduce the narrator," he challenged. I did this with enthusiasm, loading my analysis with psychological speculation, writing an essay twice the assigned length.

However, this was graduate school and the era of the New Criticism. The rules were to keep your enjoyment to yourself, learn what the teacher was lecturing about, and then demonstrate what you had learned in the essays and on the exams. So that while I always enjoyed Kafka, it took a long time for me to understand what it was I was enjoying: his work has virtually no literal cultural reference.[14] Much later, relatively recently, I had occasion to read (aloud) another work of Kafka's, "The Vulture," which I found particularly winning. Here it is, in English:

> A vulture was hacking at my feet. It had already torn my boots and stockings to shreds, now it was hacking at the feet themselves. Again and again it struck at them, then circled several times restlessly round me, and then returned to continue its work. A gentleman passed by, looked on for a while, then asked me why I suffered the vulture. "I'm helpless," I said. "When it came and began to attack me, I of course tried to drive it away, even to strangle it, but these animals are very strong, it was about to spring at my face, but I preferred to sacrifice my feet. Now they are almost torn to bits." "Fancy letting yourself be tortured like this!" said the gentleman. "One shot and that's the end of the vulture." "Really?" I

---

[13] Leon Edel, *The Modern Psychological Novel* (New York: Grove Press, 1955).

[14] Kafka's work contrasts in this sense with Arthur Miller's, for example, whose clear references to American culture were perhaps a basis of his plays and something to which I could see myself responding.

said. "And would you do that?" "With pleasure," said the gentle-man, "I've only got to go home and get my gun. Could you wait another half hour?" "I'm not sure about that," said I, and stood for a moment rigid with pain. Then I said: "Do try it in any case, please." "Very well," said the gentleman, "I'll be as quick as I can." During this conversation the vulture had been calmly listening, let-ting its eye rove between me and the gentleman. Now I realized that it had understood everything; it took wing, leaned far back to gain impetus, and then like a javelin thrower, thrust its beak through my mouth, deep into me. Falling back, I was relieved to feel him drowning irretrievably in my blood, which was filling every depth, flooding every shore.[15]

When I first read this piece, I so enjoyed its private articulation that I inserted it into a talk I was scheduled to give. To put my response metaphorically—I read this piece aloud for the first time in a public lecture in a way that lets my "blood fill every depth and flood every shore."

The act of "speaking" Kafka's literature rather than reading it let me bring out feelings of my own about my community member-ship[16] and my professional membership, a faculty member that society generally views as "an academic." Consider the latter mem-bership first. Since becoming a senior faculty member, I have spo-ken to administrators about problems of teaching and academic life. "A vulture is hacking at my feet," I said, and gave them an account of how the vulture would have gone right for my head but that I decided "to sacrifice my feet" instead. The administrators said, yes, we can help, but can you give us half an hour to get our "guns." My requests were then reviewed by three or four committees and finally turned down or so altered that the vulture went for my head after all. When I read this account of the vulture, my identification of the gentleman merged with my frustration with the bureaucratic "hacks" who I thought were arbitrarily obstructionist. My conversa-tions with the "hacks" were civil and decent, serious and respectful. But my modest proposals and their responses were the equivalent of the vulture, gun, and blood, which are the main terms of this para-ble. People said, yes, that makes sense, let me help, and then pro-ceeded to help in just the way that defeated the proposals and drew "blood" from me. As an academic professional, I follow the rules of conversation: in a polite and civilized way I present my "narrative" in the same calm that the narrator of "The Vulture" presents his. Do

---

[15] Franz Kafka, *Parables and Paradoxes* (New York: Schocken Books, 1946), 149. (German and English).

[16] Like Arthur Miller, I am an American Jew from New York.

I need to deduce or infer this narrator? As a critical project this seems superfluous, since I am already this narrator as soon as I start reading this text. My voice is activated because an East European Jew like my parents has already recorded the conversational structure, depicted its results in terms that describe my feelings as I discuss, for example, with administrators that I think teaching is being "hacked to death" in academic life.

Yes, it is only a metaphor. But here is also where my membership in the first-generation offspring of East European Jews makes itself felt. Kafka's vocabulary and style of speech was present in my childhood household, not as his but as my parents'. My friends and I made the same kind of jokes. In our talk, there had always been a conversational leitmotif in which real, or dangerous, or intolerable circumstances of life are routinely described in these deadpan metaphors of violence and death. My mother was adroit at spontaneously thinking up devastating epithets to describe villains or others who, in her judgment, behaved badly; sometimes I was the one who got the metaphor. So when someone says, "a vulture was hacking at my feet" I recognize its genre intuitively, without analysis, and I feel its meaning by virtue of my membership in my first-generation community. I don't analyze its existential meaning; I don't look for Kafka's Oedipus complex; there is no literary riddle for me to solve, no paradox. In my world, now as then, the gentleman who offers to save my life in such a way that will actually do me in is recognizable as the television ad, the salesperson, or even the local politician.

At an early age I learned what it was like to speak two languages at once—there were my parents' language Yiddish and the mainstream language English, but there was also within my English the vocabulary of the Yiddish culture, the East European culture in which both my parents and Kafka lived, the culture that was accustomed to external hostility. My parents' culture had already begun to respond to an environment whose German-speaking descendants finally did try to do us all in through a well-organized crusade of humiliation and murder. To read Kafka not only reestablishes these historic fears and dangers in my mind, but articulates my own culture's ways of naming and dealing with them through a kind of intrapersonal wit and dramatic metaphorical initiative that we Jews from New York in my generation recognize as "our language."[17] If I

---

[17] W. E. B. DuBois. This is very similar to the "double consciousness" described by DuBois for African Americans in 1903. The discussion of Black English in Chapter 2 makes a similar point from a different perspective.

claim that bureaucratic hacks[18] are injuring teaching in many universities, it seems to me like ordinary, rather than dramatized, language. If my usages and style seem strange to you, you can notice them in a public forum, so that, as I have tried to do now, I may explain and share them, then hear your responses. My liking of this author has a history and a context that existed before I did. I feel his voices within me represent a way of speaking and knowing that play a role now, in these universities, in this country, in this mix of interests. It matters to me to know whether and to what extent I am reading and thinking from memberships because I draw emotional, cultural, and intellectual sustenance from them.

Recognizing Common Memberships

But when I read the work of Toni Morrison, in spite of my expectations to the contrary, her language has a similar effect on me. On the one hand, I approach her work as a researcher: I want to know the literature of those who are living through the aftermath of slavery in today's United States. But I also overtake her narrative voice in ways that cause me to feel as if I am telling the story rather than listening to it, just as I feel when reading Kafka. Here is a group of characteristic passages from *Beloved*[19] that had Kafka-like effects on me.

> When the four horsemen came—schoolteacher, one nephew, one slave catcher and a sheriff—the house on Bluestone Road was so quiet they thought they were too late. Three of them dismounted, one stayed in the saddle, his rifle ready, his eyes trained away from the house to the left and to the right, because likely as not the fugitive would make a dash for it. . . .
>
> Inside, two boys bled in the sawdust and dirt at the feet of a nigger woman holding a blood-soaked child to her chest with one hand and an infant by the heels in the other. She did not look at them; she simply swung the baby toward the wall planks, missed and tried to connect a second time, when out of nowhere—in the ticking time the men spent staring at what there was to stare at— the old nigger boy, still mewing, ran through the door behind them and snatched the baby from the arch of its mother's swing. . . .
>
> Right off it was clear, to schoolteacher especially, that there was nothing to claim. The three . . . pickaninnies they had hoped were alive and well enough to . . . take back and raise properly to do the work Sweet Home desperately needed, were not. Two were lying

---

[18] In Chapter 7, my discussion of evaluation involves a critique of bureaucracy. The foregoing discussion of Kafka suggests an affective aspect of that critique.

[19] Toni Morrison, *Beloved* (New York: Knopf, 1987).

> open-eyed in the sawdust; a third pumped blood down the one he
> said made fine ink, damn good soup, pressed his collars the way he
> liked besides having at least ten breeding years left. (148–149)

This is one of the several accounts of the event around which this
novel turns. Beloved is the ghost of the infant daughter whom Sethe
murdered as she tried to kill all her children to prevent their being
taken back to Sweet Home by the four horsemen of slavery. As I
become the narrator and get into Schoolteacher's head, I feel a similarly outrageous (Kafka-like) irony in the evocation of the slave-
owner's unabated wishes for fine ink, good soup, and pressed
collars as he watches the infant's blood "pumped down" her
mother's dress. The language feels loaded with the same bitter double voice: Sweet Home, the site of slavery and torture; Schoolteacher, the sadistic dispenser of violence; Beloved, the incomplete
inscription on the gravestone as the name of Sethe's murdered
child, yet living in the novel as a mature, beautiful young woman;
Paul D, the somewhat cowardly apostle of masculine identity.

I do not use analytic techniques to overtake this language. If this
work portrays anguish over the history of a people, it is also a celebration of the freedom to speak, to speak out, to shout out that
anguish. Overtaking the language lets us feel our affective and historical implication in it. History and community membership provide the translation of this novel's languages into the terms of our
daily lives. Continuing with my own translation:

When I responded to this novel in November 1990[20] I cited the
following passage:

> And the Germans who flooded southern Ohio brought and devel-
> oped swine cooking to its highest form. Pig boats jammed the Ohio
> river, and their captains hollering at one another over the grunts of
> the stock was as common a water sound as that of the ducks flying
> over their heads. (155)

Here is what I wrote:

> I think this was the only mention of Germans in this book, though
> they are the ones I thought of throughout much of my reading. . . . I
> thought it was noteworthy that the Germans were associated with
> swine—here mainly as consumers of swine, I think, where Paul D
> was a worker in a swineyard, and it tells how he had to wash . . .
> offal from all over his body. When Paul D was in Delaware the first
> bit of food he got was pork sausage. Sixo went on the path toward
> being shot when he took a shoat. . . .

---

[20] David Bleich, Response given in class: Seminar preparing prospective secondary
school teachers of English.

I never read anything about how women lived in a world of Nazis[21] but this novel told about it and that is what I learned, in some ways, for the first time. I have seen countless films of the death camps in Europe, countless tellings of naked people marching to be gassed, countless narrations of how it was. Here is the same story stretched out, dedicated to the "sixty million" (instead of the . . . six million). The story seems the same because it was the group of men [the four horsemen] that brought out the truth of the atrocity that millions of people collaborated in creating, in this free country over a period of two hundred years—a mother running a handsaw over the throat of her nine-month-old child.

When I read Kafka, my Jewish membership tends to obscure another membership I have in common with him—that in the community of men. A similar thing almost happened in my reading of Morrison: I can identify with those who were once slaves, those who were victims of fascism. In addition to this identification, I am in the community of those partially responsible for Sethe's relationship with a ghost. If I identify with Paul D by feeling his betrayal of Sethe and by recounting a memory of having let my mother down, I arrive at my membership in a different community from Toni Morrison, the community of (white) men. In becoming aware of this membership and in overtaking Morrison's language, I lay groundwork for revising the masculine-identified language use and genres, a revision which, in turn, is then in position to "revise" my gender membership.[22]

The terms and style of otherness will vary from person to person, culture to culture. Consider how, in my class of white, mostly female prospective teachers, the responses show that all readers are emotionally caught up in this tale, and that none suggest this was not a worthwhile reading experience. However, how the different readers are involved tells something about what they think their own memberships are. Three readers, one male, introduced their responses with the same word:

> Wow! I think that sums up my reaction pretty well, but I think you're expecting me to elaborate on that . . . it made me realize how lucky I am. I couldn't help thinking about my life and how different it was from these characters. (Ms. D)

---

[21] Not long after this was written, Alison Owings' *Frauen: German Women Recall the Third Reich* (New Brunswick, NJ: Rutgers University Press, 1993), was published. At the least, it helps us to frame questions regarding the relationship of totalitarianism and gender ideologies.

[22] This process is discussed at greater length in Chapter 4.

> Wow! I was very spellbound by the book. I loved the characters, especially, the slow pace with the development of character. The dialogues felt very real. I do see the reason why it won the 1988 Pulitzer prize. (Mr. L)

> Wow! What a book. The way Toni Morrison quietly unravels . . . a glimpse of yet another horror, yet another atrocity. . . . We keep pushing the events behind us, not daring to feel the true impact of them, not daring to understand them, until they force themselves to the surface, and we must face the horror head on, somehow deal with it and make sense of it. (Ms. R)

For all three of these readers to feel "Wow!" is to remain somewhat separated, in the responses, from their actual implication in this novel. They are willing to report that they felt moved, but mostly the people in this novel are "others." ("I couldn't help thinking about my life and how different it was from these characters.") Of the three respondents, Ms. R is the most alert to the conventional literary statements one could make about the reading. But none of these readers identified with any character; they are wowed as if this were an adventure, the reading being the occasion to learn of the unusual happenings in the enslaved zone of American history. After observing that "it's unbelievable what happened to these people" and listing some of the novel's atrocities, Ms. R writes:

> Finally, a woman driven to kill her own baby rather than give up that baby to the system of the white slave owner. . . . A race of people forced to deny love, hope, or any other emotion, because such an emotion can be torn into bits at any moment.

In spite of the fact that Ms. R is an eager, sincere, and inquiring student of history on this occasion, she seems to write as if she were reading about "a race of people" rather than people who could be connected to her. When speaking of modern times, she mentions lynchings in the South and white gangs in the North. At the end of her response she observes that the only way out of this history is "if we on the other end stop acting in ways for which we will always have to make amends." This response shows some stake in the otherness that the novel and the author are trying to change. The "Wow!" feelings are resistances to the voices of this novel in that the readers' surprise may be the result of American traditions of detached innocence dramatized in "Benito Cereno" or of socially naive guilt portrayed in *The Scarlet Letter*. From their responses it is not possible to tell how far beyond "this race of people" they went. They stopped at the victim condition of African Americans.

This was not true of all readers, however. Other class members responded by registering a degree of discomfort both with the relationship between Sethe and Beloved and with the catastrophe of the novel—the murder of Beloved by Sethe. These responses suggest that Sethe's killing of her infant daughter on one level makes sense to us as an escape from slavery, but we hesitate about it because of our continuing acceptance of traditional family life. One can say, as one student did, that under slavery, there can be no family, and one can thereby sympathize with what Sethe did. But how many will challenge the premise of the family itself, and how many will entertain the thought that this premise is also the premise of slavery?

One reader in my class, Ms S., had this thought and here is some of her response.

> Even though *Beloved* is set a century ago, in a culture that outwardly seems totally alien to anything I know—I found myself being reminded of pieces of me and my life as I read. Unfortunately for my mom, Sethe and she have a lot in common. . . . My mother . . . blames herself for my brother's horrible death. There must have been some inherent flaw in her mothering skills, or she would have been able to save him. Women have carried what seems like the guilt of the world on their shoulders for so long—as bearers of humankind they are tied to a yoke of guilt and unfulfillment.
>
> In a sense, all women who are solely homemakers are slaves. . . . My mom, like Sethe, when we all grew up and left, felt like she had nothing. . . . She had denied selfhood in order to be a "good" mother. . . . I can't fathom the idea of not tending to my personal needs, of denying that I even have needs, of being scared to live on my own for fear the community would ostracize me like Grandma Baby's "friends" did to Sethe. . . . [My mom] talks like I would have withered and died if she wasn't there every second to watch over me, feed me, love me. . . .
>
> I'm glad I'm not my mother I'm glad I am my mother.

Ms. S poses a problem she sees in a mother's killing her child to keep it out of slavery: why does Sethe feel guilty? The novel, being taken up with Beloved's long stay with Sethe, is seen by this reader as an extended metaphor of maternal guilt. Ms. S's answer, that this is the historic lot of women, also seems to say that this novel, for her, is about the lot of women, and that slavery as we know it— racial slavery—is a special form of the universal slavery of women who are associated with domestic life and children only.[23]

---

[23] Some readers may ask if this too "looks away" from the racial basis of slavery in America. It could be, but I can't say what Ms. S's response would be.

What about Ms. S's formulation "All women who are solely homemakers are slaves"? This statement, which some would dispute, has some stylistic affinity with "A vulture is hacking at my feet." There is daring and pugnacity in both statements, yet their literal immediacy is compelling. In ordinary situations, Ms. S's view is commonly cited: I have heard my mother say repeatedly, "I work like a slave in this house"; another reader reported having informed her fiance: "I am not your slave." In a literary formulation, Ms. S's no less than Kafka's and Morrison's, we may tie together human physical pain with Ms. S's sense that a feature of society is responsible, here and now, for this pain, and we recognize this responsibility because we are inside and not outside of society.

After Ms. S's response, some of the other readers' perceptions about how distant this black community is might be seen as a reduction of Morrison's warning that there is a racial fire in the house and we are in danger of perishing. From Ms. S's perspective, a fundamental condition of slavery now exists and has existed through history. Neither Ms. S nor others who have thought like her are rejecting the need to distinguish one's own interests, one's own community, from those of others we meet in a fluid society. Ms. S believes in families and rejects slavery. Yet she saw in response to this reading, to this suffering mother Sethe struggling with an intolerable memory, to her own mother with a similarly intolerable sense of failure in spite of a lifetime of self-denial, that slavery may be the predictable result of living in a traditional family and that her own life and the lives of fellow students and fellow teachers are similarly planted in that history.

In Ms. S's response there is a new challenge to politics and to language. She writes, "I'm glad I'm not my mother I'm glad I am my mother." Ms. S, without using a period or other punctuation, is a part of her mother and not a part; the same as mother, yet not the same; part of a traditional family yet not a part. This loosening of categories is the new phenomenon, but it does not include the elimination of boundaries. Other respondents, myself included, show this element in their discourse—the declaration of simultaneous membership in several communities, participation in several societies, being a product of several histories. Our language begins to accommodate contradiction, the condition of being in and out, something and not something at once. In reading Kafka and Morrison, I experience the simultaneity of multiple memberships, the depth of several perspectives. I suppose this pluralization of our categories of social identity complicates our lives even more, since we need now examine our patterns of membership rather than just whether we are in or out.

The foregoing responses were read and discussed by their authors with one another. Readers learned about the novel and about reading of the novel by reading with and through others. The developing relationships among the students showed that they were learning to read other people's readings as well as to change their responses in response to what others were experiencing. Furthermore, this way of reading in postsecondary classrooms is something that needs to be recovered.[24] Habits of sharing and relating to others found in early childhood and in the early grades of primary school are replaced by the school system with the habits of individualism. When children learn to read, they are urged to read privately and to report their reading to the teacher. This process privatizes their language. Comparing readings and considering their distinctiveness is a low priority as compared to creating a self-contained skill at "accurate" and politically inert analysis. Recovering and resocializing is the result of reading and speaking though disclosure of memberships.

Writing and Reading as Reflexive Ethnography

Toni Morrison's critical writing shows how criticism can exercise social influence. By rereading familiar works of literature with different interests, by helping readers make "other" literature their own, readers' writerly perspectives change our memberships. Readers who are sharing their responses, who are disclosing their relation to the literature, may be said to be writing their reading (even if the sharing is oral). In turn, we wrote their readings (perhaps) into our own. We changed our memberships by admitting new issues into our discussions, our classrooms.

Writing that textualizes lived experience is ethnographic. To share this writing reconfigures our memberships and teaches us new language uses. Because of this fact, ways of ethnographic writing have gotten increasing attention from writing

---

[24] Edward Pauly's *The Classroom Crucible* (New York: Basic Books, 1990), discussed in Chapter 6, describes the kind of classroom that should be recovered, and that would accommodate the collective reading scenes I describe. Two textbooks given to the purpose of letting literary response teach writing are David Bartholomae and Anthony Petrosky, *Facts, Artifacts, and Counterfacts: Theory and Method for a Reading and Writing Course* (Portsmouth, NH: Boynton/Cook, 1986), and Kathleen McCormick, Gary Waller, and Linda Flower, *Reading Texts: Reading, Responding, Writing* (Lexington, MA: D. C. Heath, 1987).

teachers.[25] Early in this century, ethnographic writing was considered to be work for anthropologists alone. During the postcolonial period, anthropologists have become more self-conscious
about how they create their descriptions, reports, and comments
about societies in which they are not members. Some also have
begun using ethnographic techniques to study aspects of our
own society.[26] For both writing teachers and anthropologists,
the relation of writing and reading (in the sense of interpretation) to group membership became a part of the subject matters
of literacy and of anthropology. Ethnographic genres change
depending on whether their authors are writing from outside or
from inside the society.[27] For writing teachers, the virtue of ethnographic genres is that they are adaptable to different standpoints on society, but they take a perspective similar to
Morrison's—the writerly perspective, with the sense that
regardless of the degree of membership in a society or a part of
society, reading and writing that society enacts people's implications in it. Ethnographic techniques render the literate
approach to society a way of articulating degrees and kinds of
memberships in it. They thereby move toward the practice of
research being self-consciously socially generous.

Ethnographic writing, and the more general ethnographic view
of people and society, presupposes the materiality of language: the
view that to use the language places us within the context or situa-

---

[25] Attention has come in two directions: first, the improvement of research on the
classroom by using ethnographic techniques such as those outlined in David M.
Fetterman, *Ethnography: Step by Step* (Newbury Park, CA: Sage, 1989); collections
taking this approach include Judith L. Greene and Cynthia Wallat, eds., *Ethnography
and Language in Educational Settings* (Norwood, NJ: Ablex, 1981); David Bloome, ed.,
Classrooms and Literacy (Norwood, NJ: Ablex, 1989); and Catherine Emihovich, ed.,
Locating Learning: Ethnographic Perspectives on Classroom Research (Norwood, NJ:
Ablex, 1989). Second, writing teachers have begun using ethnographic genres to
render writing projects more substantive: James Clifford and George E. Marcus, eds.,
Writing Culture (Berkeley: University of California Press, 1986) is a frequently assigned
model collection that follows from Clifford Geertz's ideas of "thick description," "local
knowledge," and "autoethnography." Although these are two directions, the writing
done in each is cognate: research on the classroom relates very closely to research
assigned to students in the classroom. The problems of "writing" the research results
parallel the problems students need to solve in articulating the results of their own
inquiries. Readers may want to consult my essay "Ethnography and the Study of
Literacy: Prospects for Socially Generous Research," in *Into the Field: Sites of
Composition Studies*, ed., Anne Ruggles Gere (New York: MLA, 1993), 176–192. This
essay discusses a classroom ethnography written by the one female student in a class
of nineteen.

tion about which we are writing and is an action that affects that context as a whole. To assume the materiality of language teaches us that language loses its identity as language if it is separated from its contexts of use. The genres that could be considered to be ethnographic writing—the travel narrative, the description of customs, habits, mores, or rituals, the first-person account of lived experience, the bounded story or anecdote, or life-writing, and so on—depend on the materiality of language, on the assumption of the writer's membership—of one sort or another—in a group related to the subject matter of the writing.[28]

A recent collection of essays edited by J. Boyarin[29] presents several descriptions of language use in different societies that demonstrate language use as membership. The essays show how the materiality of language appears in living societies. This materiality is the result of the societies' assuming the unity of oral and written genres of language use. The term *reading* as used in the title of this collection means "ability to be responsive to what others are saying" rather than the more common meaning, "being able to articulate orally what appears in written texts." As presented in this collection, the meaning of reading is broad enough to describe something like "human interaction." Conversely, some of these examples cast interpersonal interaction in terms of reading. Language use as membership depends on a sense of continuity between the oral and written, on the indivisibility of language.

---

[26] Examples include: Sharon Traweek, *Beamtimes and Lifetimes* (Cambridge, MA: Harvard University Press, 1988), an ethnography of the particle physics communities in the United States and in Japan; Anne Allison, *Nightwork: Sexuality, Pleasure, and Corporate Masculinity in a Tokyo Hostess Club* (Chicago: University of Chicago Press, 1994), where the author posed as a hostess to do her ethnographic study; Julian E. Orr, *Talking about Machines: An Ethnography of a Modern Job* (Ithaca, NY: Cornell University Press, 1997). These studies are more than the application of anthropological techniques to parts of our own society: they are new levels of self-observation and self-involvement where the society of the researched as well as of the researcher stands to benefit.

[27] For example, pejorative jokes about their own group can be told among members of that group, but an outgroup member cannot tell that joke to an ingroup member. To put it another way, criticism or debunking are not just that: debunking from within is much different from debunking from without. The "within" form could be read as sedition; the "without" form could be read as "sour grapes."

[28] The ethnographies cited in note 26, above, are in this category.

[29] Jonathan Boyarin, ed., *The Ethnography of Reading* (Berkeley: University of California Press, 1992).

Daniel Boyarin distinguishes between the contemporary sense of reading as a private, silent, pleasure-giving activity and the biblical, Israelite sense as a collective event.[30] He notes the common root, in Hebrew, of "to call out" and "to read." Reading, as used in the Old Testament, often means "reading in public" and "calling the public together for the purposes of reading" (13–14). There is no connotation of pleasure associated with the reading and the calling, but a sense of noticing an occasion of collective implication. In the subsequent Talmudic era the root term ("qore" [ko-ray]) refers to "participation in the religious act of studying scripture" (17). In the societies of first-millennium (C.E.) Jews, reading and subjective privacy were unknown in the sense that they are common today, when such privacy occurs even in collective situations such as viewing a film.

Daniel Boyarin outlines how "the habit of private silent reading among laymen"[31] began in fourteenth-century Italy and is related to changes in the status of erotic behavior, especially the need for people's erotic life (24) to proceed in spite of religious restrictions. He does not discuss it, but the turn in the Reformation to authorize private individual reading of the Bible may also have helped to bring the changed sense of reading into the present as well as to enhance the potentially sinful feeling of erotic activity.

Jonathan Boyarin tells how, among contemporary observant Jews who "read" Torah and Talmud in study circles as well as in religious rituals, the biblical sense of reading is practiced: reading is something done in public, with others.[32] A modern feature of the study circle he describes is that the readers are literate, but this fact does not radically affect the collective sense of the reading. He sums up: "Text and speech are of equal priority in Jewish study" and "The task of Jewish study is to create community among Jews through time via language." These two features of study are related. The interlocking oral and literate modes enact the social purpose of engaging in language-intensive activity. The work of Daniel and Jonathan Boyarin might be combined with Susan Handelman's dis-

---

[30] Daniel Boyarin, "Placing Reading: Ancient Israel and Medieval Europe," in *The Ethnography of Reading,* ed. Jonathan Boyarin (Berkeley: University of California Press, 1992), 10–37.

[31] Cited by Daniel Boyarin from Paul Saenger's (1982) citation of Erich Auerbach, in "Silent Reading: Its Impact on Late Medieval Script and Society," *Viator* 13: 367–414. From Daniel Boyarin, "Placing Reading," 37.

[32] Jonathan Boyarin, "Voices Around the Text: The Ethnography of Reading at Mesivta Tifereth Jerusalem," *The Ethnography of Reading,* 212-237.

cussion regarding the materiality of language:[33] in Hebrew, the root of the word for *word* and for *thing* is the same: "davar" (or "dbr"). Language in Hebrew and contemporary Jewish religious culture is a material item that is self-consciously used as such to foster, continue, and preserve interpersonal and collective attachments. There is no "spirit" given as a counterpoint to the "letter." There is only the letter, which necessarily lives among people: Susan Noakes suggests that the founding of Christianity is partly based on a dispute over how to read the Hebrew scriptures, a "political struggle" that disappeared with the destruction of the Temple and left free, so to speak, the Christian ideal that the (real, oral) word comes directly from God, thus effecting the characteristic division between "the spirit and the letter."[34] Christianity needed this division to establish its authority.

These essays suggest that once reading and literacy are studied ethnographically, they are understood relativistically, recalling perhaps the controversial Whorf-Sapir hypothesis about language: because of the embeddedness of language in culture, different cultures, because of their different structures of names (symbols), have different objects, materials, or customs, even though, through translation, one may accept a certain degree of transferability of these entities.[35] The task of distinguishing the extent of transferability and the extent of cultural specificity is part of language pedagogy in multiculturally oriented classrooms.

The closeness or identity of orality and literacy appears in other non-Christian societies. Studies of Asian and South American communities describe language use mores that, while different in topical senses from the Jewish styles, share certain basic orientations around language use that raise doubts about the Western separation of orality and literacy (spirit and letter). The way the societies are described suggests repeatedly that one cannot divide language into

---

[33] Susan Handelman, *The Slayers of Moses* (Albany: SUNY Press, 1982).

[34] Susan Noakes, "Gracious Words: Luke's Jesus and the Reading of Sacred Poetry at the Beginning of the Christian Era," in *The Ethnography of Reading*, ed. Jonathan Boyarin, 38–57.

[35] Snow or bread, which seem to be the same across cultures may actually be different things in each culture because of their functioning within different symbol systems. The phenomenon is similar to the "swinging stone" being converted into a "pendulum" by using a different kind of mathematical description, as Thomas Kuhn discussed in *The Structure of Scientific Revolutions* (Chicago: University of Chicago Press, 1962/1970). A symbol system (a language-in-culture) is a worldview whose change changes the meaning of elements that under an absolutist assumption would not change.

oral and written, spirit and letter, in contexts of language use. These societies' manifestations of the indivisibility of orality and literacy strongly imply that this indivisibility in the West is suppressed and out of sight rather than absent or inaccessible. The foregoing reflections on the work and influence of Toni Morrison imply that the suppression is loosening under the influence of the cultural pluralization of society.

H. Mack Horton describes how Japan had gone through a development similar to what the Christian West had experienced.[36] An earlier period in the first millennium, C.E., in which orality and literacy were unified was followed by the second millennium in which separation was valued. In the late nineteenth century, "the gap between spoken Japanese and the language of high literature would again come as close to disappearing as it had in The Tale of the Genji of nearly a millennium before" (174). Diana Digges and Joanne Rappaport study orality and literacy in contemporary Highland Colombia.[37] Describing a certain Indian ceremony, they write,

> Ong's distinction [between word-as-thing and word-as-event] is thus challenged and clarified by the signifying unity of words, act, and image. They are inseparably woven together in an event that has retained central meaning for the Indians, despite the existence of written documents that preceded and later ratified the decision embodied in the possession ceremony. This intertwining of word, act, and image is so complete that each becomes the repository for the others. . . . Written law is merely word-as-thing and must be fleshed out, given meaning, given life, by creating the original word-as-event. (151)

In this case the real-life reference is real estate—the boundaries of Indian lands whose legal status is reaffirmed through a ritual. In Jewish practice, this is common: it is not enough to follow a written law; there has to be a ritualization that authorizes it among followers. Digges and Rappaport's discussion implies that the survival of civilizations is connected to how we approach the questions of orality and literacy: there is reason to think that an axiomatic distance between orality and literacy, an axiomatic sense of the divisibility of

---

[36] H. Mack Horton, "Japanese Spirit and Chinese Learning: Scribes and Storytellers in Pre-Modern Japan," in The Ethnology of Reading, ed. Jonathan Boyarin, 156–179.

[37] Diana Diggs and Joanne Rappaport, "Literacy, Orality, and Ritual Practice in Highland Colombia," in The Ethnology of Reading, ed. Jonathan Boyarin, 139–154.

language use, is damaging to civilization as a whole, even though, using this axiom, certain segments of a culture gain more mobility, power, and access to commonly valued materials.

Here is a formulation from James N. Baker's discussion of the Kalaodi in Indonesia:[38]

> We might say that it is the force of irony, always putting into question the presented order of things, that makes their reading of the written word an essentially oral one. But more broadly than this, we would want to say that, so long as we attend to reading as a social practice and therefore regard it within the context of real interaction and struggle, there can be no claim that the rhetorical potentials most apparent to us in oral discourse are never really displaced by the written word to begin with. (133)

This generalization is based partly on the fact that in a chant among the Kalaodi the names of certain known figures in Islamic history are repeated. Baker's informant told him, however, that according to learned oral custom, these were not the real names. Only certain privileged people knew about these other names: "The hidden names were ones for which personal responsibility must be taken" (132). As Baker describes the situation, the recitation of the public names alluded to the hidden names, which in turn alluded to territories associated with the people.

The oral information brought forth by the public names, however obscure this information may be to any one individual, necessarily accompanies the written names, that is, the names read from a written text. From another perspective, this phenomenon is so common that the only reason it may appear uncommon is that it is described as having been observed in an unfamiliar culture. Children are commonly named after others dead and living, as a matter of course. Sometimes such naming is a conscious continuation of a family line; at other times, it is a memory of a departed ancestor. Or, it aims to achieve solidarity with an aspect of public culture, as when people are named Adam and Eve.[39] If anyone were to claim that the written proper names were unique and self-enclosed, they would be considered to be out of the conversation.

---

[38] James N. Baker, "The Presence of the Name: Reading Scripture in an Indonesian Village," in *The Ethnology of Reading*, ed. Jonathan Boyarin, 98–138.

[39] Thanks to Eve Salisbury for pointing out how frequently parents (usually men) name children after themselves. This narcissism is collective and is good documentation of the narcissistic values of the society.

Johannes Fabian's reflections[40] provide an interesting take on this matter of the permanent fusion of the oral and the literate:

> Two discoveries of orality have been made, one forced on us by the absence of written texts, the other by the presence of them. However, we must keep in mind that "written texts" may be an equivocal and confusing notion. The texts of Western ethnographic discourse and the texts produced by autochthonous, grass-roots literacy, although both are written, cannot be "read" unproblematically as members of one and the same class. (92)

Fabian has two main thoughts: first, whether or not there are written texts in the studied culture, there is always an oral as well as a written locus of language interest; in both instances, the ethnographer's search for understanding unifies the oral and the written; he/she records the oral and produces one genre, and the oral is a necessary part of what has been found as written. The second thought is that the distinctions in genre between ethnographic writing and its politics and discovered writing and its politics are the categories of interest for research, assuming the continuing unity of the oral and the written. Put another way, the political status of the "texts" under study, which holds a very high priority in ethnographic research, is best understood in terms of the texts' different *combinations* of the oral and the written.

Reading, language use, and writing, understood as aspects of cultures, are connected to issues of status, authority, and power in any culture. Elizabeth Long discusses a contemporary context in America that points this up.[41] She studied a variety of spontaneously formed reading groups in the Houston area, some for women only, some of mixed gender. She notes that the ideology of the solitary reader has been dominant: the assumption that the ultimate locus of reading is individual, as opposed to social. Her survey of the reading groups is consistent with the discussions by Anne Ruggles Gere in her *Writing Groups* and in her *Intimate Practices: Literacy and Cultural Work in U.S. Women's Clubs, 1880-1920.*[42] Many initiatives were taken by women and others who were peripheral to mainstream and professional literati to create a more active sense of liter-

---

[40] Johannes Fabian, "Keep Listening: Ethnography and Reading," in *The Ethnology of Reading*, ed. Jonathan Boyarin, 80–97.

[41] Elizabeth Long, "Textual Interpretation as Collective Action," in *The Ethnology of Reading*, ed. Jonathan Boyarin, 180–211.

[42] Anne Ruggles Gere, *Writing Groups* (Carbondale: Southern Illinois University Press, 1987); and *Intimate Practices: Literacy and Cultural Work in U.S. Women's Clubs, 1880-1920* (Urbana: University of Illinois Press, 1997).

acy, including reading, writing, and discussion. Even as self-help, the reading groups were directed toward social change and the amelioration of society as a whole. Long notes that "sociopolitical allegiances condition engagement with books" (202).

Comment

Language use as membership presupposes the materiality of language and shows how genre and disclosure are necessary parts of writing. Situated as part of changing social memberships, language use is the combination of orality and literacy that enacts the materiality of meaning; it revokes the assumption that written texts must seem to stabilize reality, that language should control inchoate experiences, politics, values, and feelings. It exposes the "manly writing" values traced by Brody (see Chapter 2), and shows why they need not be the standard.

Chapter 4 considers men's responses and writing in which the values of separateness and purity are made available for classroom consideration. This disclosure shows that men are often largely unconscious of having androcentric language uses and memberships because they are the "unmarked" case. But we might also see how teaching language use coaxes unconscious masculine genres to appear in the classroom.

Chapter Four

Disclosing Unconscious Genres and Language Uses

Disclosing Genres

Men's memberships, language use, and roles in society have been part of the social scenes discussed in previous chapters. Men as a class and institutions made up of mostly men have been the "unmarked" or "standard" case.[1] In discussing the teaching of writing and language use, the consequences of men's belonging to an unmarked class need to be faced in classrooms and in society. Disclosing the genres of men's language faces these consequences by marking the genres and by teaching about situations in which they appear. This chapter considers how and why the genres of men's language[2] have not been accurately identified, and how these inaccuracies are the bases of classic failures of social relations such as violence and predatory behaviors of the privileged toward the unprivileged. The teaching of writing and language use is part of the social responsibility of teachers and schools to citizens. Disclosing genres identifies memberships and shows the relations of language use to people's experiences in everyday life.

---

[1] For many, women are considered a minority because this group is "marked."

[2] For those thinking about essentialism: we can all allow that not every member of an identified group should be considered to fall into the stipulated identity. In identifying men as a group, we are speaking of trends, styles, and tendencies rather than things that are or must be true in every case.

Because the unmarked is taken as a standard, the equivalence of men as a class to women as a class is obscured. The enhanced life-style of men is sometimes invisible because some women partici-pate in it. This invisibility appears in the writings of male students. In classrooms, when the inhibition common to the unmarked classes is reduced, some students write more candidly, permitting class members to learn about them and about their collective iden-tity in new ways. This less inhibited masculine style lets teachers raise more pointed, more urgent questions of genre.

The unmarked state of men's social identities is perpetuated in experience by the tendency to remain unaware of genre and lan-guage use. Proposing the principle of disclosing genres, this chapter first reviews some of the social and historical contexts for men's lan-guage uses and memberships. Scholars and critics have identified values that men hold about whose social effects men, collectively, are unconscious;[3] these values include heterosexuality, homopho-bia, misogyny, racism, and the tendency to violence. Because men are not generally aware of their own ways of holding these values, they participate to some extent in collective lying to oneself, to loved ones, and to colleagues. The lies appear in public as ordinary opinion or orientation and are taken as normal. Men's enhanced sta-tus in society produces collective deceptions and self-deceptions routinely. The teaching of writing discloses and studies these decep-tions.[4] Writing pedagogy is rarely understood to be responsible for teaching how to write truthfully. Yet what values could extended attention even to technical competence be serving if they were not primarily contributing to the long-term tasks of using language truthfully and responsibly?

Following a discussion of critical opinion, this chapter studies men's language uses (as reported in classrooms) that exemplify unconscious genres and social assumptions. The examples suggest that heterosexually identified (though not necessarily heterosexual) men often participate in damaged relationships, hatreds, fears, and insecurities among men and those who trust them (children and women). In social and historical contexts, the examples in the sec-tion Classroom Texts suggest that men's language use genres reflect

---

[3] This is not, of course, the "collective unconscious" of Carl Jung, who wrote that this form of unconsciousness is not only shared but inherited. Here "collective unconsciousness" means large numbers of people being unconscious of the same things.

[4] To say that some are telling the truth or lying is also to say that the genres of these tellings are accurately or inaccurately identified.

unconscious struggles that are often connected with the historically repeated excrescences of violence and killing, with the breakdowns of language and knowledge that accompany violence. To disclose these language use genres could be a step toward the reduction of violence in society.

Social and Historical Contexts

The United States Constitution articulates the right of the people to bear arms. Under some circumstances, ordinary citizens' use of arms to kill is also lawful.[5] In the army, everyone bears arms. Soldiers are trained to kill, and under some circumstances, a soldier is authorized to kill a member of his or her own army.

In the United States' Army (and other branches of the military), gay men and lesbians are not permitted to identify themselves as everyone else may; they must remain silent and "pass" as heterosexual. In civilian life, it frequently happens that no one objects to or prevents the assaulting of gay men by gangs of other men. Although recently there has been more public alertness to this crime, it is still common. At the highest levels of the military—the Joint Chiefs of Staff—and in the Congress, men say in public that gays are not welcome. While such views are homophobic and malicious, their presentation as principled views creates the window of tacit permissibility of violence against gay and lesbian soldiers. In order for this circumstance to obtain, there also has to be on the part of the military an agreement to lie about how things really are; large numbers of people have to agree to misuse the language or to permit others to misuse it in their presence. A double standard requires the collective agreement to lie and to misuse language in other ways. Teachers of writing and language use are responsible to teach how ordinary language participates in maintaining social double standards.[6]

The story told by José Zuniga[7] is an example of this situation. Although Zuniga's is an account of a gay man coming out, it represents the "coming out" of many nongay people toward values and

---

[5] As in the recent murder of a "trespassing" Japanese student who failed to respond to the homeowner's telling him to leave.

[6] This chapter deals in several ways with feelings and behaviors associated with the military. The following discussions should be considered as part of the picture of the military influence on society discussed in Chapter 7, Testing and grading, as one form of military psychology not identified as such, is a fundamental part of education.

[7] José Zuniga, "My Life in the Military Closet," *New York Times Magazine,* July 11, 1993, 40–42, 45, 58.

perspectives that, if adopted, would change society considerably. Having served with distinction in the army for four years, Zuniga was chosen for the "Soldier of the Year" award, to be bestowed by one of his admired teachers and heroes, Lieut. Gen. Glynn C. Mallory, Jr. This is Zuniga's account of the ceremony:

> As he pinned a Fifth Army Commendation Medal on my freshly pressed uniform, he whispered, "I'm damned proud to serve with you, son."
>
> Barely a week earlier, Mallory sat with me and several colleagues in a conference room watching a CNN report on homosexuals in the military. "Fags," he snorted, did not belong in "this man's Army."
>
> The words rang in my ears as Mallory pinned the award on me. I had kept my mouth shut then, and I did so now; ambition trumped my anger. I continued to smolder, knowing what I alone between us knew: I was one of the "fags" who did not belong. (41)

Under the circumstances described by Zuniga, whatever moves he might make—remain silent and stay, or speak out and leave—would seriously disrupt the life he had led until that moment. Nevertheless, the story seems to say that the moment at which that medal was bestowed by the very man who judged he didn't belong in the military seemed to him to violate something fundamental in human relations. He could not continue to admire Mallory and also be candid with him. Zuniga had to lie by not identifying himself truthfully. The values represented by Mallory, by the army, by male heroism, by patriotism, even by self-sacrifice, are shown to be sustained by fear and by lies that conceal this fear.

The fear I refer to is not of homosexual people or behavior, but of women and of a society in which there is gender equality.[8] Suzanne Pharr spells out this point:[9]

> Sexism, that system by which women are kept subordinate to men, is kept in place by three powerful weapons designed to cause or threaten women with pain and loss. . . . The three are economics, violence, and homophobia. (9)

> A lesbian is perceived as a threat to the nuclear family, to male dominance and control, to the very heart of sexism.

---

[8] The response of Ms. S to Toni Morrison's *Beloved* (see Chapter 3) suggests how the family is included in this list. Readers wanting to include a literary perspective might read her response alongside this discussion.

[9] Suzanne Pharr, *Homophobia: A Weapon of Sexism* (Little Rock, AR: Chardon Press, 1988).

Gay men are perceived also as a threat to male dominance and control, and the homophobia expressed against them has the same roots in sexism as does homophobia against lesbians. . . . They are seen as betrayers, as traitors who must be punished and eliminated. In the beating and killing of gay men we see clear evidence of this hatred. . . . For many men . . .war and sports offer a cover of all-male safety and dominance to keep away the notion of affectionate openness being identified with homosexuality. When gay men break ranks with male roles through bonding and affection outside the areas of war and sports, they are perceived as not being "real men," that is, as being identified with women, the weaker sex that must be dominated and that over the centuries has been the object of male hatred and abuse. (18–19)

Pharr reads homophobia as the transfer of misogyny to men. Her vision of history, similar to Gerda Lerner's,[10] presupposes the underlying structure of social relations as being based on heterosexuality and reproduction. However, for unknown reasons, men have acquired something "extra"—the power to "traffic in women."[11] This is a longstanding social power over women that is maintained by violence, intimidation, and economic domination, all of which entail and require psychological domination.

The socialization of heterosexual men requires education in the conservation, preservation, and perpetuation of this power. Processes of passing along the meanings of "civilization" depend, in turn, on the ideal of "compulsory heterosexuality."[12] The socially compulsory status of heterosexuality is its problematic aspect. When the compulsory feeling becomes part of young men's affective vocabulary, it urges them to convert something occurring spontaneously—namely, different levels and styles of sexual feeling—into something that has only one identity, which then is presumed, necessary, and enforced. A self-sustaining social cycle had been historically established by the forces or "weapons" discussed by Pharr and other analysts. In this cycle, heterosexuality has been idealized, relieved, so to speak, of its variations and uncertainties, and converted into an articulable social, philosophical, scientific, and religious dogma. This belief cluster is then textualized, thus appropriating the authority of literate civilization to its tasks.

---

[10] Gerda Lerner, *The Creation of Patriarchy* (New York: Oxford University Press, 1986).

[11] Gayle Rubin, "The Traffic in Women: Notes on the 'Political Economy' of Sex," *Signs* (1985): 157–210.

[12] Discussed by Adrienne Rich as well as by Pharr and others. Adrienne Rich, "Compulsory Heterosexuality and Lesbian Existence" (1980), in *Blood, Bread, and Poetry: Selected Prose*, 1979-1985 (New York: Norton, 1986), 23–75.

The process of idealization and textualization is what we today understand as education. (When we read we idealize; when we write we textualize.) As Thomas Kuhn outlines in *The Structure of Scientific Revolutions,*[13] science has been idealized and reduced to textbooks, making the harnessing or control of science easier but also misrepresenting both its history and its meaning. Similarly, and related to the usages of science, heterosexuality has been overtaken toward political ends and textualized in religious documents, which are in part the model for the science textbooks discussed by Kuhn, as science overtook religion to become the more influential factor in civilization.[14] Over the eight millennia identified by Gerda Lerner as the period of historical record, men's superior social position was maintained by portraying heterosexuality as civilization itself, natural law, human beings' greatest pleasure and greatest duty, something sacred overseen by the transcendental gods of different religions, and (in today's media) the one quality that may be associated with every human activity and especially with commercial activity.

The ideology of heterosexuality, not its practice, uses homophobia to support misogyny. Homophobia models the trope of sacrificing a small part for the preservation of the whole. Through participating in the social roles taken by both men and women, gay men challenge the rigid intrapsychic boundaries created by heterosexuality. They thus present a model of what is to be opposed so that the majority may overlook the unfair arrangements between men and women. Since the majority of women are also heterosexual, members of this majority may be deceived by homophobia into seeing themselves as part of the ideology of heterosexuality, thereby implicitly associating themselves with the interests of men as a separate gender. Even when some heterosexual women see themselves, lesbians, bisexuals, and gay and straight men as being in one political category, their reduced voices take this political stance out of play. Heterosexist ideology overrides what women think and advocate, and it often punishes them as well.

For the present discussion, the key fact to consider is this: Heterosexual men, and probably any heterosexual person, male or female, already participate to some extent, as individuals and as social figures, in genders and races other than one's single, publicly identified gender or race. Genders, like genres, are mixed. The political change

---

[13] Thomas Kuhn, *The Structure of Scientific Revolutions* (Chicago: University of Chicago Press, 1962/1970).

[14] For example, science, like religion, formulates transcendental "laws."

implied by the recognition of this fact is that it is no longer possible to assume a stable social hierarchy that requires the sacrifice of a small part of a "different" gender or race. The means of change are the education of people as to just how "my" group participates in "your" group, how "my" identity participates in "your" identity. This is the mutual disclosure of identities. Teaching ourselves to decline heterosexuality as a dominant perspective requires us to examine the cultures of other groups in society, to put them on the reading lists and discussion tables. As we discussed with regard to our memberships, we participate with those we first viewed as outsiders, aliens, or, in one way or another, not us. Such participation teaches us to stop lying to ourselves and others about the true scope of our set of social affiliations. The boundaries in practice between different kinds of people, while they exist, are not boundaries that control, but boundaries that mark: they are lines on the ground rather than fences or walls, material in their suggestive roles: writing and naming, subject to the customlike but changeable regularities of language use rather than to fixed, transcendental, underlying, law-of-nature rules.

Randy Shilts' study *Conduct Unbecoming*[15] gives historical perspectives and facts that show the participation of the straight majority in what might be understood as some mores of the gay and lesbian minorities in the military. Early in the book, he is discussing manhood, manliness, and virility, and their roles in military life:

> The futility of trying to establish virility through military service is obvious when one probes the notion of manhood in all its thoroughly nonbiological implications. Manhood is an entirely social construct. Even within the military, over time, definitions keep changing. . . . The Greek regimen produced one of the most fearsome, and thoroughly homosexual, corps of soldiers in the history of warfare, the Sacred Band of Thebes. As the popular saying of the time went, "An army of lovers can never be defeated." (32–33)

In every aspect except the acceptance of sexual intimacy, this description of the Sacred Band of Thebes[16] reflects the values of bonding that are now considered necessary for an effective fighting unit. In the army there are not colleagues but buddies. There is a definite ideal of interpersonal intimacy in the army that helps soldiers to preserve one another's lives. While the sense of invincibility cited by Shilts is only bravado, it is similar to the intensity of het-

---

[15] Randy Shilts, *Conduct Unbecoming: Gays and Lesbians in the U. S. Military* (New York: St. Martins, 1993).

[16] A description of which is also found in David F. Greenberg, *The Construction of Homosexuality* (Chicago: University of Chicago Press, 1988), 115.

erosexual fathers protecting their women and children. Just as nuclear patriarchal families have an erotic basis, so do these military families, which generate the extra motivation to fight harder and perhaps take more risks on one another's behalf in the interests of their preexisting closeness.

In his discussion of pre-Christian civilizations in *The Construction of Homosexuality,* David Greenberg cites the classical Greek belief that soldiers' contact with women may compromise their ability to fight (110). Aristocratic warrior groups in pursuit of their military ideals accepted and often promoted homosexual love among soldiers; but also, homosexual love relations between soldiers and young nonsoldiers were equally manifest (111); both forms of relationship preserved the ideal of remaining separate from women. Greenberg cites Aristotle's reports that the Celts of 500 B.C.E. "esteemed homosexuality" and then cites a first century B.C.E. source, Diodorous Siculus, who wrote of the Celts, "the men are much keener on their own sex; they lie around on animal skins and enjoy themselves, with a lover on each side" (111). Greenberg's discussion of homosexual mores in "archaic civilization" is far-ranging and helps to suggest the idea that homophobia as we know it is the result of the Judeo-Christian culture's overtaking of European civilization. At the same time this discussion shows that in pre-Christian Europe then, as now, military organizations served to create a decisive boundary between men and women; then, male homosexuality may have been the "weapon of sexism" in just the same way homophobia is today.[17]

Shilts reminds us of the strong "homosexual subtext of the armed forces" (401) and especially the Navy. Shilts makes a point of this because the "United States Navy, more than any other service, was dedicated to purging itself of homosexuality" (402). He cites both playful rituals and public sensations, as well as the total atmosphere and ways of life aboard large warships as contributing to the homoerotic subtext. Describing conditions on the USS Enterprise in 1982, he cites the end of the "shellback" ritual, at which time the sailors who were "initiated" after their first crossing of the equator were naked and "strutted around the deck. Their nudity was evidence of their having passed the test."

---

[17] This point is implied with some emphasis with regard to Enlightenment Europe in David Noble's book *World Without Women* (New York: Knopf, 1992).

> The players in the games aboard the USS Enterprise—experiment-
> ing with transvestism, simulated fellatio, sadomasochistic role
> playing, and group nudity—were not gay. Rather they were sailors
> participating in a time-honored Navy tradition. . . . After the cross-
> ing and the ceremonies, the sailor became a "shellback." (400)

Shilts emphasizes a fact about life at sea that those of us on land
most of the time might not consider: it is difficult for the young heterosexual sailors to spend such long periods of time away from
women. He reminds us of Winston Churchill's wisecrack that naval
tradition is "nothing but rum, sodomy, and the lash" (401). And
with regard to submarine life, there is "the old Navy cliche that a
submarine leaves port with 120 crew members but returns with 60
couples" (402). Rather than arguing that Navy life creates homosexuality, he is portraying something different: most sailors remain heterosexual and engage in homosexual activity. Occasions of
homosexual sex do not mean that the sailors are thereby choosing
homosexual or bisexual lifestyles in some definitive way. Rather,
homosexual activity is a part of their affective vocabulary, just as it
was in the pre-Christian era. For most, it is a minor part of their history; for some it is their identity.

This is not the Navy's view nor that of the heterosexual sailors.
The activities, described by Shilts and subsequently in *Newsweek*[18]
are understood as jokes, pranks, foolishness, silliness, things, in any
event, that *don't count.* The boundary between these activities and
the main work of sailors on warships is considered a strong and
rigid one. Considerable mental energy is spent separating the two
zones of "action." The reluctance to understand the horseplay as
itself serious and meaningful even as it is lighthearted and frivolous
is the machinery of repression: there is no reason not to acknowledge its serious elements because people's underlying sexual orientations and identities would not be changed by such experiences.
The need for repression derives from nonpersonal, political considerations—the preservation of men's superior social status. One
might speculate that because this status was secure among men in
Greek society, homosexuality was considered a contribution to that
security.

Gary David Comstock[19] considers that the recent upsurge of
violence in North America is related to the recent challenges to
men's superior status mounted by movements of the disenfran-

---

[18] David Gelman, "Homoeroticism in the Ranks," *Newsweek,* July 26, 1993, 28–29.

[19] Gary David Comstock, *Violence Against Lesbians and Gay Men* (New York: Columbia University Press, 1991).

chised—women, ethnic minorities, gays/lesbians. He observes that one of the ways in which the men in power have responded is to reaffirm the father-led nuclear family ("family values") as well as to attack "alternative life styles," i. e., those of nonheterosexuals. This view is consistent with such writings as Susan Faludi's analysis[20] of the seemingly progressive television drama, *thirtysomething*, which, she says, holds up the nuclear family as a model (160–163). She describes how many other shows, especially the popular soap operas, subscribe to the "matrimonial imperative" by raising the rates of marriage and lowering the divorce rate (158).

As Faludi and other observers of this scene have already noted, it is the preaching of the religious right that has most regularly and for the longest periods articulated the priority of family, matrimony, and heterosexuality over other possible domestic choices. This is one fact that lends credibility to Comstock's comparison of the social context of Leviticus to today's North American societies. The reason for Comstock's attention to ancient Hebrew society is that in Leviticus, the third book of the Pentateuch, are found the two oldest biblical verses that are taken to be foundational justifications for homophobic violence; these verses are understood to underlie the homophobic sentiment in the New Testament as well:

> You shall not lie with a male as with a woman; it is an abomination. (18:22)

> If a man lies with a male as with a woman, both of them have committed an abomination; they shall be put to death, their blood is upon them. (20:13)

Comstock describes how Leviticus is essentially a long list of laws and rules of human relations for the Hebrews as they prepare to move from Sinai into Canaan. Thus, he observes, "Leviticus is about defining a separate community that sets itself apart by virtue of its superior differences with others" (126). He suggests that the Hebrew concept of "holiness" is used for this purpose of communal definition and separation.

Consider the historical picture, namely, the theory that the book of Leviticus was compiled as a preparation for a Hebrew restoration, courtesy of Cyrus of Persia, who reconquered Babylon forty-nine years after the Babylonian destruction of the First Jerusalem Temple in 587–586 B.C.E. The Hebrews were living among many other nations such as the Babylonians (now Iraq) and the Persians (now Iran). This

---

[20] Susan Faludi, *Backlash: The Undeclared War Against American Women* (New York: Crown, 1991).

is approximately contemporaneous with warrior cults in Europe and the Mediterranean welcome of the homosexual lifestyle. A series of laws was compiled in Leviticus to discipline the Hebrews to live their own lives as a buttress against temptation toward assimilation to the larger, allegedly less disciplined nations. The detailed laws of Leviticus, Comstock writes, amounted to the "repeated warning against doing as the surrounding nations do" in order to "establish order and control with the authority of Yahweh's voice from the past" (129).

This account is plausible, as are Comstock's comparisons of the Mediterranean societies of twenty-five hundred years ago to contemporary societies, in spite of the historical distance. It is noteworthy that only some Hebrew formulations were taken up in subsequent Christian societies, when so much else in Hebrew law and tradition was abandoned or overruled. One likely reason for the retention of the prohibition against homosexuality is that Christianity still shares with Judaism the commitment to the patriarchal family, and in general, to the mores of male public privilege. Furthermore, if generally Jewish life today does not have as strong an antagonism toward homosexuality as, for example, the Roman Catholic Church does, this may be a result of less hierarchical and authority-driven social and religious organization with more tolerance for variations from the traditional patriarchal family.

Comstock's account suggests that violence against gays and lesbians is historically related to the practice of isolating the patriarchal family as a distinct, privileged, even sacred way of social functioning. But his account implies more than this, namely, that commitment to the family goes along with a hierarchical rule of society in general, a rule that reduces women collectively to a less privileged status and separates them generally from men, thus leading to the special violence wrought on gay men and lesbians because of their explicit challenge to the separation of genders and male rule in family and society.[21] When homosexuality is accepted, it is only because men's rule is already assured. And regardless of whether a society supports violence against gays and lesbians, an androcentric society has as a threat, and sometimes uses as a means, violence against women, including the at least tacit right to rape women.

It has already been observed that in societies such as Sparta and Nazi Germany, which encourage and honor militarism, physical culture and fitness are promoted to exaggerated and obsessional levels. Pressing one's body to its limits and beyond has become a hallmark of

---

[21] Recall again, in this context, the response of Ms. S to Morrison's *Beloved* in Chapter 3: "Women who solely are homemakers are slaves."

the ideology of manhood. One of the main zones of such activity is American football, whose constituents, under pressure to win at any cost, have been moving beyond the body's limits with steroids.[22] This one sort of exaggerated pressure is supplemented by the additional belief that one may illegitimately harm one's opponent in the effort to win, as I discuss shortly in the writings of students. We may therefore expect to find in football, a contact sport to begin with, a similar kind of homoerotic subtext that Shilts and Gelman described in the Navy.

The grounds for such claims lie in what happens in public (in plain sight) rather than in knowledge of what sexual activities are preferred by players in their individual lives.[23] Alan Dundes, in his analysis of American football,[24] reflects on this sport just as Shilts reflects on Navy rituals. Certain background facts about football are germane, such as Dundes' thought that "it is almost as though the masculinity of male alumni is at stake in a given game" (199). Dundes does not ask why football has become important, though Comstock's answer may also apply to Dundes' discussion: football, the most physically violent team sport there is, requiring elaborate protection equipment merely for normal play, has increased in importance and popularity even beyond where it was when Dundes wrote about it: the increase in interest in football by men parallels the increase in violence against gays and lesbians in contemporary society.[25]

Dundes suggests the same psychology operating in football interest as in Navy horseplay: a way to indulge one's implication in homoerotic feelings while concealing this individual psychology

---

[22] Isn't it also true that the national obsession with the Simpson case represents the collective sense that football success may have led beyond social and family limits?

[23] This value is thought to differ for men and women. A recent commentary in the *New York Times* (May 30, 1993, Section 4, p. 11) by Jill Ellen Steinberg, "Why Is It Different for Men?" claims women on athletic teams are much less likely to think about the private lives of other team members than men on athletic teams. On a team with both lesbian and heterosexual players, Steinberg reports, there was virtually no thought given to the showering and changing activity. The women did not assume that sexual thoughts follow from their physical, athletic activities. Steinberg wonders why men assume that sexual thoughts are related to athletic privacies.

[24] Alan Dundes, "Into the Endzone for a Touchdown: A Psychoanalytic Consideration of American Football," in *Interpreting Folklore* (Bloomington: Indiana University Press, 1980), 199–210.

[25] In this connection Mariah Burton Nelson's book, *The Stronger Women Get, the More Men Love Football: Sexism and the American Culture of Sports* (New York: Harcourt, Brace, 1994), has gotten media attention. Its perspective is consistent with those of Pharr and Comstock as well as those of the students whose work is discussed in this chapter: men's love of implicitly homoerotic contact and violence is a reaction formation to women's gaining political influence.

from the group of men. He writes: "I think it is highly likely that the ritual aspect of football, providing as it does a socially sanctioned framework for male body contact . . . is a form of homosexual behavior" (209). If one takes this view, heterosexuality as a value and violence as a team self-indulgence are exaggerated to the same extent that homoerotic feelings are repressed. The game's terminology, more or less, makes this case. The idea is to move the ball into the opponent's end zone. It is to penetrate the other's space. At scrimmage, the players align themselves in the three-point stance, their buttocks becoming their body's highest point and facing their own teammates, who are to be trusted not to penetrate them. Meanwhile, the quarterback places his hands in the genital area of the center, actually touching the center's buttocks, and waits to get the ball from him. The quarterback may "pass" the ball, give it off, or run with it. The ball itself, unlike other balls (but like, because derived from, the rugby ball), is elongated (a feature of the game not mentioned by Dundes but nevertheless germane to his description) and can only move forward quickly if thrown—passed—a certain way. Those catching the ball are "wide receivers," "split ends," "tight ends," and "backs." There are also such plays as "end run" and "end around." The fundamental motion of the game is painful: the opposition physically resists penetration of its space: the opposition is either overpowered or deceived, though on occasion it is outrun. Because offensive players are more vulnerable than defensive players, the latter try, covertly and illegitimately, to harm the former, and this practice is known and tacitly approved, and lied about in public. Even though Dundes calls his reading of the game psychoanalytic, it is not necessarily that, since the language itself carries enough homoerotic connotations, along with the actual contact and kinds of touching that are part of the game, for us to acknowledge the homoerotic dimension in football.

Dundes also reflects on the routine locker-room language in football, citing Kopay and Young's[26] book, which recounts the experience of one of the few football players admitting to be gay. The citations there are quite like what we will see, shortly, to be the language of undergraduates fifteen years later:

> The whole language of football is involved in sexual allusions. We were told to go out and "fuck those guys"; to take that ball and "stick it up their asses" or "down their throats." The coaches would yell, "Knock their dicks off," or more often than that,

---

[26] David Kopay and Perry Deane Young, *The David Kopay Story: An Extraordinary Self-Revelation* (New York: Donald I. Fine, 1977).

"Knock their jocks off." They'd say, "Go out there and give it all you've got, a hundred and ten percent, shoot your wad." You controlled the line and "knocked" 'em into submission. Over the years I've seen many a coach get emotionally aroused while he was diagramming a particular play into an imaginary hole on the blackboard. His face red, his voice rising, he would show the ball carrier how he wanted him to "stick it in the hole." (Dundes 207)

This account helps us to understand the connection between sex and violence in the minds of many men and also suggests how violence against gays by straights is a reaction-formation, an exaggerated attempt to deny one's own implication in the loosening of sexual boundaries and the enlarging of identities.

The Kopay story and its citation of coaches' language leads us back to the issues of language use. In 1974, Andrea Dworkin related the matter of language use and public lying to the perpetuation of sexism throughout history. She believes that a change in the role of language is essential to permit society's escape from historic woman hating.[27] In her introduction, where she considers the act of writing, and at the end, in a self-punctuated objection to the editor's insistence on standard punctuation, Dworkin surrounds her treatise with warnings and demonstrations of the abuse of language in our society. However, her remarks offer a purpose beyond the need to speak out:

Academics lock books in a tangled web of mindfuck and abstraction. The notion is that there are ideas, then art, then somewhere else, unrelated, life. . . . Because of this strange schizophrenia, books and the writing of them have become embroidery on a dying way of life. Because there is contempt for the process of writing, for writing as a way of discovering meaning and truth, and for reading as a piece of that same process, we destroy with regularity the few serious writers we have . . . it is a great tragedy, for the work of the writer has never been more important than it is now in Amerika.

Many see that in this nightmared land, language has no meaning and the work of the writer is ruined . . . we cannot talk or hear each other speak. It is the work of the writer to reclaim the language from those who use it to justify murder, plunder, violation. . . .

Those of us who love reading and writing believe that being a writer is a sacred trust. It means telling the truth. It means being incorruptible. It means not being afraid, and never lying. Those of us who love reading and writing feel great pain because so many people who write books have become cowards, clowns, and liars.

---

[27] Andrea Dworkin, *Woman Hating* (New York: Penguin, 1974).

> To keep the sacred trust of the writer is simply to respect the
> people and to love the community. (24–25)

These thoughts appear in her introduction because much of her documentation of how our culture hates women comes from literature—fairy tales, pornography, and mythology. She describes how
texts lie and how they are read mendaciously. A theme of her book
is that lying is bound up with sexism and that the hatred of women
is so deep that it has perverted the language in ways that we cannot
even see because we identify with our received language. In the
introduction and in other parts of her treatise, her use of language is
so disturbing that one cannot help but hear the thought—an alarm,
harsh as it probably sounds to many—that many ordinary uses of
language in the academy and in everyday life are perpetuating suffering and debasing society.

One of Dworkin's final paragraphs connects the inertia of the
sex/gender system with the "doorkeepers" of the "Law" of speech
and language.

> This book is about the Immovable Sexual Structure. in the process
> of having it published, Ive encountered the Immovable Punctua-
> tion Typography Structure, and I now testify, as so many have
> before me, that the Immovable Structure aborts freedom, prohibits
> invention, and does us verifiable harm: it uses our holy human
> energy to sustain itself; it turns us into enforcers, or outlaws; to sur-
> vive we must learn to lie. (203)[28]

The "immovable sexual structure" requires the education that
allows one to survive its immovability: learning to lie. Dworkin's
use of terms like "sacred trust" and "holy human energy" portray
her reappropriation of religious feeling and authority. She associates
her argument with Kafka's perspective by citing a short passage
from the end of *The Trial*,[29] where K., in the Cathedral, hears a story
from the priest (who had identified himself as the "prison chaplain"
[210]) about the "doorkeeper" who guards the entrance to the Law.
The priest counsels that the doorkeeper is to be *identified with* the
Law. K., persevering in his deluded rationality and thus relying on

---

[28] An autoethnographic note. The similarity between the term "Immovable Sexual
Structure" and the sense of the permanence of the reduced condition of women in
society was, from time to time, shared with me by mother. She recounted the views of
her mother regarding marriage: "In order to stay married, you have to be able to delude
yourself." This thought identifies the connection between sexism and lying that
Dworkin is discussing.

[29] Franz Kafka, *The Trial* (New York: Schocken, 1937/1956/1964/1968).

the ultimate authority of the truth, counters that if what the priest says is the case, then "one must accept as true everything the door-keeper says." Dworkin's citation concludes:

> "No," said the priest, "it is not necessary to accept everything as true, one must only accept it as necessary."
> "A melancholy conclusion," said K. "It turns lying into a universal principle." (220)

Dworkin's use of this passage to contribute to her argument helps to enlarge its original application (lying as the principle of sexism) by including its unconscious application: lying is a principle of masculine social identity. In the novel, the priest's counsel and behavior identifies the Law with the Church; this is almost certainly how society appeared to Kafka and to Jews in Czechoslovakia early in this century. The "universal principle" of lying is a principle that both Catholics and Jews must accept (pursuant to this portrayal in the novel). But in this same section of the novel, just before the priest brings out the story of the doorkeeper and the Law, there is the following exchange:

> "What is the next step you propose to take in the matter?" asked the priest. "I'm going to get more help," said K., looking up again to see how the priest took his statement. "There are several possibilities I haven't explored yet." "You cast about too much for outside help," said the priest disapprovingly, "especially from women. Don't you see that it isn't the right kind of help?" "In some cases, even in many, I could agree with you," said K., "but not always. Women have great influence. If I could move some women I know to join forces in working for me, I couldn't help winning through. Especially before this Court, which consists almost entirely of petticoat-hunters. Let the Examining Magistrate see a woman in the distance and he knocks down his desk and the defendant in his eagerness to get at her." (211)

The priest immediately changes the subject and moves toward the "doorkeeper" discussion. However, the foregoing exchange extends the meaning of Dworkin's use of the other passage. The priest's job is to explain to K. that no help will be forthcoming because the Law, the Church, and the doorkeeper are all locked together establishing lying as a universal principle. K., however, is always ridiculously searching for the truth. The "lying" passage (cited by Dworkin) functions in the novel to revoke the sentiment in the "women" citation, namely, K.'s persistent but self-deluded belief that he still is connected to women, though they are obviously "outside" of the Law and the Church in the novel and in society. K.'s conversation is also amusing and ironic, claiming that women have "great influence," and that

they might well "join forces" with him and help him, as if they share
his political cause. But what evidence of their political influence
does he have? The sexual incontinence of the Examining Magistrate!
K. or Kafka or both articulate that women have influence but actually
mean this influence to be the usual sexual sort. In a sense, K. vaguely
implies and perhaps even hopes that a serious appearance by women
on his behalf will catch? bribe? deceive? the Magistrate into a favorable approach to K., who partly participates in the Magistrate's
misogyny and partly retains his respect for women. The priest, by
then citing the doorkeeper story, tries to purge K. of this vain sense
that women are finally in the same community as he is. The means of
purging for the priest: the coercive power of the Law; the meaning of
the purging for K.: lying as a universal principle. Dworkin, in her
brief citation, uses the example of Kafka in the cause of exhibiting a
male figure, necessarily caught up in the perversions represented by
Church and Law, nevertheless searching for the "whole truth," the
entirety of his gender makeup rather than lying and continuing to
live in the "pure" identity of male for self, female for others.

Some male students are in this intermediary stage in their
responses to issues raised by Dworkin. The young men are trying to
tell the truth, to be writers in the sense suggested by Dworkin, yet
fail in the sense that K. does.

Classroom Texts

The Context

My advanced undergraduate course, Seminar in Writing: Telling the
Truth, presented the subjects of writing and language use as dealing
with problems of "telling the truth" in public and professional life.
One view of this issue and of language, teaching, and society was
represented by Adrienne Rich's *On Lies, Secrets, and Silence*,[30]
while the (more or less) traditional viewpoint was represented by
Lynne Cheney's reflection on then-current National Endowment for
the Humanities philosophy entitled *Telling the Truth*.[31] Between
these two perspectives, a variety of issues was considered, includ-

---

[30] Adrienne Rich, *On Lies, Secrets and Silence: Selected Prose 1966–1978* (New York: Norton, 1979).

[31] Lynne Cheney, *Telling the Truth: A Report on the State of Humanities in Higher Education* (Washington: National Endowment for the Humanities, 1992).

ing hedging, euphemism, and jargon as ways of obscuring "true" meanings, as well as different contexts that determine what "truth" is in different ways. This, at least, was the planned curriculum.[32]

Because of an accident of enrollment, this course "unconsciously" had as one of its principal subject matters what is happening collectively to men as society reexamines traditional masculine roles. Particularly, the term *unconscious* seemed to describe accurately the trouble men feel as our privileged status is reconsidered. The work of some of the men in this course shows that this trouble comes from the disclosure of the kind of discontent experienced by both Zuniga and Mallory. Students used new essay genres to explore the problems they are experiencing as gender roles are reviewed. The essays they wrote suggest the terms and pace of change in the lives of individuals and groups in connection with this gradual disclosure. In addition, we can discern suggestions about what may be happening collectively, on a larger scale in society. Some men accept the need for change in how things are said, announced, and thought about, while others answer its challenges with personal defenses, describing their own sensitivity, their history of feeling responsive to the claims of aggrieved constituencies. Many men show a new level of personal and social uncertainty, previously masked by exaggerated truculence or pugnaciousness, or by facile assumptions about self and society. This uncertainty reaches public consciousness through changes in the usual classroom genres, through feeling able to say things previously not admissible in school.

The accident of enrollment referred to above was the student population—six white men, two women (one white, one Asian), and me, the white male teacher. In their presentational manner, five of the seven men were talkative and loud; two of the men were soft-spoken and not given to interrupting. The two women were reserved, reluctant to chime in, sometimes raising their hands to speak but tending to stay silent while the men's shouting, including my own, proceeded. I sometimes interrupted the shouting and urged

---

[32] Chapter 6 considers contingency in classrooms a necessary feature in order for the curriculum to be responsive to what the students bring to class. The material presented in this chapter from this course is one of several classroom experiences that taught me how to look for, find, and utilize initiatives by students to change the course plans, concerns, and curriculum.

the two women to share their thoughts, which they did more often than not, but briefly. Here is how this situation looked to one of the two female students, Ms. P:

> Mr. G would ask Bleich about the presidential election or vice versa and suddenly there was a debate on which candidate would win and then a bet over beer was being worked out to see who could guess the winner. Someone would ask what kind of beer and the loser should buy. . . . I suddenly found myself in left field. I didn't know whether I should say something because I felt that I had been gradually pushed out of the conversation, out of the circle, out of the field, and onto the bleachers as a spectator. I was no longer a player. I was flustered because the males could introduce and carry on any conversation they wanted to and I could not. I wanted to be a participant because it was more fun.

The frustration this course had for Ms. P led to a final essay, which, through an ethnographic account of our class, prepared as her final project, disclosed the foregoing perspective through the above events and several others that frustrated her. In spite of feeling inhibited by the men, both women wrote hard-hitting ethnographic descriptions of class, and shared and discussed these accounts with the rest of the class in plenary. I often tried to make room for the women to speak, but probably too many times, as suggested above, I was part of the problem. However, Ms. P observes the following:

> I knew Bleich was aware of Ms. F's and my feelings. He was careful of what he said and more attentive to what we said. I know that Bleich was even "nicer" to us. He had raised his voice so often to the guys, especially to Mr. G. When Mr. R mumbled, Bleich would say, "Speak up!" but when Ms. F whispered like a "mouse," he either looked like he was straining his ears or he would say something in a gentle voice. I didn't mind the special treatment even though I knew it was unfair for the guys. I may have stepped into a man's shoes when I saw the unequal treatment by Bleich yet I did not say anything; in fact I liked it. It was great to be on the other end for a while. I had the desire to agree with Mr. S vocally [about the unequal treatment] but I also thought it was unfair at the same time how once women or non-whites get preferential treatment, it becomes so obvious and white men are quickly up in arms.

Into this atmosphere class members were invited to "tell the truth" and explore the ways our language use conventions help us to conceal "true" things from ourselves and others. People treated one another with respect, but the men perceived the women as secondary in some sense; men's respect for women in the sense of courtesy did not lead to eagerness to hear the women's thoughts. I tried to insure that the women had the chance to speak and that their work was studied. At the same time, the men did feel that they could learn in public, that the atmosphere was finally safe for them to "be themselves." The women also felt it was safe to share thoughts and feelings that do not normally emerge for discussion in school. Each class member considered all the others to be trustworthy. In the following discussion, I consider the work of three male students, trying to show what genres of disclosure encouraged discussion of unconscious masculine psychology: how the allegedly normal masculine identity presupposes violence, misogyny, and homophobia, all connected with one another but not acknowledgeable as values associated with this identity.

Euphemisms for Love and Sex

Mr. B was one of the soft-spoken members of this class but was close friends with the others, especially with the loudest and most politically conservative in the class. He was from a well-to-do family, and he went to a good high school before coming to this university. Mr. B had an offbeat life as a student: he was particularly proud of his ability to present himself as an African American rap artist. In a sense, Mr. B was already bilingual or bicultural in that he could easily shift back and forth between a white and an African American voice persona. In his essay on hedging and euphemism, which was presented in a traditional analytical genre, Mr. B conceptualized hedging and euphemism as linguistic tropes which, in the contexts he described, acted as forms of lying.

Mr. B first cites an episode of *Star Trek* that presents a fictional society of genderless people:

> Anyone who claims to have the feelings of either the male or female gender is quickly arrested and "cured" (brainwashed) of their "problem." As the show progresses we see one of the alien people begin to express female feelings. She expresses an attraction for one of the male heterosexual members of the Enterprise. (Reiker, for all you Trekkies.)
>
> At one point, she reveals her oppressed feelings to the man. She describes how she lives in fear of her own people. She describes how she has no control over her natural desires and how it is unfair that her kind is persecuted. During this scene, she is identified as the heroine of the show. The audience sees the message that people should not be punished for the sole reason of having different wants and needs.

Mr. B reads the reversal of sexual orientation identities in this episode as a "euphemism for the plight of the homosexual in the world today." Why is this reversal to be understood as a euphemism instead of just a metaphor? He explains:

> In accordance with the government's FCC laws of censorship, we can see a man and a woman kiss on television, yet, we cannot see a man and a man kiss. Therefore the episode is able to show us a heterosexual relationship much more easily than it could show us a homosexual one. The show hedges around the issue by being able to give a positive heterosexual example of homosexuality. Instead of disregarding the issue, the show uses hedging in order to discuss it within the censorship boundaries. . . .
>
> By using euphemism, the viewer is not only able to hear an opinion from the homosexual point of view, but is also able to see an example of the ugly persecution that goes with it. The euphemism is able to draw upon a common theme in humanity.

How about the phrase, "a positive heterosexual example of homosexuality"? In *Star Trek,* Mr. B judges, heterosexuality is a euphemism for homosexuality. What might this mean? Well, "passed away" is a euphemism for "died." "Settled your account" is a euphemism for "paid your bill." "Internal revenue" for "government's taxes." And so on. In each case, a euphemism refers to the same thing as the item it replaces. If you read heterosexuality as a euphemism instead of as a metaphor—that is, instead of as a reversal—we would think that heterosexuality, like homosexuality, can be understood as one social identity genre among others and that it is neither more nor less right for all people than is homosexuality. The *Star Trek* metaphor/reversal calls attention to the assumption of a predominantly heterosexual television audience. Its use begins to overcome the habits of ignoring an important social fact.

Reading heterosexuality as a euphemism made it possible for Mr. B to announce a sense of the social equivalence of the two categories rather than their conventionally perceived unequal status. Mr. B describes another instance of hedging and euphemism in the same essay: a reading of his own language use in high school.

> In high school I met a female named Marge. She and I began to see each other regularly. I had sexual intercourse for the first time with Marge. In fact, we had it regularly. During the time we spent together (one and one-half years), Marge and I bonded closely.

Mr. B relates in the next few paragraphs how he would try not to admit in public, when asked by his friends, that he was seeing Marge regularly "because I was not mature enough to be able to deal with a relationship that included love and sexual relations." He felt he had to pretend not to be involved. He writes,

Over time, this pretending grew. Shrugging off responsibility and claims to my serious relationship made other immature males think I was some kind of "stud." Euphemisms for love became rampant. My false show of apathy turned me into a cocky bastard. I began hearing questions like, "Are you fucking her?" "You bet I'm fucking her," I would respond. Even though this answer seems harsh to me now, it was definitely a euphemism (for my male friends) in high school. "I'm fucking her" was a much more acceptable and prevalent term than "I love her." . . . My entire nonchalant attitude in front of my friends was a sexist euphemism for love, something I could never publicly express for fear of being ridiculed.

It had not occurred to me to read men's bragging about sex as a euphemism. Yet many have observed that men have trouble acknowledging their feelings of tenderness. If Mr. B's account is to be believed, heterosexual men's harsh speech about sex and women often functions as a euphemism for what to men are more difficult tasks: describing feelings of tenderness, dependency, and vulnerability.

Mr. B's juxtaposition of instances is suggestive: he observes that both heterosexuality in the *Star Trek* episode and heterosexual bragging are euphemisms for homosexuality on the one hand and for tender feelings toward women on the other. This conclusion is consistent with Suzanne Pharr's discussion[33] of how sexism, violence, and homophobia are "extra" concealments of the sexually "mixed" character of men's social identity. Mr. B's insight came from an inquiry into the ways hedging and euphemism appear in public contexts. He was considering a familiar language use style, and he found instances in both popular culture and in his own life that, first, changed slightly the sense of what a euphemism is, and, more distinctively, enlarged its meaning in a way that gives insight into how sexuality could be changing its identity in society: feelings of understanding and tolerance for homosexual behavior and respect for tenderness in heterosexual relationships have been concealed in similar ways for similar reasons. Young men, including privileged white males like Mr. B, can, by interrogation of their own language use habits along with their own cultural texts, find enough space in the classroom to participate in movements of social change. Because Mr. B is himself somewhat unusual in addition to being a member of the most privileged group in America, he is in a position to influence his less understanding friends.

---

[33] Suzanne Pharr, *Homophobia.*

Perhaps another, if uncertain, index of change in the gender identity consciousness in young men could be the unusual announcement
by Mr. B of "the first time" he had intercourse, an announcement I had
not seen before in student essays. Mr. B's work demonstrates what
Dworkin claims about how writing functions. Here, in a public place,
private feelings and insight about a "frontier" issue in social change
have been rearticulated, changing the meanings, slightly, of received
terms in order to express Mr. B's changing knowledge of self in society.

Mr. B's writing shows something about which men are mostly
unconscious and women are mostly conscious: the possibility that
heterosexual men will become physically violent toward women and
with each other when communication doesn't yield quick solutions,
and sometimes for no apparent reason. Something pertinent to the earlier discussions of homoeroticism in the military and in sports
emerges in reading the students' work: to men violence has an erotic
component in heterosexual and homosexual situations. The language
cited by Mr. B—"Are you fucking her?"—suggests this feeling, as do
other slang words used in the same situation, like "banging," "pok-
ing," "nailing," and so on. Consider this passage from Robert Cormier's
The Chocolate War,[34] which characterizes Emile Janza, a bully in the
all-male parochial high school that is the main scene of the novel:

> For instance, when he went to the john at school he seldom flushed
> the toilet—and got a kick out of picturing the next kid who'd go in
> and find the mess in the bowl. Crazy. And if you told anybody, it
> would be hard to explain. Like how he sometimes felt actually
> horny when he roughhoused a kid or tackled a guy viciously in
> football and gave him an extra jab when he had him on the ground.
> How could you tell anybody about that? (42)

That he "felt actually horny" and the tacit sense that this feeling
can't be told show male sadism, which is pleasure in another's pain
as well as sexual pleasure experienced in the act of inflicting the
pain. In this instance, the pleasures are homoerotically sexual, and
the inflicting of the pain is, in a sense, a sex act, a fact that bears on
the feelings involved for men in war and sports. As a rule, such
admissions are found mainly in fiction, but students also tell their
own experiences in ways that, if identified by classmates and readers, teach new language and new social awareness.

There is reason to understand heterosexual men's tendency to
violence as a repression of homoerotic feelings—in the novel, the
repression is evident in the sense that violence "can't" be explained

---

[34] Robert Cormier, *The Chocolate War* (New York: Dell, 1974).

or is otherwise "crazy."[35] Male heterosexual violence results from
repression—and perhaps from conscious suppression—of one's feelings of tenderness or vulnerability, as in the case of Mr. B. This tender
feeling, in turn, is related to homoerotic feeling: tenderness is felt by
and toward both sexes, as when parents and siblings have the same
kind of tender feelings toward family members of either sex. The case
of Emile Janza suggests that male physical strength is used violently
on others in order for the individual to conceal from himself the
socially unacceptable fact that he may have tender feelings for both
sexes. In the novel, Janza has affectionate feelings for other young
men in the school's ruling junta. That one should become sexually
excited in the act of inflicting pain on someone else is the perverse
outward manifestation (in men) of believing that it is perverse to be
tender and more perverse to feel tenderly toward other men. With this
sense of men's psychology, consider the discussions of the language
of football given by Mr. F, another student in my Seminar in Writing.

Sports Language

In a loose partnership with Mr. S, another student in the seminar, Mr.
F wrote his discussion of language use in high school football. The
two explored "two sides of the coin," namely, Mr. F's discussion of
the language used by coaches to motivate teams, and Mr. S's discussion of how he and his father conversed around their many games of
tennis with one another. Their common introduction cites the following exhortation as being ordinarily given by coaches of male athletic
teams: "Be a *man;* don't play like a damn *pussy.*" This is the same language cited by Kopay and Young,[36] as well as by other students who
have reported on locker-room language in football from first-hand
experience. Kopay and Young have the following interpretation:

> On one level they [heterosexual teammates, coaches, the sport's
> ideologues] would insist on the complete absence of homosexual-
> ity among them. On another they are confirming its presence—in
> their minds, at least—by the endless banter and jokes about it. (51)

The coach's exhortation combines the two sides of F's and S's study:
the urging toward physical bodily violence described by Mr. F, and
the conscious, almost passionate, attempt by Mr. S's father to use
tennis to separate himself and his son from the three women in their

---

[35] The Cormier passage is pertinent to the considerations given in note 25, above.

[36] David Kopay and Perry Young, *The David Kopay Story.* The reader is also referred
to Jill Steinberg's commentary "Why Is It Different for Men?"

family. This semicollaborative study suggests that the disclosure of interpersonal physical violence, misogyny, and homophobia is a part of the curriculum of writing and language use. The focus, in addition to those on euphemism and truthtelling, is on how some genres of language use are unacknowledged partners in maintaining rationalizations and other self-deceptive practices: for example, "boys will be boys."

Mr. F is a biology major and respects the standards of detachment that are used in writing descriptions of work in the biology laboratory. He reported most things with a minimum of comment and let the "factual" narratives speak for themselves. First he describes his coach, "a good ol' boy from Oklahoma, with a pack of chewing tobacco in his pocket and a really big mouth," as a man whose own athletic career was ended with an injury in high school. He then cites several of the principles of motivation regularly given by this coach and which, after six years, "remain embedded in my mind": "If they don't score, we don't lose!!!"; "Go out there and knock his jock off"; "I want you to rip them some new assholes!!"; "If he holds you again, rip his fucking head off"; "If they score one more touchdown, I'm gonna run your guts till you chuck [vomit]." At the end of his account, Mr. F observes: "I realize this may seem a bit violent or hateful, but when I was on the field during a game, I wanted for the other team to lose and hurt more than I wanted to win. This was not my normal attitude, but . . . football changed my mind-set." Perhaps a surprising thought in this group of comments is that the fear of the shame of losing motivates more than the pride of winning. It is as if winning were normal and losing were a corruption of this normalcy. To think this way is to begin to lie about the meaning of winning and losing. Men's sports programs, from the professionals to the major colleges, require winning to remain viable: people do not pay to watch a losing team. If winning is achieved by action beyond the rules, one is lying about what winning means. This situation in society helps to create the coach's desperate exhortations. In sports, economic coercion, humiliation, and masculine gender identity are tied together.

Mr. F describes how the individual player, himself in this case, learns that it is not only permissible but required to hurt others to maintain the sense of normalcy. Mr. F comments on the need to avoid losing:

> During the game the main threat [to cause us to lose] was their quarterback. . . . My chance to end the threat (take the quarterback out of the game) was given with the coach's play call . . . [in which] the two defensive ends [would] crunch the quarterback; I was one of these defensive ends. As the ball was snapped and we rushed in,

the quarterback noticed the other defensive end first and this exposed his back to me, I couldn't resist, I speared him in the lower back with my helmet and I could hear a grunt leave his lungs along with the rest of his air. As the trainers came on the field to help the quarterback off, with his now broken rib, my coach and fellow teammates were ecstatic. I just seriously injured another person and my peers were saying, "Nice fuckin' hit!!" I must admit, I too was happy with my performance, I realize how violent it was, but I so loved a *"Nice fuckin' hit."* I was a very violent player.

The essay from which this was taken was long and breathless: uncharacteristically for Mr. F, there were repeated comma splices, as if he could not contain his excitement enough to punctuate according to his usual standard—this was his final essay in the semester. The narration of these events recreated the excitement generated by the combination of pleasing the coach, avoiding humiliation, and gaining the admiration of the team. Something was gained in high school; something is gained now by Mr. F in this retelling. For a moment Mr. F recovers the sadistic pleasure of having produced the grunt, the loss of air, the broken rib, in another person. Spearing (hitting with one's helmet) is against the rules. Yet the coach's counsel was to do anything to avoid losing. Players tacitly understood that any penalty was less damaging than risking letting the "threat" of losing remain in the game. Mr. F's account suggests that, unrecognized by the fans, football is governed by standards and practices that are outside the accepted rules. These standards and practices, in their lawlessness, are like those of war and the opposite of what we take to be sports.

Mr. F was also the victim of this style of behavior on the field. Here is his account:

> The game was against the defending state champions . . . an all black team. . . . We were playing an away game in a stadium that was by far filled predominantly with African Americans. Anyway, he [the opposing defensive lineman] started the little chat while waiting for the snap of the ball, "I'm gonna run your ass over cracker!!" a cracker being a derogatory term for white people. So I responded in my usual instigating manner with an extremely racist offensive remark, "Isn't your mother my maid?" Needless to say, this pissed him off and with his forty pound weight advantage, he proceeded to "knock my ass off the ball" along with snapping my head back with his forearm. I decided not to instigate verbally again.
>
> Reflecting upon the racist comment I made, I realize that my language use had again changed because of football. I was in no way racist and his mother did not look anything like my maid because we didn't have a maid at the time, but something inside my head told me to piss this guy off and I guess my statement did just that.

Of course, Mr. F is not an innocent victim. His account implies that many, if not most, of the players are participating in the regular practice of violating the game's rules by practicing violence to avoid losing: hurting and disabling the opposition, not simply defeating it.

Mr. F's remark was sexist as well as racist: it alluded to the reduced position held in society by many African Americans, as well as the characteristically subordinate place of some black women. Mr. F knew this would "piss off" his opposite number because of their common understanding that the terms of battle are for men only: having an opponent's mother as one's maid implies having dominion over "their" women. The real-life fate of black women is not on either player's mind. The issues are who has power over whom, and who has power over whose women.

Mr. S's comment on this part of Mr. F's essay is also noteworthy:

> Mr. F claimed his language went through a change when he spoke to the opponents during the game. It was his tactic of motivation to insult the other team. This was his justification for "slipping" when he retaliated to his opponent. But I believe his reply "Isn't your mother my maid?" implied more than just a change of scenes. It indicated the constant reminder of the unconscious racism that plagues our society. Although he said these words in the heat of battle, it was his way of gaining the upper hand on his black opponent. This easily could have been done without answering with a racial comment. He could have said, "You overweight piece of shit. I'm goin' to knock you so hard you're not goin' to know what hit you. You slow mother-fucker."

Mr. S's presumably better strategies for insulting the opposition include deriding his body, and his physical ability, and calling him a "mother-fucker," a term that implies a shared sexism between the two players. In proposing this term as a point of solidarity between black and white men, Mr. S expressed feelings of unconscious sexism, while he correctly identifies Mr. F's unconscious racism. To further document his point, moreover, Mr. S might have commented on what can only be a sudden lapse of logic on Mr. F's part: would the opposing lineman's mother have actually had to look like a particular person for Mr. F's wisecrack to have had its effect?

Sports, Family, and Men

As Mr. F did with his discussion of team language use, Mr. S wrote a description of family life that describes his struggle to remove himself from the coercive feelings often experienced by male athletes. However, neither writer paid attention to the frustration they may be having; both gave their accounts with a sense that they are now enlightened and beyond the struggles of their youth. Mr. F coped with his struggle by moving out of football, through water polo and its female coach, to finally settle on weightlifting, where the cheering is only of the encouraging kind. Mr. S dealt with his family and gender identity struggle by paying attention to his relations with African Americans, demonstrating that he had no history of racism and had been speaking the same hip-hop language of his black friends on the basketball court. While both Mr. F and Mr. S presented materials that showed masculine gender identity as troubled, neither fully faced this trouble in their work in this course: but if you asked them, they would say they were candid to the point where they overcame whatever trouble they may have had in the past.

Here is how Mr. S describes his relationship with his father:

> My relationship with my father revolved around sports. We never talked about the world. We never conversed about my education except with grades. And, we never, never talked about the family. That was the forbidden topic. If I brought something up with relation to the family, I was crossing over the boundary. I learned to keep quiet when I had a problem. My confusion had to be solved with my own intelligence.

Mr. S is the youngest child in his family. He recounts that his father was aggrieved because, having had two older children who were both female, he had to suppress all of his previous interest and thinking about sports within the family. When Mr. S was old enough, he attracted his father's strong attention, but mainly with regard to his being a partner in sports and in conversation about sports: "I guess he believed sports were men's games. Women could try it but they could never be good, I mean really good." Because of this principle, Mr. S's father did not involve himself with his daughters, either in sports or in other ways. He reports that his sisters longed for the father's attention, but instead the father's attention was on him, Mr. S, though only in the one narrow sense: the path, through sports and competition, toward separating female family members—referred to as "family"—from the world of men and male sports.

As Mr. S describes it, even when this separation was achieved, it was, in a heartbreaking way, itself unsatisfying, itself marked by the frustration felt by the rest of the family with his father. Mr. F had observed that "it seemed as if my IQ dropped about fifty points when I was in the company of my teammates" with his speech "filled with curses, slang, and yes, a more violent tone." Similarly, Mr. S wrote that "I always said 'ain't' when I wasn't around my mother. I acquired the habit from my father who, although very well educated . . . [at] Cornell University and Harvard Law School, seemed to use the word frequently when talking about sports." His mother, correctly perceiving the origin of Mr. S's changed speech habits, "took it upon herself to blame my father for my bad habits." However annoying his mother's reminders may have been, they were additionally painful because conversations between himself and his father were themselves troubled:

> The conversations between my father and me usually lasted for about two hours but they always ended on a bad note. Whatever topic we were on, it always led into my tennis game, and this was my forbidden subject. I hated talking about this particular sport because it represented more than a game. It involved my entire family. . . . It resembled gambling in the sense that my father neglected his other responsibilities in life for his selfish pleasures [of playing with his son and paying large sums for his tennis lessons and training].

Mr. S cites several telling instances of conversation between his father and himself in which his father's tone and approach to Mr. S sound like Willy Loman's:[37] "You never see a Jimmy Connors looking up before his hits. You're not going to get anywhere playing the way you are." Although Mr. S's father pays cash for his son's expected athletic achievement, the ideal is no different from Willy's hopes for Biff's athletic stardom. For Mr. S, his father's financial sponsorship of his own wishes for his son contributes the element of coercion that sullies this relationship. In addition to the sense of obligation established in Mr. S by his father's sponsorship and idealism, yet another factor damaged the integrity of Mr. S's athletic identity:

> "Dad, do we have to talk about tennis? I'm sick of hearing about it." My voice would begin to rise every time the subject of tennis was the focus of conversation. I become very impatient talking about the game that dominated my life since I was seven. I wasn't sure why, but I refused to take criticism from my father . . . I felt I couldn't enjoy the game if he was part of it. It took something away from my advancement in the sport. . . . My progress was so hindered by his involvement that I contemplated quitting the sport. But also, I hated the idea that I was better than him. . . . It was difficult to think of my father in a less than dominant role. It

---

[37] The self-deluded protagonist of Arthur Miller's play *Death of a Salesman* (1949).

was too fantastic of an idea. How could I be better than him, the man who governed my life? . . . My skills were being hidden to appease my father.

Mr. S describes how "the game . . . dominated my life" and that he could not imagine his father "in a less than dominant role." There was a close government of Mr. S's life by his father through sports talk and playing tennis. While this government did not overcome Mr. S, the space of his own autonomy was small and emotionally reduced, a reduction marked by reduced language—a stutter ("sometimes it took me three or four times to get out the first word when I was conversing with my family about sports"), the use of *ain't,* and his own abbreviation, "bees" for *because.*

Mr. S reports how his mother responded to this reduction.

> My mother . . . wasn't bothered by my stuttering as compared to the misuse of my language. She seemed to accept the fact that the stutter was a lack of maturity. But I didn't understand why she didn't put forth an effort to analyze it. . . . I became embarrassed by the thought of stuttering. I found it easier to avoid any discussion that involved sports. . . . The only time I felt free was at school and on the courts with my friends. That was the only place where I talked all the jargon [including hip-hop, or Black English, in this case] without hesitation.

Mr. S believed that his mother did not connect his stutter to his relationship with his father, to whom she connected his other language reductions. But he seemed to feel that all of his unconsciously prompted language usages were bound up with the habits of servitude in sports to the ideals of his father.

I noted earlier that in responding to Mr. F's essay, Mr. S considered the inertia of Mr. F's racism but did not reflect on the sexism that accompanied it. His essay suggests that, in addition to his struggle with his father's narcissism, he senses that there is something else wrong at home that he can't quite identify. This issue emerges in his telling of two moments in his family where the sports imperative conflicted with another social event. The first moment came when Mr. S was about to see the Rambo movie, *First Blood*, with a few of his friends, but his father reminded him of a previously scheduled tennis date he had with him.

> I was confused by the thought that I couldn't do my own thing. I wasn't happy with this obligation to my father. At that moment, I felt more like a puppet than his own son. He was pulling the strings and I had no defense. His presence was too great for me to revolt. There was no way I could change the things that corrupted the house.

His sister observed his agitation, and when she asked what was
disturbing him,

> I yelled at her to relieve some of the frustration. My mom always
> hated when I treated my sisters in this way. She said it was just
> another influence from my father. To take the anger out on the
> woman.

Although Mr. S knows not to get angry at innocent people, he told in
his essay of events (the second moment) that took place six months
before his essay was written. These events involved the same sister,
who had been about to graduate from a highly regarded undergraduate school. His whole family went to the graduation:

> My parents were most proud of her accomplishment. But their dis-
> play of joy was short-lived when I decided to play basketball at the
> gym. My whole family followed me to the courts and on my sister's
> graduation weekend, we watched me play basketball. It was true
> that we were all bored, but this was obviously not the answer. It
> was an exact replica of how things were. I was the center of atten-
> tion trying to impress everybody who watched, as my sister looked
> on, wondering how this was possible. She graduated from one of
> the toughest schools in the country and she wasn't even acknowl-
> edged for her accomplishments. . . . Her emotions were controlled
> by the familiarity of the situation. The scene was so depressing. . . .

Although Mr. S knows he helped to create this situation, one cannot
discern from this account just how disturbed he is by what happened. It looks as if he had his own response to the boredom, did
not himself demand that everyone follow, but unconsciously understood that his father would follow, his mother would follow his
father, and then so would his sister. The women would not take an
initiative, as Mr. S did, on their own, without first consulting the
others. I offer this reading of the narrative because of Mr. S's
repeated mention of the familiarity of the situation, his sense of its
representative character, and his belief that his sister was able to
cope with it because she was prepared for it by experience.

This is a demonstration of how the family was unconscious of
"the things that corrupted the house." Mr. S is unconsciously inhibited from opposing his father. I say unconsciously here because he
did not need to oppose his father in this story. Because of this inhibition, described earlier, in the paragraph about the film, it looks as
if he is acting on his own to relieve the boredom. But being unconsciously fixed in the "exact replica of how things were," Mr. S seems
to have re-created how things were by enacting the male trope of
separating himself from the women in the family. His understanding
of his sister's needs was not enough to change anything. He implied

in his essay that one need not worry about how badly his sister may feel because "She no longer needed a father figure. She had adapted to her situation. She had no more expectations." What a remarkable claim: to observe that his sister "looked on, wondering how this was possible" and to declare that she had adapted to her situation.

It is not enough to view Mr. S's father as the corrupting aspect of Mr. S's house. Mr. S is receiving his father's heritage and using it, and the other family members do not or cannot change the situation. Mr. S is unconscious of his role in perpetuating the corruption that he otherwise finds so disturbing. His playing basketball at that moment is the result of the momentum of his adolescence; it is the result of his habitual use of the athletic field, with its reduced language demands, its freedom to use other languages to build solidarity with black men his own age so as to escape home and family. Mr. S wants himself and us to understand this interracial bond as a progressive step against racism. But he is not aware that this step is, in turn, the ground for remaining unconscious of Mr. F's sexism, and of his own responsibility to become a different kind of a person on behalf of his sister with whose needs Mr. S is able to identify and sympathize.

What Was Accomplished?

It could be that B, F, and S are thinking along lines that can help them grow toward less troubled values and futures. The interpersonal and political conditions that these writers disclose are their special combinations of insight and inertia, self-examination and smugness, that cause many men to feel discontent without knowing why. These combinations of feeling and perception are each oriented to uses of language, things that had to be consciously thought through and written. Both the language genres reported and those used were significant. Mr. B reported literary and boys' group languages; then in analytical style interpreted those languages in order to read a received term, *euphemism,* in new ways. He changed the genre of euphemism by showing how it applies in the literary, social, and personal situations. Mr. B also changed himself: he recognized the mixed character of heterosexual identity and the obfuscating function of men's harsh descriptions of sex and sexual feeling. He made his individual understanding available to other students, who then could pick up the insight, using it toward a changed approach to society.

Mr. F and Mr. S had more complicated and troubling stories to tell, but they too started in awareness of their own uses of language in specific interpersonal experiences, and used modified ethnographic narratives to air their struggles and, even if in small ways, make them less demanding. Mr. F could find the language to eschew the violent aspects of his love of athletics. Mr. S could reread the languages of his family to spot their participation in the painful situations that these language uses sustained. He could at least begin to note the relation of his uses of language to his placement in his family. As genres, his abbreviations, his "low" talk marked memberships that took him out of his family, just as the violent talk represented a membership that won Mr. F respect among male peers. These connections of language use, genre, and membership are fundamentals in the teaching of writing.

Telling the Truth

Attention to oral and written language is likely to guide us to the struggles, some of which are unconscious, taking place within ourselves and between one another, struggles now increasingly common in the teaching of writing. The ideal of "telling the truth" urged by Andrea Dworkin and José Zuniga refers to a common purpose of writing and speaking: to "speak out." The teaching of writing means learning to "speak" in public, to achieve an ability to discern how our language tells the truths of history and experience in our lives as they affect our involvement in a subject matter. If writing teachers teach how language use discloses people's implication in knowledge and learning experiences, the collective meanings (such as those associated with the struggles of Mr. B, F, and S) of previously unconscious genres and feelings become appropriate, appealing features of writing curricula. If these meanings also alert us to previously unexamined actions of academic, athletic, military, or domestic memberships, we have perhaps told more of the truth about how our subject matter contributes to society.

Chapter Five

Collaboration[1] and the Discomforts of Disclosure

Is Classroom Discomfort Necessary?

The collaboration of Mr. F and Mr. S mentioned in Chapter 4 brought out several speech genres found in different relationships among men. Mr. F's citations of how coaches and players speak to one another showed adolescent language use tropes of competitive sports among men. Mr. S cited how fathers' speech to sons showed the kind of struggle many fathers and sons experience with one another. Each writer, enhanced by the presence of the other, saw his own story as germane to the other's; this led them to combine their essays into one statement, which suggests that the genres of one zone of masculine social life may relate to the genres of other zones. To our class the juxtaposition of language uses helped to conceptualize wider gender identities.

These two students were prepared for this collaboration by having engaged in some of the conversations described by Ms. P in Chapter 4. A certain amount of dispute accompanied our class discussions, and as one can see from Ms. P's account, a certain amount

---

[1] Sally Reagan, Thomas Fox, and David Bleich, eds., *Writing With: New Directions in Collaborative Teaching, Learning, and Research* (Albany: SUNY Press, 1994); and David Bleich, guest ed., "Collaboration and Change in the Academy," *Journal of Advanced Composition*, 14 (no. 1, 1994). The twenty-nine essays in these two publications show a wide variety of situations for collaboration; in almost all of them, the kinds and number of memberships of all classroom constituents is a major factor in how the collaborations work.

of discomfort[2] was experienced by both women and men because of the disputes. As a small group of nine people, we did learn to collaborate more than we might have in a larger course. The stage for focused collaboration was set by the high level of exchange in the regular class meetings. Class members articulated their memberships seriously and taught each other how their language use styles acquired a greater weight if they were understood as a feature of their memberships. It does seem that some classrooms can tolerate and benefit from discomfort emerging from people's mutual disclosures. The questions for this chapter are, How does classroom discomfort work in the teaching of language use and writing, how much is helpful, and when does it endanger people and learning?[3]

As Kenneth Bruffee has discussed,[4] the philosophy of classroom collaboration has evolved from peer tutoring toward conceiving scholarly work as a continuing "conversation" among teachers, researchers, and students. Many of today's graduate students are more ready to create cooperative classrooms because they have been classroom group members in high school and college. Those of us who prepare teachers are proposing a growing variety of practical moves regarding how to organize classroom groups, how to encourage thinking and planning with one another, and how to formulate projects that depend on cooperation.

The questions that come with experiments in collaboration come from several directions. Successful individual-centered teachers view writing as having to be done alone. This is the ideal of the "independent scholar," a value whose practices are criticized by Patricia A. Sullivan and by Judith Entes, but which is viable in the hands of many good teachers. In the same volume,[5] Sally [Reagan] Ebest describes how difficult it is, even for graduate students interested in change, to shed the habits and expectations of a purely individualistic pedagogical philosophy. And as I note further in Chapters 7 and 8, the administrative bureaucracy does not give formal credit to collective work.

---

[2] In Chapter 1, the boundary between discomfort and personal danger is considered.

[3] In regard to Chapter 6, discomfort is one of the contingencies that should be expected to influence how a classroom agenda changes. As a contingency, however, it has this, its own chapter.

[4] Kenneth A. Bruffee, *Collaborative Learning: Higher Education, Interdependence, and the Authority of Knowledge* (Baltimore: Johns Hopkins University Press, 1993).

[5] Patricia A. Sullivan, "Revising The Myth of the Independent Scholar"; Judith Entes, "The Right to Write a Co-authored Manuscript"; and Sally Ebest, "Collaborative Learning in the Graduate Classroom" in *Writing With*.

Other hesitations about collaboration are produced by clashes of styles between new school populations and traditional practices already in place. Increasingly in schools there are differences and distances, brought into school from society, among students as well as between students and teachers. Working with their colleagues under these circumstances has taught many students that sharing often is not safe or pleasant and that hostility, malice, and withdrawal, when appearing in collaborative situations, can stifle productive schoolwork. Regardless of how culturally homogeneous a group of students and teachers may consider itself, collaboration requires more than opening up or expressing ourselves; it demands the patient, gradual buildup of trust and understanding. Because each site of collaboration is different, and because forms of disclosure are multifarious, often nonverbal, there can be no fixed instruction for every group or class, no one technique that will guarantee the absence of conflict and discomfort. The classroom and scholarly populations themselves must be understood by their constituents as bases for finding their own modes of collaboration, always bearing in mind that, for any one group, working together and exchanging consequential thoughts may not, finally, be the right thing.[6]

The term *collaboration* may not be comprehensive enough to describe the importance for class members to understand how each person's history, membership, and language use genres play roles in how and what we know. One can learn with and from others without cooperating or collaborating with them. But it is probably not possible to understand the otherness of any other person without some form of engagement with that person, over a period of time, where one of the acknowledged purposes is to see a subject matter of common interest to all parties from the individual and collective perspectives of others.

Disturbing Complacency by Recognizing Membership

In the past, many teachers believed that it was an ordinary part of teaching to disturb the complacency of students through "ideas." Students dealt with their intellectual discomfort by repeating the unpleasant knowledge on essays and examinations, and then ignoring the materials to the degree demanded by their vocational lives

---

[6] The condition of fundamental difference for every classroom is discussed in Chapter 6, with reference to Edward Pauly's *The Classroom Crucible* (New York: Basic Books, 1990).

after schooling was over. Lately, however, classroom discomfort is taking different forms as students and teachers feel more directly implicated in the disturbing knowledge. Just as teachers are beginning to recognize the political character of some students' discomforts, students cannot cancel the political weight of the teachers' and other students' senses of how things are. These new kinds of classroom discomfort are not easily overcome; they reverberate in the university community as a whole; they are not easily relieved by the curricular move of "teaching the conflicts" without changing traditional classroom social relations, and they present yet one more challenge to objective knowledge as an ideal. Classroom discomfort involves the students' feeling disturbed by historical processes about which they came to school to learn. If their discomfort is discounted, the exchange of views on which school is predicated is defeated, and school continues to be unresponsive both to its constituents and to the history it is trying to teach. There is reason to think that classroom discomfort, felt, disclosed, and explored by students and teachers proceeding cautiously, is to be treated as a source of understanding well adapted to what students want and need.

Instances of such discomfort have been announced in the *Writing With* and the *Journal of Advanced Composition* essays cited in note 1 of this chapter. Several teachers and students discussed the emergence of classroom discomfort during their experimentation with different forms of pedagogical and scholarly collaboration. The discomfort derives from the new kinds of questions that arise out of the new mix of students created by the increasing numbers coming from parts of society that are first starting to send their children to college.

Perhaps a good way to get an accurate picture of such new populations is to examine, before returning to postsecondary discussion, a scene in a ninth-grade classroom[7] in an urban school in Rochester, New York, that prefigures what we may now be facing in university classrooms with regard to unexpected memberships. Then I describe how some teachers (myself included) met in a yearlong group to think about what this class was saying to us. We took the events of that class as something of a warning of what to expect down the road. Third, I describe a more public sense of curricular discomfort in a university setting. I further consider how discomfort motivates thinking and adaptation in postsecondary writing and language use situations, how unexpected memberships emerge, along with other surprises that come with teaching through the exchange of disclosures.

---

[7] This is the same class cited in Chapter 2.

The Ninth-Grade Classroom from Another Viewpoint

The population of this class of about twenty students was mostly African American with several students of Anglo, Hispanic, and other "hyphenated" (that is, mixed) backgrounds. There were two white teachers (themselves descendants of the "hyphenated" forebears): one female, the "real" teacher, and one male, myself, the twice-a-week guest teacher. We planned to teach works that the students would not consider alien. We assigned, and the students read with interest, Zora Neale Hurston's "Sweat" and "Story in Harlem Slang" (also referred to as "Jelly's Tale"). While the latter story was difficult in that the students had to use the glossary of Harlem slang that Hurston includes, the students had few complaints about using it to gain access to the story.

Their understanding was different from what we expected. The students read with and through a sense of membership in ways that urged us teachers to recognize our status as students in this class. We failed to anticipate which memberships (in the fall of 1990) these students would evince. There are two senses in which this was the case—gender and race. Here is Ms. T's essay:

> In both stories by Zora Neale Hurston ("Sweat" and "Jelly's Tale") I identified with the women. Following is my explanation of why I identified with the women, how I felt about the two stories, and why I thought one story was better than the other.
>
> The reason I identified with the women in both stories is because I felt I could relate to their situations. In "Jelly's Tale," the woman is being told a pack of lies so that she'll pick one of the "men" to go to lunch with her. And in "Sweat" I identified with the woman because of her rebelling spirit and want for a change.
>
> The feeling that I had when reading the story "Jelly's Tale" was that I felt sorry for the "men" because of how they tried to be bigger than the other and for the woman who had to listen to their boasting. In the story "Sweat" I felt happy for the woman who finally decided to change her life for the better.
>
> I think both stories were the same. This is because the stories are both about women rising above what the man are saying to them and going on about their business.

Here is another comment, by Ms. G:

> Now comparing the men in "Harlem Slang" I did not like that Jelly-sex [*Jelly* is defined as *sex* in Hurston's glossary] bragged so much about what he has and is gonna get, and I don't like the way they wanna be pimps. But the men talk alike to the woman; they go off on them and use ugly language towards them.

A year after these remarks were written, Rosemary L. Bray, an editor of the *New York Times Book Review*, offered the following observation:

> In the quiet and resolute spirit she might very well have learned from Sunday school, Hill confronted and ultimately breached a series of taboos in the black community that have survived both slavery and the post-segregation life she and Clarence Thomas share. Anita Hill put her private business in the street, and she downgraded a black man to a room filled with white men who might alter his fate—surely a large enough betrayal for her to be read out of the race.[8]

Ms. T and Ms. G, both about fourteen years old when they wrote their essays, anticipated Anita Hill's point of view. With two white teachers, many black students, male and female, and several white students, male and female, in the room, these two students spoke up as women and as black women in ways we teachers did not anticipate. Both respondents observe the manipulative and "ugly" language of the men, who tried to bum a meal from a woman who would put them down. Both identify with the women who defeat men. Neither fears the teachers or the opinions of the other students. Two adolescents, without the public backing for their sentiments and attitudes that came a year later from Anita Hill, speak a language of informed membership. We teachers were somewhat uncomfortable: we did not speak in that genre.

The students had not heard of Hurston until we brought her stories to class. The students put the readings in a new perspective. Some white people are fascinated by the Harlem slang of the 1920's,[9] but are less likely to see Jelly's talk as "ugly" or to identify Delia, who could not save the life of her mean-spirited, disloyal husband, as a woman with a "rebelling spirit." The students' language of response signaled a membership we did not expect to emerge in school. It did emerge because there was a constituency that already existed in the language and society of the students but that we did not notice. This caused us discomfort.

These students then taught something else unexpected. Here is an essay presented by Ms. G after our two weeks' study of the Hurston stories:

> 23 November 1990: Reading these stories I found them to be irrelevant to my learning ability for an English class. The stories themselves not only offended me but it offended my entire race.

---

[8] Rosemary L. Bray, "Taking Sides Against Ourselves," *New York Times Magazine*, November 17, 1991, 94.

[9] Mr. B and Ms. S in Chapter 4 reported learning to speak "hip-hop."

I don't appreciate reading or writing about the low class of my people. The main part of our race we look at is our doctors, lawyers, famous speakers, inventors, etc.

Far as pimps, hoes, drug dealers, street-hangers, and gangs, we don't look down on them because they come in all different colors including the Caucasians. If you want to discuss my race let's talk about people like Martin Luther King, Jr., Malcolm X, Nelson Mandela, Louis Farrakhan, Frederick Douglass, and many, many more.

The majority of the vocabulary words that has been used are offensive and stereotypical of the black English. I've asked three generations of my family and none have heard of those words [in "Harlem Slang"].

I don't understand the purpose of the story and how it can educate me by putting down my race. Actually I was unable to comprehend what the story was trying to explain.

Maybe after class you can explain the story to me.

PEACE. P. S. remember "BLACK IS BEAUTIFUL"

This essay is responding, partly, to our having brought Hurston's stories to class. Ms. G reads our action as "wanting to discuss my race." This reading changes what we thought we were doing into something we did not think too much about. We did not expect to be told that we wanted to discuss *the students'* race. We forgot that we are seen (by some, perhaps many, black students) as representatives of the white majority rather than of the unspecified entities "teacher" or "society." We did not consider that these students know very little, if anything, about the public discussions of the canon, and that they are not interested in how politically forthcoming we are. They think that if "race" is the topic, or even if "pimps and drug dealers" are discussed, then all "races" involved in these activities should be considered.

Ms. G's two responses show the conflicts posed by the positioning discussed by Bray in her reflection on Hill: the simultaneous membership in the groups "women" and in "black people." Ms. G's list of people to discuss includes only men; to Ms. G, Hurston does not seem to belong. In response to white privilege, Ms. G wants to discuss black leaders and public achievers. When white privilege is less in the forefront, Ms. G and Ms. T are members of "women," without special attention to their racial identity.

These voices come from students who go home and tell what is happening in school. This is one reason Ms. G wrote her second essay. She reports asking three generations of her family if they had ever heard of Hurston's language, Harlem slang. No, they had not. Other black students in class wondered what it meant that white teachers brought these works into English class. One student wrote that he thought the stories were written by white people to diminish the status of blacks. For most, it was not plausible that the reason we brought these works in was to learn about them ourselves as well as to present what are at least unsettling accounts of life in the history of African Americans in this country.

Because of the way nonwhite students know society is already structured, white teachers are not always reliable members of the classrooms in this school. True, in this school many white and black teachers have good relations with one another. But the ground of these good relations is that their respective social memberships remain unquestioned: they stick to their common membership in the economic middle class. This group of students discussed the more uncertain and potentially turbulent feelings about gender and race only when a black teacher joined us and participated in the discussion. And this happened only for one thirty-eight-minute class period. On a deep level, everyone's membership in this class is uncertain, often conflicted, and always multiple. Both black students and black teachers distrust individual efforts by white people who have not yet learned that "race" can apply to everyone or to no one but not just to one group. As difficult as it may be, teachers within schools would have to collaborate with each other and disclose their own languages and memberships in order to produce a self-perpetuating level of collaboration that then students could trust.[10]

Teachers' Disclosures and Exchanges

In spite of our skepticism, we teachers tried to work together to teach ourselves more about teaching in multiethnic classrooms. I and six teachers at this high school, responding in part to events in this classroom, making use of our three-year association with one another and our wishes to contribute more realistically to the students' experience, decided to form a yearlong study group. A certain level of disclosure-enabling trust had already been developed among us. We therefore thought we could share our responses to literature in ways that might help us explore our own senses of membership. One member of this group proposed that we read Anne Moody's *Coming of Age in Mississippi*,[11] her autoethnography and account of the beginning of the civil rights movement in this coun-

---

[10] Edward Pauly's *The Classroom Crucible*, discussed in Chapter 7, also shows how the way government funds are distributed to schools discourages collaboration among teachers.

[11] Anne Moody, *Coming of Age in Mississippi* (New York: Dell, 1970).

try. In addition to our interest in her accounts themselves, we group members were contemporaries of Moody. Many of the events in her story are also part of our common historical memory. Our readings were shared in order to disclose and relieve previously unacknowledged social discomforts. Our discussions helped to bring out new senses of membership and new terms for us to consider as we sought to follow up on what the students were saying. In citing briefly the responses of four of us—two white men and two black women—I consider how our own readings and discussion taught us about the experience of daily life for Anne Moody and, to some extent, for the students in this school.

Mr. D, who has been a socially committed teacher for more than twenty years in urban schools, copes fairly well with and sometimes closes the distance between himself and his students. Here is what he responds to in the text:

> Fear of physical harm must be the most degrading, dispiriting mental state. Time and again, Anne comments that she feels "sick," "nauseated," "choked," at the news of murders and savage beatings. . . . She ridicules Martin Luther King, Jr. as a dreamer, removed from the realities of rural Mississippi. But Anne's anger is kept carefully in check. . . . The smart retorts to whites, the bold condemnations, are thoughts, not statements.
>
> I can recall being poor, but with great differences. When I slipped a piece of cardboard into a worn sneaker to protect my big toe from the hot pavement, it was with a sense of annoyance, but not shame. . . . Most of all [in my home town] there was no constant fear. Avoiding or confronting a neighborhood bully is far removed from taking on the brutal power structure of the South.

Mr. D sees the difference between his shame and Moody's fear. Daily life for many African Americans is living in fear that prevents the attempts to overcome poverty. Because they do not sense the daily action of fear in students' lives, white teachers are challenged in this and similar schools. This fear spontaneously goes into action when white teachers take initiatives that seem suspicious to the students.

My response to the book also stressed this theme:

> Finally, after two hundred or so pages, I start to see a terrible point. . . . Anne's frustration with her own communities—the fact that the majority [in her community] is governed by the fear imposed by society in the United States as well as by the local terrorism in Mississippi. . . . This, I decide, is her coming of age: the realization that the injustice and fear can go on indefinitely. . . . The ruling minority is scared, but nevertheless always willing to use its guns to keep things as they are.

My path to this understanding is through the memory of my community of postimmigrant Jews. The sexuality among Jews of my parents' generation was damaged by the burdens of having to survive in a hostile environment.[12] Moody's book uses sexual terms and sexual talk, but sex for her seems like wearing a nice dress, looking dignified and attractive rather than sexy in the popular television sense. Being familiar with this "meaning" of sex, I was able to identify with Moody through the path of feeling frustrated with my own communities and their own attempts to mold lives that insulate against fear.

The responses of the African American members of our group dealt with the hierarchy of color,[13] a theme unfamiliar to many white people. Ms. J writes,

> Because of the shame inflicted on blacks by whites, some African Americans found themselves making distinctions among other blacks based on the pigment of their skin. Anne Moody often referred to how the "high yellow" blacks acted "uppity" compared to darker skinned African Americans. Older people were more guilty of being "color struck" than most blacks of my generation. I remember telling my grandmother about my high school sweetheart. . . . Her response was: "what color is he?" I quickly replied, "what do you mean? What difference does it make what color he is, if he is good to me?" I can recall people of color making statements like "Get out of that sun before you turn black as smut." Some blacks, much like Miss Josephine in *Rainbow Jordan,* opted to use bleaching cream to be more like whites because they looked and were treated better in that land where skin color defined self worth.

Ms. P, born in Jamaica, also responded to this theme in Moody's narrative:

> Anne's reference to blacks who were "yellow" made me reflect on certain happenings when I was growing up. I thought this reference was common to so called Third World countries because colonial influences had lingered in these areas longer. In the late and early sixties many people in Jamaica found themselves given jobs

---

[12] This theme appears in an essay of mine that discussed my responses to Toni Morrison's writings at greater length than I do in this chapter. The idea is that for outgroup men sexual activity is affected by being in a reduced social status.

[13] Some people may not have known that different shades of black may matter in social ways. The responses helped to teach this fact. Readers may want to consult "What Color Is Black: Science, Politics, and Racial Identity," *Newsweek,* February 13, 1995; and David L. Wheeler, "A Growing Number of Scientists Reject the Concept of Race," *Chronicle of Higher Education,* February 17, 1995, A8–A9, A15.

because of the color of their skin. People who were not of mixed [background] or somewhat fair in complexion would never get jobs as host/hostess on an airliner, bank tellers, or [other] visible positions. The darker complexion Jamaicans found themselves behind the scenes constantly. Many people found lighter complexion partners to ensure that their children would not be a darker shade of black. Marriages were also forbidden as children were told that he or she is too black for you. . . . I was amazed to learn that in a developed country like America this issue also was very much alive.

Mr. D and I were both not well informed about the color hierarchy among some nonwhite people. Though we had read about it, this was the first time we had been present in an oral discussion about it with African Americans. This topic seemed withheld from nonblack contexts because of its admission that the acceptance of the superiority of whiteness, or at least of less color, is an issue in black communities.

Ms. J's story reveals how much of an assumption this was for her grandmother, who simply assumed that it was better to marry lighter and lighter, until, presumably, one became completely white. Perhaps, they thought, this was the only peaceful way out of the fear. Ms. P's remarks meanwhile suggest, analogously, that the color hierarchy was part of a colonial situation associated with industrial underdevelopment. But to her surprise it is no different in America.

This color scale seems related to the wish to cast off the status of fear. On this occasion, it also suggested gender issues. Because color is affected by reproduction and perhaps its social identity through cosmetics, it may represent a female technique of working for change. Male techniques, historically, have been more in the news. The moves toward accepted, dignified citizenship that are not violent, such as Martin Luther King's, are still dramatic because they demand immediate change. However, the lightening of one's skin gradually through marriage or immediately with bleaching creams (construable as cosmetics like any others) may be part of a gender-specific feature in black and African American culture. They are quieter, not revolutionary, and governed by the feeling that eventually they will succeed. In the situations we explored we found mixed memberships. By focusing on fear and color, we got beyond the obfuscating commonality of middle-class membership. We thought about men's roles in the perpetuation of fear, and we considered women's approach to the psychology of color.

Students take the multicultural membership of each class seriously; because they are young, belonging and gender identity are on their minds. They need demonstrations that mixtures of perspective are possible among teachers, that teachers want to know how their lives really are. Exchange, disclosure, and study in classrooms and among teachers identify truer patterns of social membership and the directions they may be taking. Ms. T and Ms. G may learn to include Hurston in their list of exemplary figures; teachers can learn to expect new constituencies that may be taking shape during each new classroom gathering.

Discomfort from Student/Teacher Politics

In 1994 students who were entering college would be about the age of Ms. G and Ms. T. The following events do not involve those students, but they may well have. The political consciousness of the ninth graders in 1990 affects how the students view received knowledge in 1994. Recently at my university two first-year African American students came to me with a problem. For the most part, African American students are not acutely uncomfortable because many do speak up fluently in adverse situations. On the other hand, there is an ongoing collective discomfort with the kind of administrative unresponsiveness played out in the following incident.

Many faculty members construe learning as being one-way: the faculty can teach the students, but the students can't teach the faculty. This means that faculty may tell students what counts as knowledge, but students may not tell the same thing to faculty members. Because of this imbalance, disclosure does not matter in such situations, since faculty members will not change in response to students' differing politics of knowledge. While one-directional teaching has gone on for centuries, students with different values and styles of understanding—such as the ninth graders we discussed above—should be invited to contribute what they know to the subject matter. In the following case in psychology, their claims were not heard, but they had some effect.

In the fall of 1993, several African American first-year students complained about the following question in the first-year psychology textbook's Study Guide:[14]

24. Minority (especially African American) children's:

    a. self-esteem is finally catching up to that of European-American children

    b. academic achievement equals that of non-minority children if teaching styles are matched to learning styles

---

[14] Study Guide to James W. Kalat, *Introduction to Psychology* (Pacific Grove, CA: Brooks/Cole Publishing, 1993), 95.

    c. self-esteem was higher than European-American children's in the mid-1950's

    d. parents rarely help them with their homework

Because the allegedly correct answer is (a), the African American students said that this question implied that all African American students' self-esteem is lower than that of all European American students. The choices are related to individual statistical studies mentioned in the main text. The textbook emphasized studies that dealt with choice (a). However, what those hearing the complaint did not understand was the challenge to the implied premise of choice (a) regarding the reduced self-esteem of African American students. The response of the instructor was to defend the textbook on the grounds that it was only citing a study. But the complaining students believed that both the textbook and the study itself assumed the false premise that, in general, African American students have lower self-esteem than European American students. This presumption is so common among white researchers on such topics that the instructors could not hear the African American students rejecting the presumption more than they rejected the results of the study. This unresponsiveness is reconfirmed a year later by a memo I and others involved in the original complaint received.

    In the fall of 1994, the Herrnstein and Murray study of intelligence, *The Bell Curve,* appeared,[15] again bringing up the question (in the psychology course just discussed) regarding the study, by white men, of racial differences. The principal instructor in the psychology course decided to bring the contested question 24 into juxtaposition with the complaints by the African American students of 1994 about *The Bell Curve.* Presumably trying to "teach the conflict," the instructor writes in a memo to faculty that this arrangement "presents an excellent teachable moment":

> Our students, particularly our students of color, will look to us for support as they work through this issue that is personally and vitally important to them and about which there is much confusion and emotion.

This statement suggests the instructor's separation of himself from the complaint. His patronizing tone suggests that he did not need to learn something new from the discomfort of the African American students: it is them and not us (faculty members) for whom this is a

---

[15] Richard J. Hernstein and Charles Murray, *The Bell Curve: Intelligence and Class Structure in American Life* (New York: Free Press, 1994).

problem. One might also note how "emotion" is being blamed for the trouble this issue is causing: a scapegoat that diverts attention from the main problem.

The alternative "bonus" assignment this teacher used overlooks the contested premises of the intelligence issue, namely, whether human intelligence is one measurable thing and whether the accuracy of its measurement can be established.

> Read one of the many articles about *The Bell Curve* as well as the material in [the psychology textbook] on intelligence,[16] then develop and argue for a position on either (1) the use of IQ tests as the primary criterion in making decisions about who should be encouraged to succeed, or (2) the use of an average difference in IQ to make decisions that affect an entire group of people.

While this question permits a challenge to the premises of IQ testing, the task includes other questionable premises, namely, that some people may decide whether to encourage others to succeed, and that some people may decide the fate of entire groups of people. The question is disturbing because it implies a level of openness to the thesis of *The Bell Curve* that is unresponsive to the outrage felt by African Americans and others who are agitated that such a book would appear at all. The opposition to this study is not about how valid it is but about its return to the justifications for colonialism and slavery: for generations, "science" has been used to justify the assumptions of the inferiority of others to shore up social and economic domination.[17] The authority of science and measurement is so fully taken for granted that it occurs to very few that this is a case of the political misuse of this authority. The objecting students responded to something substantive in the curriculum and, from one standpoint, were in position to teach (try to persuade to take a different position) those who thought the work of scientists was politically neutral. A more sensible approach to this situation would have been to take the opportunity for collaboration between teachers who "know" the traditions of social science and students for whom these traditions are posing problems. The forms of interaction—the "assignment," the presumption of the one-way "teach-

---

[16] Note the comma splice. In itself, it is unimportant. But this teacher and others like him demand "excellence" and "drill," and so on (see Chapter 2).

[17] As discussed in Stephen Jay Gould's *The Mismeasure of Man* (New York: Norton, 1981).

able moment," are sources of discomfort for many students who otherwise might collaborate with faculty members in speaking and thinking from positions of acknowledged membership.

Discomfort as Motivation: Five Scenes

Disclosure desentimentalizes writing groups, teaches the discipline of interacting with others, and adds collective achievement to what can be learned in school. Disclosure makes it clear that the sites of language and writing are collective. Cooperative classrooms started with peer revision groups.[18] If peer critique is given without self-disclosure it may or may not help. But when given with and through self-disclosure, it is more likely that the critique will be understood and helpful. In instances where the collaboration is extended (for example, after twelve weeks of working with one another and interviewing one another), and the students perceive one another's language use style as a function of their history, culture, and vocational identity, the interactive discourse changes. Individual accomplishment gains independence by virtue of its implication in the perspectives of others; the collective accomplishment is that dependence and relatedness are acknowledged as part of what one knows, including but yet advancing beyond the individualist standard.[19]

The discomfort that can emerge from collaboration can teach about the connection of the subject matter to the not-school world. To consider this proposition, I outline five scenes of disclosure and collaboration, where the disclosures may seem dangerous or potentially harmful to the total classroom situation. Eventually, the scenes tell us truer terms of membership in the classroom and in society. The discomfort felt by the students motivated their use of instructive speech and writing genres. The discomfort people felt was related to how things are said and written, when, to whom, and in what tone. Sometimes things were not said when they should have been. Sometimes the "right" thing to say or write took time to

---

[18] Kenneth Bruffee, *Collaborative Learning*.

[19] David Bleich, "Extended Collaboration," in *Writing With*, 179–196. I refer to this instance because of its salutary outcome: each group member was oriented toward cooperating with one another and with the agreed-upon stipulations that there were few differences that could lead to discord. It could be accurately observed, however, that because these students were Protestant, Catholic, and Jewish, and white, born in America, and academically oriented, that cooperation would be expected and that disabling differences would be understood as personality conflicts.

emerge. In the teaching of writing and language use, the following situations suggest materials for the regular curriculum and contribute to what is discussed in Chapter 6, The Contingent Curriculum.

The situations are identified by modes of disclosure, with the understanding that such kinds are not limited in number and character, and that these are only examples I am using now, in this book. They are: (1) head-on antagonism; (2) differences of affective style; (3) opposition to covert racism; (4) differences within a presumed cultural homogeneity; and (5) the disclosure of previously unannounceable knowledge.

Head-on Antagonism

Tom Fox, in Chico, California, teaches and supervises basic writing classes in which there are frequently different kinds of white, African American, Hispanic, and Asian students. The student groups are supervised by a master's-level graduate student who directly tries to teach the students how to work with one another. Fox, not present but supervising Laurinda for the following exchanges, recorded some of the sessions and wrote about them in his essay "Race and Gender in Collaborative Learning."[20] The teacher in the group is Laurinda, who is Anglo. There is a new member, Mike, also Anglo; Lorena and Jorge are Mexican American. An early exchange between Mike and Jorge is as follows (this is real hostility, not kidding around):

Mike: Let's see the ol' green card, Jorge. Come on, let's see it.

Jorge: Shut up.

Mike *(laughing):* What, not gonna show it?

Jorge: Will it give you a hard-on to see it? *(Reaches into his wallet and takes the card out.)* Here. *(Throws it at Mike.)*

Mike: Oh . . . it has your picture on it. It's even green.

A week later, the following exchange takes place:

Mike *(to Laurinda):* How old are you? What do you do on weekends? How come I never see you at any parties?

Laurinda: I go out with my friends, go to Bidwell Park, and do homework. I don't care for those parties.

---

[20] Thomas Fox, "Race and Gender in Collaborative Learning," in *Writing With,* 111–122.

Lorena: *Se entretenido. (Jorge laughs.)*

Mike *(flustered):* What'd she say?

Jorge: She said you're a nosey son of a bitch.

Lorena: I did not!

Jorge: No, she called you nosey. I call you a son of a bitch.

Fox says that these exchanges show that in classrooms one should expect the re-creation of ethnic antagonisms present in society. He observes that the first exchange closed down the group altogether for that session, but that the atmosphere of male combat was established, particularly by Jorge's rejoinder about whether seeing his green card will excite Mike. Further evidence of this development is Mike's attempt to flirt with the Anglo female teacher, thus, in a sense, seeking two sorts of ascendancy, sexual and ethnic. Lorena's remark then defeats him on both counts. A woman "answers" his efforts by speaking Spanish, taking him out of his superior status by using another language to ostracize him. Ethnic and gender solidarity, activated by a language use initiative, defeated Mike's disruption of the group, though it clearly did not secure the peace.

Events like this contribute to disclosing the underlying classroom situation. As time goes on and if the atmosphere improves, the curriculum has been opened to kinds of language not previously considered part of what should be taught: obscene language, male language, peremptory shift to Spanish (here, an in-group language), flirtatious language, ganging-up language, including derisive laughter. The foregoing instances are conventions worthy of study. But could they have been studied in Laurinda's class? Perhaps, but only after she and Fox have disclosed the antagonisms, understood them through analysis, and then, in advance, worked out a contingent strategy of letting the class' language determine the curriculum. Laurinda herself was not prepared for the events described. But if expected, they become a good basis for teaching the use of language, even including the use of local ("second") languages by groups in reduced status in the society at large. Someone observing in urban high schools might well want to find a way to use Black English as part of the language curriculum (as I discussed in Chapter 3). But unless the ethnic antagonisms can be acknowledged within the curriculum, unless the expressions of antagonism count as a form of individual and collective self-disclosure, the curriculum remains in its narrow state, and collaboration can neither ameliorate antagonisms nor teach writing and language use.

Differences of Affective Style

Differences of affective style, which appear in the foregoing account, are different ways of allowing oneself emotional release—anger, in particular. In some instances, the differences are cultural or ethnic; in others, gender. The following situation seems to have mostly to do with gender but the issues are intertwined. Donna Qualley and Elizabeth Chiseri-Strater describe this case in their essay "Collaboration as Reflexive Dialogue: A Knowing 'Deeper than Reason.'"[21]

The group, all white, is made up of Serena, Emily, and Avery, who is biologically male but has concealed from the group that he considers himself a "trans-gender" person: psychologically female and not gay. The significance of this identity is that because of presenting as female in manner, Avery as a child and youth was an object of ridicule and thus had a history of feeling ostracized and discriminated against. However, only the teacher of the class knew this fact, and the authors of the essay did not announce it in the essay either: Donna Qualley allowed to me, over the telephone, that this information could be cited here. The following thought may apply: Avery exercised styles and choices available to both genders as currently understood. Recorded communication among group members took place through memos and journal writing, and these are what the authors cited to reflect on this collaboration.

The substantive issue for discussion in this group was racism, a topic strongly urged by Avery; Emily, a high school valedictorian, considered herself ignorant of the topic, and Serena was cautious about it. In contrast, Avery thought this was *the* issue, as if to say, what else would one discuss in this class, in school?

His opening statement quotes Sister Souljah's view that racism is "synonymous with white supremacy" and writes: "race (white skin) + power = racism" (122). In partial answer to Serena's more interrogative approach to racism—"Why should I have to pay for the mistakes my ancestors made"—Avery writes,

> How many more riots and how much more violence do we have to see before changes actually occur. . . . Sister Souljah is angry and radical . . . her goal is not to comfort liberal whites and tell them what a good job they are doing. (122)

---

[21] Donna Qualley and Elizabeth Chiseri-Strater, "Collaboration as Reflexive Dialogue," *Journal of Advanced Composition* 14 (no. 1, 1994): 111–130. The page numbers for the quotations that follow are from this essay.

Qualley and Chiseri-Strater place equal emphasis on the substantive issue of racism and on the contrast between Avery's style and the more reserved styles of Emily and Serena. Furthermore, the way they describe the situation suggests that it is already seriously burdened by preexisting differences:

> Unlike Emily . . . and Serena . . . Avery's interest in pursuing this topic does not seem to be related to his ignorance or confusion. He has specific ideas about what the problem is, why it is a problem and what can be done to solve it. The information will not be new territory for him. . . . From the start then, the students' different and unequal knowledge positions affect the dynamics of the dialogue. In many ways, Avery already owns the position the women are seeking to understand. Since he is much better read and informed, his role in the group becomes one of shepherding others, sometimes quite emphatically, toward a specific (politically correct) understanding of racism. . . . However, this kind of strong, vigilant stance does not invite the kind of shared, open, exploratory inquiry that occurred in [another] group. (122–123)

The authors of the essay are trying to report the simultaneous effects of several forces. In the foregoing paragraph, they portray a male student in a socially masculine role occupying a strong position with the justification that it is only right that others less certain of how society is configured must be told in no uncertain terms about the long reach of injustice. The authors consider it important and of some concern that Avery thinks society is configured according to traditional gender roles. They note how sharing and exploration in mutually respectful styles is inhibited by these traditional roles. Furthermore, the authors imply that men—and here, Avery—actually perpetuate their positions in power by overtaking the custody of causes that all may want to support. So they—the authors—are asking, perhaps, Is Avery aware of how he may be undercutting his own attempts to "teach" by his use of speech and language styles characteristic of the position he opposes?

At the same time the authors have sympathy with Avery's claims that he has "been on the receiving end of prejudice and discriminatory harassment more times than I care to remember and I want to get across to you that such verbal abuse hurts." The authors observe, but do not explain in their essay, that Avery is "intentionally ambiguous because he is not comfortable enough to share the specifics. As a result, Serena and Emily misinterpret his anger as 'rudeness' or 'unreasonableness'" (124). Even though the authors understand why Avery is not fully disclosing the bases of his feelings, their observations suggest that regardless of the reason, his withholding of this explanation left his anger, in a sense, to fend for itself, and in that role it inhibited discussion and offended his colleagues. Lacking a specific locus for identifying Avery's anger, Serena and Emily gave it a gender identity. It may or may not have helped for Avery to disclose more about his history; what he did disclose led, regardless, to collective engagement of an issue as germane as the ones that did not emerge.

This difference reached acute proportions in this group, when, in an informal lounge meeting, Avery shouted at his colleagues phrases like "How many times do I have to tell you?" At that point, the matter of shouting and anger became the issue that helped to show more of what was taking place among these students. As the authors describe, Avery explains himself by reminding

> the group [in his memo] that their topic is an "extremely sensitive, controversial, incendiary issue: and it is only "natural" that they will get "angry or impassioned about certain points." Furthermore he believes that "when people get angry, they tend to be honest about their true feelings." Indeed, Avery writes that he has previously been so "quiet, reserved, and passive [that] it truly feels liberating when I blatantly tell someone how I feel. . . . If I raise my voice . . . it is not a personal indictment of you or your views." (125)

On the one hand, Avery does not detail his history and the grounds on which he identifies with oppressed groups, and thus the grounds for his "true feelings." On the other hand, the class and the group have become a suitable occasion for him to acknowledge his anger through antiracist advocacy, which, itself, does not reflect, and in fact may be helping to conceal, the actual grounds of his anger, namely, discrimination on the basis of his unusual gender identity in childhood and youth.

In her response to Avery's explanation of the role of anger in his personal history Emily reaches understanding by contrasting it to her own personal history:

> Because of my upbringing I always assume that once people start to yell while they're arguing, that means they have stopped listening and that they no longer care about what the other person has to say. Avery explained to me that in his family they get their point across by yelling and raising their voices. That really helped me see where he was coming from. I'm not saying that I won't cringe if we start a screaming match again. (126)

Whatever else is the case, a certain level of the disclosure of family history that called attention to the language use traits that were involved in the dispute stabilized the styles of exchange and helps us to understand the relationship between Avery and his colleagues.

The authors generalize about the exchange between Avery and Emily and Serena in this way:

> Avery doesn't realize that many (white, middle class) women have been socialized to feel that anger is not natural or honest, that it is a personal indictment of them, and therefore, it is always to be avoided or prevented. (125)

The process of communication itself came under the authors' scrutiny. A specific way of speaking was identified both individually and politically as inhibiting collaboration. To contrast styles of speaking highlights gender styles and, through the students' interest in racism, calls attention to ethnic styles as well. Avery had cited Sister Souljah's anger as being one element with which he is identifying. The subject matter about which he is especially exercised is the treatment of black people by whites. However, even if it is clear that Avery is identifying in two or more senses with women and African Americans, the conflict in the group could also be identified as being over language use, which, in turn, was understood by the authors as gender-marked. Subsequently, Qualley and Chiseri-Strater describe the levels and styles of self-enlightenment that took place after the ironing out of the communication inhibitions early in the group's functioning. One of the experiences Serena reports having had toward the end of their collaboration was of having observed, at a meeting of the Black Students Organization, that

> I wanted to be fluent in two cultures like they are. Where they are able to switch from "white" English to "Black" English without thinking, I only know one language. (126)

The descriptions in this essay suggest that perhaps if African Americans know two (or more) languages, then women do also, and that Serena just had not thought of her language use styles in that sense. We may all know two or more languages, but because of the custom of single-culture self-identification, we are not prepared to recognize our many languages. Scenes of collaboration and disclosure, bearing the discomfort they often have, can help us toward such recognition.

Opposition to Covert Racism

Carrie Leverenz at Ohio State University reports on a collaborative scene in which literature and writing both play important roles, where ethnicity is the main site of conflict, but where the collaboration took unexpected but instructive turns. In her essay[22] Leverenz reported observations of a classroom having a female African American teacher, referred to as MJ.

Students in the class were divided into peer response groups to react to each other's literary responses. The students were to form habits of writing for, listening for, and expecting critique from colleagues doing the same work. This particular peer response group had three female members: Carol, an African American sophomore honors student; Patricia, a Korean American senior history major; and Beth, "a white woman who was a senior majoring in English" (171). (Her ethnic background is not further identified.) Leverenz describes Beth's role:

> Because Beth values the power of literary texts, it is not surprising that she uses her knowledge of literature to construct herself as an authority in her writing, providing as support for her arguments textual evidence gleaned not only from the texts assigned in class, but from texts she has read elsewhere, texts that are often unfamiliar to her classmates. Significantly, she did not seem to see her approach as one option among many, but as the "right" way to write about texts. (172)

In some contexts Beth might be unremarkable: the "A" student, conversant in New Criticism techniques. In MJ's African American Voices class, her role asks to be studied. In spite of what she may think, her authority is no longer constituted by her academic performance alone. To some extent, she is deceived by the indulgence of her role by the teacher, who is eager for her groups to function and may not be able to monitor the social psychology of each group. Leverenz tries to describe this group's political psychology: an account of how Carol, with the help of Patricia, subverted Beth's authority, which at first seemed to dominate the group. Although this outcome is good in some sense, it remained undisclosed in that classroom, and it is only in Leverenz's essay (and here, I hope) where the result may do its teaching.

Beth was acknowledged by Carol and Patricia as the group authority; Beth had taken the university's peer response tutoring course. Beth, who took the role in the group as the one who knew how to respond to and instruct the others in their writing, "established herself as an authority whose advice must be obeyed" (174). She did not contribute her texts for response, but she told her part-

---

[22] Carrie Shively Leverenz, "Peer Response in the Multicultural Composition Classroom: Dissensus—a Dream Deferred," *Journal of Advanced Composition* 14 (no.1, 1994): 167–186.

ners what response she was going to do later. (That is, she was unprepared *now.*) Beth steadily maintained the concept of literature as dealing with "universal human experience" in contrast, for example, to "issue-oriented experience." Regardless, Beth received the highest possible grades on her papers and responses. Leverenz presents her as an especially irritating presence whose own formulas for academic success were constantly under challenge, even if the challenge was not overt or confrontational. It seems a plausible conclusion, as Leverenz entertains, that "Beth's distress over the loss of her authority in the class as a whole contributed to the strength with which she asserted her authority in her peer response group" (181).

As the group moved toward its final project, there was class discussion of the first Rodney King verdict, and Beth tried during that discussion to view racism toward black men as being confined to the male sector of society, thus removing her own responsibility for coping with the general event. Because of this move, Beth lost some respect in the class, and particularly with Carol, one of her partners. At the same time, her other partner in the group, Patricia, had some sympathy with Beth's distancing, since her (Patricia's) parents owned a grocery store in South Central Los Angeles that had escaped harm in the riots following the verdict. As Leverenz describes, therefore, Carol had been isolated as the course came toward its end.

The final project was read only by the teacher. Carol used this situation to recover her own voice, as Leverenz describes:

> In spite of Beth's attempts to fit Carol's writing to the established mold of academic writing, Carol managed to resist Beth's authoritative voice in her revision and to continue writing "differently." This difference emerges in Carol's choice to support her generalizations not with more textual references to the poems but with additional references to Rodney King and to her own experience as an African American university student. (183)

This description refers to the ongoing tendency of Carol to integrate accounts of lived experience into her critical commentaries and responses, as contrasted with Beth's style of referring everything back to a text. Unlike the friction between the two men in Fox's example, the fight here was not fought in public. It is possible that this dispute could well have been aggravated by the collaborative situation and that Carol's personal conviction enabled her to get around the adverse established values. On the other hand, the class as a whole was different from most classes, and Carol had the implicit support of the teacher and of the predominant style of teaching in the class, supports that Beth, as an individual, did not have; Beth only had the more abstract support of the university's customary ways, which helped her get good grades.

Carol's victory did take place accompanied by an interesting move. Earlier in the class, Patricia had mistakenly(?) judged that in Paul Dunbar's "We Wear the Mask" the *we* can refer to the oppressor, and this reading was vigorously corrected by Beth, who insisted on the obvious. Here is Leverenz's description of what happened in Carol's final essay:

> In Carol's revised essay about the continuing effects of racism, she wrote, "In the poem, the oppressed group of people are wearing the mask. However the poem can be interpreted to read as the oppressor wearing the mask. Racism can cover itself from being seen as it really is and can dodge confrontation, by wearing a mask."
>
> In the margin next to the sentence, MJ wrote "Good point," and at the end of the essay comments, "This essay is much better than the first one. Your tone is more confident. I love your use of masks as worn by the oppressors. That is quite innovative."
>
> In spite of enormous pressure to conform to traditional conventions of academic discourse, in her revised draft, Carol clearly produced a different kind of discourse, one that challenged the narrow standards of text-based academic writing by relying on African American experience and by openly interpreting a piece of literature in ways that served her larger purposes. (183)

From one standpoint, this account says that the African American student, in spite of the collaborative classroom, the African American teacher, and the significant African American enrollment in the course, could not pursue her intellectual inclinations directly because of (1) the local politics of the group, (2) the bad luck of having Beth in the group, and (3) the continuing authority of a narrow, text-based standard of authoritative discourse. If it weren't for Leverenz's reporting, how many people aside from Carol and MJ would really be able to learn from this significant set of classroom events?

On the other hand, the events in this class demonstrate that there are new trends at work, one of which is the reduction of the authority of Beth's work style and its basis, grades. Also, the form of the reduction is interesting: Carol in a sense rescued her Korean-born partner's imagination by appropriating it to her own cause. However, Patricia herself did not benefit from Carol's support. Leverenz had reported Patricia's silent leaning toward the "white" perspective. The more we think about this account, the clearer it is that we need to know more. Yet two things may be said: the collaborative scene permitted the emergence of new voices; and the problems and frustrations that appeared in this group might have been fewer had group members felt more ready to disclose their perspectives to one another: the new voices might have been able to teach one another new genres.

Differences Within a Presumed Cultural Homogeneity

An instance from one of my own classes took place in the spring of 1993 in a course entitled Literature and Jewish Identity. It was the first time I had taught an academic course in which my ethnicity was part of the curriculum. This background was related to the issue that I discuss here, differences within a presumably homogeneous cultural group. There were thirteen students in the course, twelve women. One student was not a Jew. One student had converted to Judaism in grade school. The first writing we did was the "Jewish identity autobiography," which was energetically taken up by the students: class members, myself included, felt more than the usual comfort and license to disclose our senses of orientation as Jews, women, and men. The autobiographies had been distributed in advance, but the day on which we were to discuss them in class, I was absent. I asked the students to meet without me, which they did. As the course went on, about five different students gave me private accounts of that class meeting, and two students recorded their accounts and their readings of it for their final projects.

During the day I was absent, several members of the class had responded to one passage of Ms. J's essay and had prepared to engage it in class. This is the passage:

> I so desperately want to fill the void of knowledge concerning my heritage. However, I delay my study until a later date. I feel that date may be sooner rather than later. In [six months] I will be married to John C., a Lutheran. I tell you that he is a non-Jew because I know you will ask me. I ask, you ask, we all ask. For some, I think, the response is more important than to others. I never dated a Jewish man. I find them great as friends, but generally self-consumed and needing the constant nurturing they received from their Jewish mothers.

Many of the women could not quite put their finger on the problem this passage posed for them, but it had something to do with implying that a dating relation between herself and Jewish men was put out of reach in advance by Ms. J. However, Mr. P, the one male student engaged this passage by asking to substitute *black* for *Jewish* in the passage to see how it sounded—not dating black men because of

the "constant nurturing they received from their black mothers."
(This report is taken from the ethnographic account of this class by
Ms. D.) Ms. D writes,

> That kept Ms. J quiet for a while but I could tell that she resented
> Mr. P's criticism. From her paper I could tell that she prided herself
> on being sensitive to racism, sexism, and homophobia.

Ms. D, herself agitated by Ms. J's judgment, offered that Ms. J's

> decision to marry John was probably connected to her negative
> feelings about Jewish men. . . . It caught me off guard when Ms. J
> then asked me what I thought of Jewish men. . . . I responded that
> in my experience all men were pretty self-absorbed and expected
> women to be their mothers.

At the end of the paragraph, however, Ms. D observes about her
behavior in class, "I think I responded dishonestly because I didn't
want to admit that, deep down, I thought there was something to the
stereotype [of Jewish men]." Ms. D prides herself on her political
responsiveness in the same way that Ms. J does. One very interesting feature of this exchange is the intimation that "democratic" feelings don't operate so smoothly on this question of dating and
marriage among these Jewish women. Ms. D thought it may have
been dishonest of her to invoke the immaturity of men in general in
order not to identify herself as giving credence to the stereotype that
Ms. J (who in her essay did not worry about political correctness)
announced. Ms. J's personal candor may have been a step or two
ahead of her academically sophisticated classmates, but she was a
step behind in political alertness. The configuration in this group of
political and personal candor thus came out immediately. According to Ms. D, the real critique of Ms. J's judgment by most of the
women in the class pertained to her decision to get married so
young, not to her plan to marry a non-Jew.

The foregoing discussion was, I would say, in the realm of the
optimum level of serious exchange, where the students' feelings were
stirred up, somewhat antagonistic, but nevertheless within the range
of what one would hope for when a discourse of self-disclosure takes
place. However, that is not where matters ended, as Ms. D further
describes:

> The class discussion took a turn for the worse when Ms. X stated
> emphatically that, as a rabbi [which, as she announced in her auto-
> biographical essay, she aspired to be] she would never marry a Jew
> and a non-Jew. Every intermarriage, she claimed, "destroys a
> branch of the tree of Jewish life." Predictably, this led to the tears
> Ms. J had been about to shed all morning. I felt really bad when she

started to cry because I realized that, despite all the self-assurance she attempted to give off in her paper, she was (like all of us) just a kid. Mr. P and I immediately ran to Ms. J's rescue (ironically, since we were the ones who started the discussion). It was ludicrous, we declared, to make such a judgment on another person. We wanted to know what qualified her to judge another person's experience of Judaism. I got even more pissed with Ms. X when she declared that, as a rabbi, she would marry lesbian Jewish couples. Although I agree that lesbians should be allowed to marry if they want to, it seemed to me that marrying someone of a different faith was a hell of a lot more common than two women getting married. Plus, a heterosexual couple is more likely to reproduce than a homosexual couple—so if we're worried about the survival of the Jewish race, we ought to have a way of dealing with intermarriage.

"A hell of a lot more common . . . we ought to have a way of dealing with intermarriage." In her autobiography, Ms. D explained that her father was Protestant and her mother Jewish, and that they had just been divorced. Thus, when Ms. D contributed to the discussion, the class knew her circumstances.

The class also knew my circumstances, since I too had been married to a non-Jew, had been divorced, and had my own opinions on this topic, which were, more or less, in considerable sympathy with Ms. D in her attempts to sort out, with the other class members, how to reconfigure the different opinions, histories, and actions so that they all make more sense in *our* lives. Yet Ms. X had represented something that each class member wanted to consider: what does it take to maintain the health of the "tree of Jewish Life"? What will it take to balance the social, sexual, family, feminist, and religious features of Jewish life in *our own* adult lives? Ms. X did not disclose to the class the sources of her own show of certainty. Her reluctance to disclose may not have been so visible had her early judgment that brought Ms. J to tears not produced such disturbing effects at that time and subsequently.

In fact, in this class, the level of disclosure was similar for all class members, as best as I can tell, except for Ms. X. In retrospect, her "sermon" did represent a feeling of solidarity about Jewish life for which every Jewish member of the class had at least some respect. Yet because this sermon did not speak the language of disclosure as other class members' judgments did, notably as Ms. J's did, Ms. X's important views could not become an active part of the classroom attention, and did not for the rest of the semester.

Regardless of the specifics, this class demonstrated how disclosure and collaboration go together, even if it had, like the other classes I cited, a risk of dysfunction that threatened the academic and pedagogical health of the course. It is not surprising to me that I should find these terms in this class dealing with the historical problem of Jewish assimilation. This is my problem, what I brought to the class from my individual history as well as from my academic imagination, from my experiences and frustrations, from my wish to belong to a safe culture that can deal with the idiosyncratic as well as the personal and the collective. Because I was able to say that I had some of the same problems as students who were younger than I, I was able to persuade them that, on that level, I was also a student and a colleague of theirs. I relaxed my usual professional self-presentation; through my autobiographical contributions, and through the writing itself—its tone, its vocabulary, and, I hope, its authenticity—I brought out the terms of my membership in the students' community, my implication in the issues that evoked their strong feelings.

The one class member who was not a Jew (Ms. T) was already friends with several of the class members and knew, more or less, what was on people's minds. She was ready for the political turn of our discussions and was especially conversant in the disputes lately arising between feminism and religious orthodoxy. The students could see, with Ms. T's help and through the interrogatives of Ms. D and Ms. J, the relation of difference within to difference between.

This class had many, perhaps all, "outsiders": one who had converted, one from an intermarriage, one an immigrant from the Soviet Union; another grown up in South America, another grown up in the American West; one concerned with sexual orientation; one the child of a Holocaust survivor; some with divorced parents and some with parents who stayed together; those with skin disorders and those with eating disorders. And so on. The longer one viewed each individual, the clearer individual difference became. Each new essay brought a new degree of disclosure, a new alignment with others, and a new thought about what was a new work for each of us.

The Disclosure of Previously Unannounceable Knowledge

A year later, I taught a somewhat revised version of the same course, Literature and Jewish Identity, which this time enrolled seven upper-level undergraduate students: two men and five women. One man was Protestant and planning to be a minister; one woman had grown up in a Roman Catholic home in South America. The other students were Jews. The central issue of this course continued to be the assimilation, and its literary treatments, of Jews in Christian society, in a perspective of European and American history of the last one hundred fifty years. We tried to let certain works of literature evoke our feelings about the assimilation of Jews in American society.

The situation I present was instigated by an unsettling assignment I have used over the last fifteen years, one that has usually required pedagogical and interpersonal vigilance. About two-thirds of the way into the course, I asked the students, in round-robin fashion, to write about the portfolios of the student sitting next to them, in order to learn to immerse oneself in the perspectives of one's colleagues. Class discussion was then to compare the prestudy understanding of each person's perspective with what emerged after study of the portfolio of writings. The present instance proved so emotionally taxing that during one class session the Catholic student from South America, Ms. L, ran out of the room in tears. The occasion was the discussion following her reading and writing about the portfolio of Ms. J, a Jewish student from a small city on the East Coast. Subsequently, the matter was settled through many students speaking to one another and to Ms. L and Ms. J in and out of class. The final essays written by both students, while not finding Hollywoodesque happiness, did reflect collective alertness regarding the depth of this issue.

In her first essay in this class, her autobiography, Ms. J had written,

> I feel as if I was a "silent Jew." I never mentioned that I was Jewish to anyone unless the topic was brought up; I ignored all Jewish jokes; I would never wear a Star of David on my chest, and I would never comment on the one friend who slipped me a Christmas card instead of a Happy Hanukkah card . . . I went from being the proud Jewish girl to the proud but disguised Jewish girl . . . it was all inside of me. There was something telling me that I was different and that I should keep that difference to myself . . . being Jewish meant remaining quiet.

In her response to Ms. J's portfolio, in which this matter of self-concealment appears repeatedly, Ms. L wrote,

> Her feelings of self-identification with Judaism scare me. She would never only claim: "I am a Jew, so what?" She behaves indifferently to Judaism, but her true feeling is completely different: she should be angry with the social rejection [of] Jews. She claims that "one important aspect in Jewish history is never to forget, but always remember the past." These words mean to me that she should never forget the Holocaust, jokes about Jews, and the social rejection because there is a Jewish feeling in her blood which society cannot control. . . . If she is proud and sure of who she is, why doesn't she fight against society to propagate her culture? She claims that "Anti-Semites . . . never try to discover the truth about the Jewish race," [but] in my opinion . . . based on her papers and class discussion, she does nothing to show that truth.

Since Ms. L was the "minority" in the class, however, it was she and not Ms. J who cried and left the room when students in the class responded to Ms. L's challenge. For her part, the darker, Mediterranean-looking Ms. L had learned at home in South America that Jews were all blond and blue-eyed (oddly enough, all the Jews in this class had blue eyes!), owned beauty salons, were always well-off, and "stuck to themselves," refusing to become part of the majority culture.

Underneath the expectable stereotypes is, we see, the real question that got to Ms. J and stimulated the class' defense of her, leading to Ms. L's attempt to escape the collective criticism: Why must a person who claims to be proud of their heritage hide it? Aren't you too a coward? Ms. L, unaware of the Catholic Church's history of opposition to Jews, yet herself rejecting its androcentric authoritarianism, did not know enough about Western history to see herself as a person who had to hide her womanhood in ways that Ms. J had to hide her Jewishness. Our question is, though, did the discomfort we all felt teach us enough to justify it? In this case, possibly so, since class members tried to enlighten one another with materials that spoke directly to each person's zones of ignorance. I had to play an active role—holding private conferences with all students—in order to dissolve the gang effect that brought us to the brink of failure. Some Jewish students understood the partially unjustified mutual antagonism and played a mediating role, while disclosing the existence of gradations of opinion within the Jewish group, gradations rarely acknowledged and often immediately lost in identity politics disputes.[23] Yet it is also clear that, in principle, individual classes are good sites to risk discomfort that must come from the real candor needed to provide all class members with an accurate feeling of what is involved in the idea of assimilation, which might otherwise have remained an examination-friendly formulation rather than a difficult human experience. Not everything people feel ready to disclose can or should make its way into the curriculum, which was, topically, how literature plays a role in problems of Jewish identity and assimilation. But in this, and in the other classrooms I mentioned, the discomfort accompanying disclosure of membership and collaboration provided an air of realism that encouraged the living involvements in academic inquiry.

---

[23] These gradations of opinion are comparable to the color scale among African-descent Westerners discussed by another Ms. J earlier in this chapter.

Comment

The discomfort in the foregoing classrooms derived from things said and written and were resolved with things said and written. These instances suggest that where there are articulate students eager to speak out, the problem of choosing what to say and how to say it is not reduced in scope and interest. In courses offered by other disciplines, similar connections of membership, disclosure, collaboration must be taken into account when matters of writing and language use are engaged. Interestingly, from some of the foregoing examples silence emerges as a part of language use. Class members had to choose not to speak. In some of my classes, what was said in public was scripted—arranged in advance. That too is a genre and should be recognized as such.

Discomfort occurred because people placed or found themselves in the presence of an "other" who posed a challenge to their identities, as when Ms. X made the remark about the branch of the Jewish tree, or when Mike asked Jorge for his green card. Many may claim that such friction does not belong in class, but these instances show not that friction was deliberately brought in but that it was there by virtue of the student population, the nature of the course, the teacher, the immediate writing and speaking situations. These feelings are just there, and we who supervise classrooms can convert them into occasions for thinking.

Classrooms hold rich possibilities for becoming sites of learning grounded in mutual understanding and the sense of mutual implication in one another's life situations. This does not mean that everyone must like one another. But we can teach ourselves and our students what the juices, feelings, meanings, and struggles of working seriously and professionally with others are. Individual and collective self-disclosure changes the vocabularies and the discourse styles of our classrooms, provides the bases in human experience for identifying political interests and for enacting their practical needs, provides unambiguous addresses for individuality while showing the implication of each individual in a series of groups, communities, societies, and political constituencies. If we hold this ideal, discomfort is inevitable. Heretofore, schooling has ruled out social and political discomfort as an important part of the teaching of subject matter. Recognizing the memberships that all individuals necessarily have means speaking up and out, writing up and down, and letting these rereadings and rewritings make new memberships from the old discomforts.

Chapter Six

The Contingent Curriculum

Contingent Knowledge of Writing and Language Use

One answer to the question of why the same complaints about students' writing have appeared for a century is that we are teaching people to become involved in the subject of language use, which is growing along with them. To teach through disclosure, genre, and membership is to recognize that the scenes of teaching are continuously changing in unpredictable ways. If one expects a generational cycle, the feeling of teaching the "same" thing repeatedly makes sense even though the new contexts render the "same" things "new." However, postsecondary writing pedagogy takes place in the academic context, where linear, progressive technological change is the quiet standard that leads many to expect succeeding generations to know more about writing than previous ones.[1]

Our subject is not available to articulation in formulas and laws that can be accepted or disproved; "old" knowledge of language use does not become obsolete but stays in a category of lore—"the accumulated body of traditions, practices, and beliefs in terms of which Practitioners understand how writing is done, learned, and taught."[2] An instance of knowledge-as-lore is the return of classical rhetoric, which is contributing to the theory, teaching, and practice of writing and language use. Change appears in the details of writing

---

[1] Chapter 7 considers some of the ideological retardants to the understanding of writing pedagogy.

[2] Stephen North, *The Making of Knowledge in Composition: Portrait of an Emerging Field* (Portsmouth, NH: Boynton/Cook, 1987), 23.

pedagogy; it is present in individual efforts, in each classroom, in new scholarly contributions. Genre, disclosure, and membership let us think of writing and language use as a subject that is changing as we teach it. Because language use is so decisively tied to living people and societies, it necessarily is a changing subject.

This chapter discusses how the writing and language use curriculum can and should be understood as contingent on the people in classrooms, on the personal and social circumstances of classrooms and schools, and on the critique of public values that takes place in academic and popular culture. The contingency of the curriculum is based in part on historical considerations, on a different sense of classroom phenomenology described by Edward Pauly, on initiatives already taken by some postsecondary teachers, and on examples of results that have taken place when the contingencies of classrooms were the basis for encouraging new initiatives on the part of students.

Historical and Experiential
Bases for a Contingent Curriculum

In 1918 the National Educational Association promulgated "Seven Cardinal Principles" of schooling, which, many observers agree, have characterized the ideals of secondary education since then: "health, command of fundamental processes, worthy home membership, vocation, civic education, worthy use of leisure time, ethical character."[3] These principles moved the focus of secondary education away from an exclusive attention to subject matter and toward a comprehensive approach: seeking a full menu of capabilities for each student. As historians in the Ravitch-Vinovskis volume detail repeatedly, this philosophy has gradually led to students' ability to get through school with a certain lack of discipline and accomplishment. Academic courses were not demanded past a certain point, and other courses, like typing, physical education, shop, music, became part of the accepted curriculum, which has been so wide ranging since these principles were promulgated.

By and large, this style of curriculum has not changed since it began, though there have been different emphases, different schools, different concentrations of subjects made available to students of various talents and various social classes. There was maximum

---

[3] Diane Ravitch and Maris A. Vinovskis, eds., *Learning from the Past: What History Teaches Us About School Reform* (Baltimore: Johns Hopkins University Press, 1995), 13. Other essays in that collection cite this list repeatedly.

choice for students, but few ways to vary the total curricular offering. Proposals for educational reform and improvement concentrated on the administrative structure and the delivery of resources:
there were those whose job it was to see that students could prove
that they took, and learned from, the courses in which they were
enrolled. Because of the curricular variation, per student, standardized tests[4] per subject matter became attractive. In New York State,
for example, standardized tests (the Regents exams) still are given to
attest to the fundamental, or common denominator, competence of
students. Because choice and well-roundedness were important in
the schools themselves, the task of cultivating and disciplining students in the subject matters as presented by the teachers was essentially taken out of the hands of teachers: the tests were the means of
certifying students. Teachers had to teach for the tests. Teaching
itself was, for a large part and in many cases for the most part, taken
out of the hands of teachers. As Deborah Holdstein has recently
detailed with regard to college writing at her university, the teachers
and assessors of writing are working at conflicting purposes.[5] In fact,
standardized tests (discussed in Chapter 7) are *the* way of deciding
on just how much a student did and will achieve. A wide-ranging
curriculum that encourages individualism also requires standardized tests, which discourage imagination and creativity, thus more
or less producing mostly compliant, unadventurous students. Many
capable students with different cultural backgrounds could barely
hope to learn the standard and destigmatize themselves.

   Others[6] have previously maintained that the classroom should
not receive curriculum from above but should be a site at which anything delivered to a class—by students and teachers as well as by
curriculum planners—can be brought into the curriculum. Under
such circumstances, curriculum is contingent on the needs, values,
interests, backgrounds, and social viability of class members. But
Dewey-period ideals along these lines were overwhelmed by the
wide-ranging liberal curriculum and its administrative apparatus.

---

[4] The ideological function of testing is explored in Chapter 7.

[5] Deborah Holdstein, "The Institutional Agenda, Collaboration, and Writing
Assessment," in *Writing With: New Directions in Collaborative Teaching, Learning,
and Research*, ed. Sally Reagan, Thomas Fox, and David Bleich (Albany: SUNY Press,
1994), 77–88.

[6] Dewey and the progressivists of the 1930s. One obstacle to the success of this
movement, in addition to the endemic ideological opposition, was the accepted
authority of school administrations, which would have had to change their "spots" in
order to enact the proposals of the progressive educators. I discuss shortly how the
same situation obtains today.

Recently attention has again been paid to the problem of what counts as curriculum; some documentation as to the nature and scope of school system inertia is available in Pauly's recent book *The Classroom Crucible.*[7] Pauly's explanation of the failure of the liberal curriculum is a new perspective that suggests how and why every curriculum should be anticipated as contingent on the population of schools and students. He shows why curriculum should be variable and responsive to who the students are and what they need, and should not be prescribed by those distant from the living circumstances of students, teachers, and communities that support schools.

The starting point of Pauly's discussion is a 1966 report by James S. Coleman, *Equality of Educational Opportunity,* commissioned by Congress in 1964. Being part of the Great Society initiative, the commission sought insight into the different levels of achievement by students from different ethnic groups. The conventional wisdom had been that the quality of the school was the single most important factor in individual achievement: Black and Hispanic schools were not as good as white schools. Coleman's finding went against this view. According to Pauly, Coleman found that students' achievements were unrelated to which policy or program was in effect. Rather, he discovered, variations within schools and classrooms explained different levels of student accomplishment. The finding that variations internal to classrooms and schools were the salient factors affecting students' performance went against the conventional assumption that the school as a whole was responsible for how each student does or does not achieve. From an administrative standpoint, the "school makes the difference" perspective is easier to cope with: allocate money from the congressional pipeline to districts whose schools need help. But if the Coleman finding is accepted, how are allocated funds to be used in different parts of the same school? Given the way school funding takes place, differential distribution of funds within a school does not seem possible. Federal help for schools was misguided, if the Coleman report is accurate. However, the problem is even more difficult, since help was needed for parts of both "good" suburban and "problem" urban schools. There was no way to conceive of problems on an intraschool level. The Coleman report announced that this failure to understand the shape of school problems was the case nationally. To help schools, it said, attention had to be paid to *differences within* them.

---

[7] Edward Pauly, *The Classroom Crucible: What Really Works, What Doesn't, and Why* (New York: Basic Books, 1990).

When the report was issued, the educational policy machineries were very strong. Pauly maintained, however, that centrally generated educational policies have no effect on the ability of students to do well in schools because the policies are prescriptive: they demand and enforce specific ways of teaching. If the policies failed, new centrally generated remedial steps were required, which, because they were prescriptive, also failed. Pauly understood prescription as an ideology, which is a way of saying that it was ineligible to be questioned or changed. As a result, the policy of prescription required a great deal of oversight, which created disabling levels of intrusion into the efforts of teachers and students to work within the parameters of their own situations, needs, and personalities. Prescriptions required repression and compliance, and endorsed the view that classrooms must be alike. Pauly is surprised that few thought to question this way of using governmental resources to help students.

The "ideology of prescription" is Pauly's identification of the cause of failure of educational policy. In a hierarchical situation, a system imposed by the funding source is supposed to help schools. The vocabulary in Pauly's description of the help—"enforcing" regulations and curricula, "testing," "monitoring," "compliance," uniformity of classroom identity—suggests its imposition. If, furthermore, in primary and secondary schools teachers are mostly female, and administrators and policymakers are mostly male, this imbalance—that is, money and authority are gender-coded to the advantage of men—could be retarding the effects of government help. The result described by Pauly is a stalemate: there is no effect of policy on student welfare. The official voices of educational policy are able to describe the history of school reform, but they do not view schools through their classroom identities.[8] Yet most teachers, including postsecondary teachers, know that the social, interpersonal, and political character of classrooms affect how teachers and students work together to learn or fail to learn.

Official education policy treats teachers the way the policymakers expect teachers to treat students. The policymakers assume a chain of command that, while not military in intention and urgency, resembles

---

[8] Diane Ravitch and Maris A. Vinovskis, eds., *Learning from the Past*. None of the essays in this otherwise interesting volume considers the classroom experience for either students or teachers. Thirty years of failed policies did not seem to suggest to this group of mostly male authors what it suggested to Pauly and many of the researchers he cites: classroom phenomenology and social experience is fundamental to understanding how to motivate students. The Shachar and Sharan experiment, discussed in Chapter 8, suggests, with more "data," a similar point.

the military in structure and behavior. Orders are given to teachers to give orders to students, and then tests, monitoring devices, and superimposed repetitive remediation takes place when the policies fail to help students. In such a system, no one person or clearly identified group seems to have responsibility—it is always those higher up on the chain of command. Students and teachers do not know if they are working with each other or with some abstract policy (usually in the form of curriculum or testable standards of performance). Time is taken from what a teacher may consider essential in order to prepare students for demands made outside of the classroom by those who want students to "become like us, the standard people."

Policymakers in the educational bureaucracy[9] want intellectual uniformity and conformity. Some policymakers mean well; others condescend to teachers and consider them incapable of independent teaching. Pauly has described how teachers have counteracted the negative effects of superimposed educational policies and curricula. The use of the term *prescription* may be somewhat euphemistic. It may not be prescription that is taking place: as Richard Ohmann implied,[10] it looks too often like indoctrination and pacification. If education were able to function as freely as business, we could expect teachers to know how to use federal funds to help lower the percentage of students dropping out, lower the percentage of the unmotivated and disaffected.

Pauly's inquiry into studies following up on the Coleman report led to the fact that classroom differences, rather than school differences, most clearly account for differences in students' performance. His book cites the literature that showed this fact. He then suggests that this literature has not been acknowledged by policymakers because "in order for a body of research to be discussed, it must be understood and restated in the language of prior research" (33). Pauly notices that whereas policymakers speak the language of "prior research," teachers speak the pragmatic language of differential problems within schools, and neither group understands the other. The current education policy paradigm has no room for teachers' experienced-based information. The data cited by Pauly are anomalous and require a new explanatory paradigm to recognize their importance, yet there was no such paradigm. In its absence people could not assimilate the thought that most education policy research was useless. The explanatory paradigm proposed by Pauly is that

---

[9] Chapter 7 considers the bureaucracy factor in universities' inertia.

[10] Richard Ohmann, *Politics of Letters* (Middletown, CT: Wesleyan University Press, 1987).

classrooms determine students' performances the most, and that classrooms are indefinitely contingent. Especially, the same good teacher teaching a new group of students can become a mediocre teacher, because the contingent mixture of students has so much influence on how the total classroom performs. The same class and teacher but, say, with only five students replaced by other students, can similarly change its total character in such a way that the same students may suddenly not do as well in the newly constituted group.

These findings bring the phenomenology of classrooms to the forefront of thinking about teaching. The actions of principals and superintendents are also not to be understood as crucial (35). These figures are facilitators, conveyors of resources; they could[11] even be thought of as teachers' assistants. Some of the more interesting data in Pauly's book are the various descriptions and testimonials about the classroom that show its feel and suggest why its collections of people and relationships are the foundations of both its successes and failures. There are few work scenes quite like a classroom, where many are thrown together for longish periods of time.[12] Classrooms are places where

> everyone is constantly aware of the people around them, respond-
> ing to and being deeply affected by them. This pattern of crowded,
> intense intimacy is the setting for daily life in classrooms. (40)

Here is Pauly's list of classroom features he found to describe K–12 classrooms, but these may be applied with some adjustment to describe postsecondary classrooms as well:

> 1. Each person in the classroom can affect how the others are
> treated. There is no teacher or student unable to gain the attention
> of his or her classmates and to impinge on their lives and work; and
> every person is at the mercy of the other people in the classroom.

---

[11] And some think, *should,* like Shachar and Sharan, whose experiment is discussed in Chapter 8. However, I do not discuss their recommendation for school administration, which, briefly, is that the administration must be in a cooperative, nonhierarchical relation with the teaching staff.

[12] Susan Miller, "New Discourse City: An Alternative Model for Collaboration," in *Writing With: New Directions in Collaborative Teaching, Learning, and Research,* ed. Sally Reagan, Thomas Fox, and David Bleich, 283–300. Miller suggests that we would do well to think of collaborative projects in a more urban vein, where perhaps the assumed distance between individuals is great, but there are so many people that what relationships form is not predictable.

2. Teachers' and students' actions are continually exposed to examination by every person in the classroom, in an unrelenting mutual scrutiny that gradually reveals each person's sensitivities and limitations to everyone else in the classroom, and greatly increases their susceptibility to influence by their classmates.

3. Teachers and students know that their contact with the other people in their classroom will be lengthy and sustained. For the whole school year, the quality of teachers' and students' lives is controlled by a single group of people, those that make up their classroom. They are always *there*. (40)

In discussions of postsecondary classrooms, facts such as these are rarely brought out.[13] In college classrooms the sense of proximity is also great. For example, it remains true in college that any member of a class can get the attention of any other; each person's actions are exposed continually, though many in college have good means of concealment; each class member knows that these same people will be in this same class week in, week out. The "school" character of college classrooms is not that different from the classrooms described by Pauly.

These regularities are classroom contingencies that affect how people are going to think and work individually and collectively.[14] Under these circumstances, the classroom population is necessarily more important as a group of potential initiators than most of us have acknowledged.[15] With this much mutual looking and checking, with this ability to engage others, there is a significant degree of varied intelligent energy to be called upon for classroom projects. To ignore this energy is to waste it. Class members' energy is a sign of knowledge and history already present. Students' alertness to one another is a sign that they will also learn from one another, that they are ready to relate their interpersonal mutual uptakes to the deeper exchanges that will take place about the class' subject matters.

The principle of "lengthy and sustained contact" is important to postsecondary writing classrooms. There is a curve or cycle of familiarity that grows from the "stranger" phase of the early meetings to

---

[13] Thanks to Ted Quimby for pointing me to Pauly's book.

[14] These and the other contingencies I describe suggest bases for changes in classroom functioning that can reduce many postsecondary teaching frustrations.

[15] In my publications I have made it a habit to cite work by students to show that their searches for understanding, their perspectives on school and teaching, should be "trading" with our "professional" claims. The present book presupposes that students' contributions are and should be acknowledged as a main feature of changes in teaching and in the teaching of writing.

the understanding phase toward the end of a course. During a year-long course, the level of familiarity is great enough at the beginning of the second semester that unprecedented levels of action, thinking, writing, and initiatives may be expected. Although the togetherness begins in an accidental way, its necessity forces a pragmatic adjustment, the key element of which is the need to cope and manage through communication and understanding; at the same time students are studying the subject matter of communication and language use. Survival as a social figure in a writing classroom means, in part, integrating classroom social relations with the study of language use in the course.

Classrooms, Pauly observes, create a sense of vulnerability for their constituents. This feeling is observable in some students through the unwillingness to speak in class discussion. However, the feeling is probably universal owing to the social architecture of classrooms. Because each person is exposed, one may interpret behaviors other than reluctance to speak as being responses to the sense of vulnerability. For example, someone who speaks too much or tends to dominate may be trying to fend off a sense of vulnerability to the "mob" of other students. Recognizing this feeling provides a basis for encouraging cooperative interactions: "For both teachers and students, their vulnerability forces them to turn to one another for the agreements, assistance, and consent that they need to get what they want in the classroom" (Pauly 49).

The use of power in university classrooms may be the other side of the feelings of vulnerability that class members have. Many of those thinking about classroom social psychology are resigned, though with some irony, to the necessity of the ultimate power of teachers. An appealing instance of this came in my class from a first-year student. Ms. S took my first-year writing course, which was graded on the A/B system: B for doing all the work, coming to class, and participating with reasonable conscientiousness; A for distinguishing oneself in some way. Ms. S wanted an A, since she was going to be a computer scientist and had high standards for herself anyway. Members of this class knew and felt they were encouraged to invent vocabulary and express opinions, regardless of how bizarre, in writing projects. At the end of the course, Ms. S commented on their alleged "liberties":

> . . . if I were being strict and formal, I would not make up words nor would I make opinionated comments concerning other classes.
>
> However, I am not sure that I would take such liberties if I were taking another course. I think that the type of course that this is allows me and other students to take certain liberties. Bleich has actually encouraged us to take liberties such as straying from the suggested topics and making up words where there are no existing

words to describe our point. Although it seems as though the students are taking liberties they are endorsed by the teacher, so are they really liberties?[16]

Ms. S has a point, and many of my graduate students have similarly noticed that if I "give" them the power to act in certain unorthodox ways, there is still doubt about whether they "really" have power. Ms. S's opinion comes partly from her acceptance of the status quo in school. Her aspirations and accomplishments to date stemmed from her ability to adapt to the system as it is. This means that taking liberties is not really part of her school paradigm. Nevertheless, she adapts well to *whatever* the school of her choice proposes. She then "takes" the liberties, but in the evaluative commentary on the course, she justifiably observes that if the system is constituted through traditional teacherly authority, what meaning can it have that liberties are taken at all? She means, If I take liberties, that will help me to get an A, which also means, If I do what the teacher proposes, I will get an A. There is doubt about whether she really had liberties. On the other hand, if the system varies the ways of accrediting students,[17] each teacher can have a different approach to power arrangements, and the students' experiments with different styles of liberty taking will be more authentic.

Pauly's discussion of "reciprocal power" in classrooms approaches this issue of classroom power in terms that may authenticate students' liberty taking. First, even in the most traditional classrooms, power necessarily resides in both teachers and students. Here are some teacher comments to that effect, cited by Pauly:

> As a teacher, you can't just go in with your own agenda and ignore what's going on with them. Because it doesn't work. Because if you did that Monday, you'd still see them Tuesday, but Tuesday they'd be a little bit angrier at you, and they'd be a little bit more resistant to what you're doing, and by the time you hit Friday it would be a disaster. I guess it's good, in that it forces you as a teacher to be more responsive to the students, and it forces *them* to be responsive, too. (51)

> They make the rules. They have made all the rules in the room. Anything that happens in the room, it's them. (51)

Such comments make the word *power* seem somewhat exaggerated for describing classroom events. *Power* more commonly describes large-scale politics; local scenes seem more to have a politics than a

---

[16] Ms. S's work is discussed in my essay "Evaluation, Self-Evaluation, and Individualism," *ADE Bulletin* (Spring 1992): 11.

[17] This issue of evaluation is discussed in the next two chapters.

power configuration in the usual sense. In the classroom, *responsibility, responsiveness, rules,* and *authority* are more pertinent terms.[18] These excerpts from teachers who were asked to describe their local scenes give contingencies and impressions. The first paragraph gives a baseline of the students expectations: in each classroom, a tacit teaching expectation must be that the students will be heard at some level. What they demand, say, and need has to be accommodated by the teacher's action. The balance of authority is to be found in the juxtaposition of the teacher's agenda and the students' sense of what is OK in *this* classroom.

The second paragraph, quoting a different teacher, may seem indirect, metaphorical, or exaggerated. But in some sense it is accurate. Students uphold rules that they think are in effect in school. Should teachers violate these rules, say, with a series of excessive demands for work or behavior, their viability as teachers is reduced. One such class I had in high school found the teacher often whirling around quickly trying to catch the chalk thrower while he was writing on the blackboard. The class came to a halt because the teacher had overstepped the known rules of class and school. Unless teachers understand students' rules in the sense of the permissible and impermissible deportments in class, the class can become disabled.

Pauly characterizes classroom situations as being supported by "reciprocal power," which refers to the fact that any one person's exercise of power over others implies that these others can exercise power "back," so to speak. This principle appplies to students' effects on each other and on teachers as well as to teachers' effects on students (57). Although Pauly speaks about *power,* it may be more accurate to substitute *authority* in most of the places where *power* is used. To the extent that Pauly is alluding to classroom behavior, *power* could be somewhat more appropriate. But if instead we read the passage as alluding to the authority each person has by virtue of having a personal and cultural history, by virtue of having struggled through certain family problems, by virtue of having learned things in urgent circumstances, by virtue of having been hurt or humiliated, or of having achieved something through work or luck, then the reciprocity of "power" becomes a reciprocity of knowledge and experience that can be assimilated to the class' subject matters. Each person needs to know something of what every other person in that class knows. What each person, including the teacher, already knows is part of the curriculum, whatever the materials handed down from

---

[18] Pauly's discussion and data accept this view, but he still uses the term *power,* I imagine, because it is in the prevailing jargon.

administrative sources. Just as teachers take the liberty of changing a received curriculum, so may students, with knowledge, readings, experiences, and questions they had on entering the class. Necessarily together for a long period of time (a semester or a year), students need to discover what each other person knows and to judge what use that other person's knowledge may be to their own efforts at asking and answering questions. As much as students obviously influence one another in terms of clothing, deportment, and talent, as much as there is extended mutual scrutiny by everyone in a classroom, these same influences apply to the power—the authority—that each person has by virtue of having grown, thought, remembered, and understood to date. In a classroom, everyone is subject to the authority of everyone else's knowledge, understanding, and experience. This reciprocity is a fundamental contingency that has not yet been recognized as a new key to making all classrooms fulfilling for all their constituents.

Classroom groups are unavoidably provisional and contingent. Pauly suggests that tacitly accepted classroom rules of social interaction function in the way treaties between nations do: all parties must find them in their interest. The rules are provisional in the sense that teachers and students can change them if they apply enough pressure. The contingency of authority is that it can and does change so long as authoritarian styles do not take over.[19] The usual presumption of civilized democratic deportment recognizes popular authority. However, in the classroom, the provisionality of the balance of authority lies in so many factors having to do with the actual people in the classroom that unless such personal factors are faced, teaching and learning remains accidental. Pauly describes how reciprocal power helps to create distinctive classrooms despite external pressures to prescribe their activities:

> Teachers' and students' on-the-spot inventions have the effect of redesigning teaching and learning in their classrooms. (73)

> One teacher summed up the way that daily classroom interactions control teaching and learning:
> The give-and-take that goes on, things that I end up responding to, altering the lesson plan, changing what I do because of what a student does or something that happens among the students, or something that happens between me and a student that everybody is watching—that happens a lot. (73)

---

[19] The discussion of Mary R. Boland's classes in Chapter 8 also makes this point. See Alison Warriner, "'I Didn't Think They Had It in Them': Students Learning from Students," *Journal of Advanced Composition,* 16 (no. 2, 1996): 325–340.

The sum of Pauly's thought about the classroom is this: even now, under conditions where official policies and administrative rules, style, examinations, and beyond-the-classroom standards seem to hold sway, the influence of the interpersonal contingencies in the classroom nevertheless supervenes to produce the results that are seen from the outside.

The task for those of us wanting to recognize what really happens in classrooms is to reduce the national, collective unconsciousness of how the classroom and its phenomenology influences how people learn and know, to face the classroom differently, and to plan and expect teaching and learning to change under the guidance of classroom knowledge we now seek in new ways.

Postsecondary Recognition of the Contingent Curriculum

The foregoing, and other of Pauly's citations of teachers' perspectives and characterizations, refer to classrooms in grades K–12. In postsecondary classrooms, the collective interpersonal experiences are also the bases of how students learn. Recently disruptions in humanities curricula have been taking place in colleges and universities. Poststructuralist approaches to language and knowledge have given the traditional humanities subjects a more political accent. Junior faculty and graduate students have helped to change postsecondary classrooms by responding to the contingency of feminist and postcolonial programs. In effect, there has been a new humanities "curriculum," which has been grafted onto traditional university teaching—lecturing and grading. Often the theory and politics that teachers have advocated in class are at odds with the underlying styles and rules of universities. As a result, there is agitation in many classrooms, deans' offices, and central administrations.

"Conservative" faculty members advocate the "proven" effectiveness of the combination of a "classical" curriculum and the traditional style of university teaching. Other faculty members like the traditional classroom teaching style but insist on a socially and politically informed reading list. Still others have encouraged new and mixed genres into their classrooms, and have used new genres of writing to teach students to try new voices, new opinions, and new inquiries into others' opinions. In writing classes, there has been perhaps the most experimenting with the teaching formats, the curricula and reading lists being the most experimental in the humanities. However, these academic differences have produced exaggerated mutual irritations and polarization. Some have begun to question whether tenure should be curtailed so that faculty can be held "accountable." This curricular unrest is an aspect of university life that links it with the increasing polarization in society: tradition for the secure group, diversity for others.

In these disputes over the curriculum very little has changed in the university teaching structure. As in secondary school curricula (as observed by Ravitch and Vinovskis), the postsecondary curriculum has been the same, more or less, for about a century. Subject matters in all disciplines are responsive to developments in industry, politics, society, medicine, and education. When new books come out and are reviewed, they enter a public discussion, and courses are given to study these books. University curricula are fluid and responsive to changes in society. In their wide range (as well as their longevity), they are similar to the "liberal" secondary school curricula. The political advocacies that are taking place are only reflecting the new voices of women and minorities in society. Any long-term member of a university community will attest that change is very slow, and there are relatively few women and minorities in faculty positions. Furthermore, many female and minority faculty members are not busy advocating but are, rather, teaching their subjects. Women's Studies and African American Studies programs remain small and underfunded, and most students are not politically active.

Curriculum functions as Robin Lakoff[20] described it in her "narrow" field of graduate linguistics:

> My department is at it again.
>
> Every five years or so we go through it, only to undo our work, like Penelope, with perfect regularity some five years later. We are fighting about revamping the department's graduate program: how many courses, and which, and in what order, are to be required for the Ph.D. It always turns out to be a long-drawn-out process, entailing almost as much internecine acrimony as our all-time favorite fighting issue—hiring of new colleagues. And the real conflicts, the things that fill a simple process with dissension, are never brought out into the light of day: they remain covert, while we debate superficialities. (141)

The series of core courses and electives are the superficialities. The "real conflicts" in curriculum and requirements situations involve the subject matter; what features of it shall be valued over others. These conflicts are implicated in the professional lives of faculty

---

[20] Robin Lakoff, *Talking Power* (New York: Basic Books, 1990), 141.

members, their list of publications, their friends at other universities, their ability to advance their careers, and perhaps their domestic lives and the welfare of their parents and children. The depth of these conflicts is too great for committees to face. Lakoff's view is that academics conceal the real conflicts from themselves and refuse to acknowledge them in formal contexts. Instead there is fighting and acrimony, which keep questions of the connections among the subject matter, the faculty members, and society off the table when the curriculum is considered.

Things don't change much in academic departments because the basis for change is the same as the bases for change in the classrooms described by Pauly: the constituents. Most faculty members remain tenured. Each year a few are hired on, a few leave, and a few retire. After five years there is *some* turnover, but not that much. Values in society haven't changed that much in that period either. For the most part, the list of courses taught in a university is not determined by a Platonic principle of curriculum, but by the interests and abilities of the faculty. Even traditional curricula are located in the faculty, and however they may change in response to what deans request and the university needs, the slow pace of change among the faculty accounts best for the slow pace of curricular change. Since I was an undergraduate forty years ago, additions to the curriculum include computer science, environmental studies, women's and minority studies, and lately, history of technology. For the most part these are *new combinations,* new genres with *new mixes* of courses. They also reflect the change and expansion of interests of existing faculty, responding to changes in society, reading new books, coming up with new ideas, trying them out in new courses. Deans usually have funding for such course development, and faculty members avail themselves of these funds sooner or later. Thus, curriculum growth is tied to faculty growth and change. There is novelty in the courses, and there are the continuing teaching and thinking styles of the faculty members as they grow older and become something other than what they once were. The slow growth of women's and minority studies programs is due to the slow hiring of those who can teach in them, not to the lack of demand. The status of any department, any program, any curriculum in almost any postsecondary institution can be understood best and most quickly with reference to the history of the faculty in that program or that university. The curriculum is contingent on society and on the faculty. The "society" influence, in a sense, takes care of itself. The influence of the faculty on curriculum is, as Robin Lakoff suggests, not considered and actively avoided.

Gerald Graff's "teach the conflicts" proposal[21] has gained some credibility as a response to the rapid growth of political advocacies in the humanities. Because it is a curriculum proposal coming from *outside* specific universities it looks new. Here is one of his formulations:

> In addition to reviewing the periods, genres, and approaches it covers, a[n English] department might ask itself what potential conflicts and correlations it harbors and then consider what curricular adjustment might exploit them. (251)

For example, when Sandra Gilbert's and Susan Gubar's anthology of women's literature was criticized for being too political, Graff proposed that the question of its political weight become a part of a course on women's literature. Instead of arguing the conflicts, he offers, participants in the argument should create a forum in which the different takes on the conflict are aired as part of the classroom scene:

> The pedagogical heart of this proposal is this:
>   Do the purposes of liberal education require that the teacher *resolve* this controversy before proceeding with his or her task? One can imagine a teaching situation in which one would not have to decide which side of the feminist controversy one thought was in the right, for one could bring the controversy itself into the classroom and make it part of one's subject matter. I can even imagine a situation in which the teacher is unsure which side of the controversy to side with and arranges the course dialectically in order to form an opinion. . . .
>   The feeling that we have to decide between the humanist and the feminist positions in order to teach literature stems again from the assumption that students should be exposed only to the *results* of the controversies of their teachers and educators and should be protected from the controversies themselves. It also assumes that since it is out of the question that different courses might be correlated, the issue will need to be resolved in the same way for every course. (260–261)

Graff's proposal[22] has some affinity with Pauly's sense of the classroom in that to teach the conflicts means not to expect stable results from one's teaching, since all members of the classroom have different views and one cannot predict who will decide what is "right." Graff also questions the assumed need for faculty

---

[21] Gerald Graff, *Professing Literature* (Chicago: University of Chicago Press, 1987), 251.

[22] Elaborated since that time in Gerald Graff, *Beyond the Culture Wars: How Teaching the Conflicts Can Revitalize American Education* (New York: Norton, 1992).

members to offer stable, resolved knowledge, presumably in declarative form, "this is the case."[23] To propose teaching the conflicts themselves is to suggest that classroom curricula should reflect the knowledge-making process, the transiency and contingency of knowledge. In the teaching of science, however, over the last fifty years, there has been no such change: the results are still taught, as can be seen in the contents of textbooks in, for example, classical mechanics.[24] Whatever else is taught about this subject, its "laws" continue to be presented as fixed truth, altered only by relativity—the wider more general law of physics. Graff's proposal is applicable to any form of academic subject matter destined for the classroom: resolutions and results are not what classrooms need. Rather, the means of exposing *issues* are needed so that students may entertain different possible results and thus learn to participate in the uncertain paths to understanding in all subject matters.

Graff's proposal is about how to develop a curriculum contingent on the issues alone. Pauly's considerations suggest that the curriculum is as contingent on the classroom population as on the issues. For issues to live, they need an interested population to articulate them. This point applies to the example that Graff gave about teaching women's literature: it matters which constituency takes this or that on the political weight of the literature. Graff's discussion needs to be oriented around living constituents even if the classroom is not considered as an ultimate site where the conflicts are taught. Teaching the conflicts is not any less a political choice than teaching the facts or teaching the values. Conflicts may be taught alongside facts and values, but the grasp of whose needs are entertained both in the critical community and in each classroom met by a teacher still must be achieved if, as Graff hopes, teaching in the academy is to be revitalized.

Graff's second point takes more account of students' needs. To combine courses provides class members with multiple perspec-

---

[23] Something also noticed by John Dewey in *The Quest for Certainty* (1929). From the standpoint of individual psychology, the collective demand for scientific certainty is related to the need of teachers, like doctors, to appear authoritative in order to maintain their protected status in society. Graff's work has achieved authority by aiming to state "both sides" of conflicts. However, this too is a simplification of situations that have more than two sides.

[24] Sharon Begley, "The Science Wars," *Newsweek*, April 21, 1997, 54–56. Notice is taken in this report that, increasingly, challenges to traditional scientific stability are being admitted, but mainly with the consideration of new views rather than through an underlying sense of the contingency of scientific knowledge.

tives. This experiment, going by the name of "linked courses," has been tried repeatedly in the pursuit of interdisciplinary goals. If an appropriate effort is made by the teachers, such courses are appealing to students and teachers alike. But the key again is "appropriate effort." Linked courses require a common student population as well as considerable preparation on the part of the faculty regarding just how the courses are to go together. The two linked courses in which I participated were similar in subject matter. One was biology, psychology, and language, and the other was physics and language. These sequences, both lasting a year instead of only a semester, provided a good variety of perspectives on the issues from the readings and from the faculty members. These courses can be an important factor in revitalizing the teaching of writing.[25]

However, linked courses cannot become a solution to the problem of having an open-ended classroom forum until there are changes in the status of postsecondary teaching. If the postsecondary employment system were different, linked courses might well flourish. First, most faculty members do not want to teach such courses because to prepare them is to take time away from research, publication, and other activities that will get tenure, promotion, and salary increases sooner than creative teaching will. Second, those who do want to teach them discover that it takes a few years of teaching a linked course to learn how it works to benefit students and faculty. This means a few years of extra teaching time, and not just a summer. Third, the structure of requirements in the universities generally discourages many students at all levels from taking linked courses. The distribution requirements are more important to more students than taking an experimental course just because the ideas seemed interesting. Fourth, insofar as Graff is suggesting that graduate courses be linked, this too is unlikely because of the social psychology of graduate education. The idea is to prepare for the comprehensive examinations and not indulge in new experiences. Furthermore, graduate students feel in competition with other graduate students, both for the approval of the faculty and for the jobs that are presumably in store for them later on. Individualistic behavior in graduate programs as they now work seems to be the most prudent path.

Linked courses, like teaching the conflicts, will improve academic teaching if the practical structure of university education

---

[25] An example of students' achievement under these circumstances is discussed in the last section of this chapter.

changes. If, as Pauly recommends, classroom needs become higher priorities, then the administration of universities and colleges will begin to play the roles Pauly recommended[26] for principals and superintendents in the primary and secondary schools: facilitators for those wishing to take initiatives in the classroom. This can be done, but teaching in its many forms must become a primary means of achieving tenure.

Electronic Facilitation of the Contingent Curriculum

Perhaps unexpectedly to some of us, another credible path toward classroom and interpersonally centered reorientation of teaching and curriculum is increasingly reported by those using interactive, computerized classrooms, supplemented by e-mail. The classrooms themselves are acquiring a new status, a new position in the thinking lives of students. At the same time, teachers who are aware of the secondary character[27] of the technology are most likely to use it responsibly to let it contribute to changing the social relations of classrooms. In a recent essay,[28] Sheila Ruzycki O'Brien of the University of Idaho observes the following:

> Although conferencing via e-mail can be a tool to effect a more student-centered environment in the classroom, the technology itself does not create this result. I have found that e-mail facilitates my own pedagogical approach . . . which . . . balances student concerns, my own suggestions, and course materials. (79)

The foregoing principle distinguishes O'Brien's report from others that tell "how I use the computer." It is further significant in that she is describing a literature class rather than a composition class (in the "composition" journal), suggesting the versatility of teaching style she is advocating. E-mail ("asynchronous communication") permits the following to take place:

---

[26] Edward Pauly, 126ff. *The Classroom Crucible, Pluralistic policies* is his term for the latitude that should be the official policy of schools and school systems.

[27] Secondary in the sense of being a tool that serves the social processes of classrooms rather than a substitute for these processes.

[28] Sheila Ruzycki O'Brien, "The Medium Facilitates the Messages: Electronic Discourse and Literature Class Dynamics," *Computers and Composition* 11 (1994): 79–86.

- Enlarged working (professional) identities. Unlike some situations where a fictional name is permitted,[29] O'Brien requires the real names, and permits anonymous contributions in cases where the writer presents material that could be embarrassing.
- The contribution of response and opinion on-line, before the class meets in person. For each meeting, each class member knows at least something about how others understood the literature. There is knowledge of different perspectives as well as their sources. Students' perspectives become part of the course's subject matter.

Aiming to achieve routine, disciplined, and cooperative opinion sharing among class members, the teacher used the technology to *habituate all class members to this principle:* Each class member is responsible to contribute his or her own, and to learn everyone else's, perspective. As a result, the teacher's role changes as all class members' interactions become the basis for public, plenary discussion, which contrasts with the traditional discussion class in which the teacher on the one hand and the student group on the other are juxtaposed categories. Networking permits students the same out-of-class autonomy enjoyed by teachers; while this arrangement does not enforce discipline, there is much less need for enforcement (even though it remains the teacher's responsibility) and many more instances of improved motivation to participate. O'Brien emphasizes what a difference it makes that "I'm not alone in knowing students' interests and what disagreements have occurred" (83). While dissemination of students' work in classrooms has gone on in the past, especially in art and creative writing courses, the combination of the principle of dissemination with the ability to do it quickly, easily, and frequently moves toward an epistemologically collectivized classroom without indulging in the fantasy that the teacher is just another student.

O'Brien's technique is also a way of letting the curriculum be responsive to the contingencies of class members' developing opinions and abilities.[30] Dan Quigley, using classroom networks and e-mail, suggested the "online evolving syllabus," and reported how

---

[29] For example, as in Lester Faigley, *Fragments of Rationality: Postmodernity and the Subject of Composition* (Pittsburgh: University of Pittsburgh Press, 1992); Chapter 6, "The Achieved Utopia of the Networked Classroom," 163–199, and a sample transcript of students communicating under fictional and humorous (frivolous?) names, 170–178.

[30] Any teaching philosophy that finds new ways to discover how students may take initiatives in their own courses might be described as using a contingent curriculum.

customized assignments, along with new collective readings, geared to questions and issues appearing on-line, can be improvised as responses to significant class member disclosures.[31] The bases for students to contribute to the syllabus, curriculum, reading list, or other course plans should be in response to articulated interests, just as the course plan reflects the instructor's professional interests and judgment. If the principle of availability to change is assumed in course planning, then a changing curriculum can take place through individual initiative and collective agreement:

> It is the potential of the online syllabus to remain malleable and responsive to individual classes and even individual students that demonstrates most clearly the concept of an evolving syllabus. Although initially an online syllabus may lay out a best-guess image of the course, in practice it must evolve with the course, taking shape as does each class. The syllabus, which cannot be complete until the class is complete, thus provides an accurate record of what each class becomes and the work it accomplishes, whereas still fulfilling the requirements of the school's administration. Such a syllabus also provides a more accurate picture for the teacher's self-evaluation. (170)

We could add that it provides a better picture for anyone's evaluation of the course, of the teacher, and of its substance, without risking the teacher's job and reputation. Furthermore, with this step the opportunity for initiative and the reduction of testing and grading are accomplished at once. There is enough information in the on-line course records to overcome the reductionism characteristic of the existing techniques of learning of students' responses to a course.

The reports by O'Brien and by Quigley are familiar to many of us. In teaching relationships and classrooms governed by the principles they describe, there is no need to grade or to rank the students' performances in order best to serve the students. In these classrooms two features are salient: the long process of students' development in a course is on the record; and the practices of mutual disclosure create a portfolio of work for each class member—both success and failure are related to self-understanding and collective opinion rather than to a ranking of the total membership. This is a teaching approach that welcomes, cultivates, and integrates each class member's contribution; it does not penalize anyone in order to honor

---

[31] Dan Quigley, "The Evolution of an Online Syllabus," *Computers and Composition* 11 (1994): 173–179.

some and reject a few. Electronically supported classrooms can contribute experience and advice that might greatly increase students' motivation and involvement.[32]

A Classroom Instance of Curriculum Change

The idea of a contingent curriculum can also be shown through ethnographic accounts of classroom experiences. In the description that follows, I was not the actual teacher, but I was supervising the two teachers of this course to observe how the curriculum was adapted to a contingency created by the growing relationships among the students, along with the influence of the two teachers. The course had been meeting for a year, and I had been the teacher of this same section the previous semester. This course, Science, Language, and Gender, was the writing component of the linked courses (the Venture). The course with which this one had been coordinated was in women's studies and concentrated on the history of women in science.

It was about one third of the way through the second (spring) semester. The eight students had been together in this class and in the Venture since the fall. They had become familiar with one another considerably beyond what one may anticipate in a first-year university class. All their essays had been shared with one another to that point. There had been Venture social events. There was closeness and distance among them. There was a more "in" subgroup and a more peripheral subgroup. However, in spite of all of these nonsuperficial variations, the group had remained together, and, in fact, new relationships among the students had begun to take shape. I want to discuss one of these. While no individuals should be understood as typical, in some sense I think that the work of these two students shows that university students are coming to school more involved in the burdens of collective society than I or most others of my generation were when we entered school.

S and T wrote a twenty-two page paper together, entitled "Our Real World." They presented it (as usual, to the class) in response to the assignment, which they thought was vague. They had first responded more literally to the assignment, but when they met to help each other revise their essays, "We realized that we didn't want to hand out the bullshit that we had written when we could,

---

[32] These issues are considered in the next two chapters: they are fundamental to any proposals for changing the teaching of writing, language use, and other subjects.

instead, learn from both of our experiences and share them with others, just by talking about what was real to us." S and T found a space within the course to contribute to the class certain private concerns distracting them while previous work was done. They related these concerns to the assignment.

Early in the second semester, one of the teachers, Ms. M, had distributed to the class long excerpts from her journal. Some of the passages dated from when she had been in college, fifteen years before this class met. These passages were quite intimate, and I was surprised that she shared them with the class. However, they finally had their effect: S and T took up the "challenge." In their final paragraph, they explained:

> We're using the journal idea from Ms. M; she so bravely showed us her side of the truth in her first essay. The questions "Can the truth ever be . . . bound up in strong feeling and still be true?" is answered in a form with her personal account of her struggles with finding herself, her writing and her own definition of the "truth." I had been springing from my own version of truth and language for a while now, but it has taken someone else to make both of us realize where our personal integrities lie: "The truth there is that someone you love will die while you hold them. The truth is you never let go. The truth took hold long before language or reason" (Ms. M).
>   And that is what's real to us.

The two first-year students carried around with them experiences that corresponded to the feeling of the citation from Ms. M's journal. Prematurely, they each had encountered personal challenges that were never announced by college students when I was in college. If perhaps they had wanted to announce them, this was not welcomed by the curriculum, the instructors, or the institutional psychology.

My college was the Massachusetts Institute of Technology, a university dedicated to science and engineering. My having gone to this school made it possible for me to help teach this Venture course, which studied the languages of science. The subject matters in this course, language, truth, and "what is real," are issues in the contemporary critique of science. Each of the students in the Venture was involved in science and math courses as well, and each was motivated to look into the underpinnings or presuppositions or premises of science, all of which we discussed. The beginning of the essay by S and T says (without directly identifying to whom *me* refers),

> Recently, we have been reading some things dealing with the issues of IQ, intelligence, and equality. New concepts have been talked about and words thrown out that have forced me to think hard, learning about some of the things that are most important to

me in my life right now. . . . Our [my and T's] casual talk turned
serious as the hours slipped by, and we realized that we didn't
want to hand out the bullshit.

T, also not explicitly identified, then writes,

> This paper is a breakthrough for me. Last semester in Ventures I had
> a goal in my writing. What I wanted to do was analyze the hell out
> of everything. Not this semester—not now. I've been talking to S all
> night and we've learned so much about each other. . . . This semes-
> ter I want to show you, my classmates, and everyone, more about
> myself. I want to write about what is important to me. . . . It seems
> as though it was a different side of me writing all those pages last
> semester, and I would let myself peek out every now and then. I do
> not regret it because I developed an aspect of my writing that I can
> continue using, but I don't want to be that way with you guys any
> more. Last semester . . . I was trying to show that I was up to "Aca-
> demia," that I could confront the challenges of "intellectuals." . . .
> Okay, that's fine and wonderful, but let's be *real* when we do it. I've
> known you guys for a whole semester and lived with you, com-
> pletely engulfed in the same environment. It's such an incredible
> advantage to be able to speak openly with the class so often.

The analytical style and formal vocabularies of science, while interesting the first semester, seemed to weigh more heavily on these two
students as time went on. It is impossible to say what caused what.
But in the second semester, one of the topics that caused a stir was
the IQ controversy aroused by the publication of *The Bell Curve*.[33]
This discussion created a blur regarding what things were "real." By
repeatedly reading the word *intelligence,* the students became more
than usually self-conscious about what "intellectuals" do. The writing assignment that followed from this topic had to do with jargon
and truth: Does the specialized and conventionalized vocabulary of
science tell the truth? What could the difference be between the
measure of intelligence and intelligence itself, as understood in ordinary conversation? If you are in the "academy" do you become an
"intellectual"? So, starting out contemplating these questions, which
are interesting to most people and to the students in this class, the
abrupt change of "handed in/out writing," represented by S and T's
long collaborative essay, entered the picture of the class. When others in the class read this essay, *they all revised their original essays
and wrote one more like "Our Real World."* Reading this essay said
to other class members something like, We will now, temporarily at
least, follow the leadership of our peers and not our teachers.

---

[33] Richard Herrnstein and Charles Murray, *The Bell Curve* (New York: Free Press, 1994).

It was not a sudden frustration with the formal agenda of the class, but the subject matters of the long essay that urged the students to break away from the predominantly academic thinking style of the class. These excellent students did all the essays, came to class, went the extra mile throughout the previous and the present semester. "Our Real World" and the class' responses to it were not moments of petulance or defiance. Just the opposite: suddenly, two students who already had a great deal on their minds decided to say, We have a great deal on our minds and those things are so real that, if real is what we are going to think about together, let us say what is *really* real.

For T, the topic of jargon led to the topic of "labels," which in turn brought up the story of her sister's coming out as bisexual. From here came the descriptions of T's two friends, one with bulimia, one with cancer who died a few days after this paper was distributed in class. "Right now I am thinking of the deaths of young people." An additional item in "labels" for T and her sister was that they were Latino, a culture, T reports, that has a strong response to the presence of nonheterosexual members. Here is a "real" place reached by T:

> What upsets me most of all is the tentative language used in hospitals or around sick people. People are afraid when they enter hospitals. Why? Could it be because of the connotations? When I visit my friend, I don't want to talk to the cancer, I want to talk to her. I don't want to speak to my friend like she's the bulimia, it's her! I've known her forever, and this is a part of her that she has to learn to control. That's where I feel reality gets lost in these words. I don't want anyone treating them like a disease. Suddenly the person disappears and they become the "cancer victim" or the "bulimic," but people forget who they used to know. The words scare them off because they haven't been exposed to these aspects of people. Yes, they are scary, but we can't forget about the person. The person is the most important thing—he/she is what's real. He/she is why we're here. Because we're all real and they need us to be real.

The assignment sheet for this departure was a four-hundred-word reflection, including a definition by Raymond Williams, on the definition of jargon and established vocabulary. Here, first, is a sentence of the assignment at its most off-putting:

> What kinds of changes would be required in scientific vocabulary—or even our daily vocabulary—in a culture that was nonhierarchical (egalitarian), noncompetitive (cooperative, compassionate), not patriarchal (either gender-neutral or matriarchal)?

This is what S and T, and the rest of the class afterward, decided *not* to think about. But the assignment sheet also had the following on it, toward the end:

What is the effect for you of being confronted by jargon? . . . Can
truth ever be subjective? Or be bound up in strong feeling and still
be true?

I do not know which of the teachers wrote this assignment sheet: the
names of both are on it. The assignment sheet inadvertently participated in and then encouraged the students' initiatives. The students
discerned the different values present in the long statement—perhaps they immediately perceived it as a mixed genre and picked
certain subgenres for their own use. However one reads the hand-
out, they did the assignment. It looks like a departure because *they
changed the genre:* in their essay, they included poems and letters,
and almost completely personalized the academic issues related to
their reflections. Each change in genre changes the mood of the
speaker, signals memory and feeling, and presents new voices.

Part of the poignancy of T's writing is the attempt to defeat the
illnesses by defeating their power to reidentify a healthy person as
someone else. While the illness may still be there, T wants to take
away its naming power and reinstate the individual's "original"
identity. The relation of T to her friends is "real" and existed "forever." With this set of events and her responses to it, T "reads" the
idea of jargon into a genre of reflective historical anecdotal narrative:
"cancer victim" and "bulimic" are jargon.[34] The words convert the
two friends, the two principals in human relationships, into members of a class of afflicted people, "victims" perhaps, all of whom
require treatment. From one standpoint, we do not permit this con-
version of our loved ones; we stand by them in the hospital, with the
situation seeming rational enough. However, T contributes these
thoughts not to the hospital but to the classroom. Her key move is
not in having the thoughts themselves, but in transposing them from
their private venues into this new forum, where they meet, for the
first time, the preinstalled issues of the Venture, the curriculum, the
official genres of "material" and "assignment sheet," and the expectation that a certain kind of essay, written in a relatively stable or
uniform genre and duly distributed to other class members, is usual.
However, the class took up the challenge and overturned these
expectations. The whole class changed the curriculum.[35]

---

[34] This reading of *jargon* is comparable to Mr. B's use of *euphemism* in Chapter 4. In
order to make their points, speakers and writers change incrementally the
conventional meanings of words as well as of genres.

[35] As I have mentioned, all the other students rewrote their original responses to the
assignment, along the lines given by this essay.

In this essay S's voice is also prominent, reaching differently in its use of language: S, but not T, included her poems. However, like Ms. M, the teacher, S reached back into her own diary/journal to remember a passage already written, suggesting her identification with T's sick friends:

> [March 1994] I have sores all over my head, bandaids on my face, pain in my lower back and a dull ache in my stomach, bruises all over my legs and my gut hanging out in pain. There is a big ball of phlegm in my throat and tears in my eyes. I am okay. I am at my worst today, my worst because I have little hope and light for the future—I am so depressed and down. But I am okay because I have you looking out for me, right, and the sun and all of my precious memories. That is all that keeps me goin'. I need people to help me, Lord, I don't ever want to ask, but I need it.

> [February 1995] I'm just covering up the real S even more and I want to see my piano again and go to that summer keyboard and really stretch my imagination and play whatever I want and almost cry where are all my four-leaf clovers? . . . I feel bad writing on Ventures class time. . . . I'm so afraid and wishful and sloppy and I have no control of what goes into my body—just as I have no control over my mind. . . . I need to chill for *real* and not do another stressed weekend, putting more harmful things in me. . . . Music makes me feel full and alive and I'm so sorry that I hurt every guy I touch because it makes everything tough—stand up goddamnit! Where is T? . . . I'd love to be anorexic and a bag of bones but think nothing of it.

Among other things, S has Crohn's disease, a stomach disorder aggravated by anxiety. S is articulate, and orally the same sort of talk emerges, often with a dramatic sense of humor. S is an athlete and a musician as well as a student. However, the foregoing excerpts record the points of connection, during this course for the first time, with T, and perhaps with other students. S is the person that T wants to remain "real." T will help her to stand up.

Even though S is good-humored and conscientious in writing and supporting the class, she reported in conversations in my office that she was often in pain from her stomach disorder. The social aspect of this class was a significant contribution to her life: it created for her a cohort of sympathetic students who were both fun-loving and serious about their work. The 1994 passage is more alarming than the later one, perhaps because it seems somewhat more orderly and more lonely. S was an adopted child, and on top of everything else, she was in the midst of searching for her birth parents. She was looking for a rational connection to the society from which she felt excluded, perhaps from the beginning of her life. T, meanwhile, now needs to de-school her public identity, so to speak, to declare to others, to colleagues what a "real" person she is. During their conversation, S became one of T's "real" people. T says,

> We've been sitting for hours reading out of her journal and discovering things that keep popping up in her life. Things that are important to her—things that are real to her.

To S, T became a newly valued point of connection with the Venture, with school, with someone else, perhaps, who has and understands pain. For T as well as for S, it is the pain of social exclusion on top of physical pain and illness. T is a member of a minority that has lower status in American society. Her and her sister's attempts to accede to some ideal of intellectuality are partly related to the drive to raise that status. However, pursuant to her success in this cause during the first semester in this course, T becomes motivated by the search for real, socially grounded solidarity in the Venture, to announce the premises of her seriousness as a student—through the important people—her sister and her two sick friends, each of whom is identified also as a member of a stigmatized group. This set of disclosures enlarges her role in the class from an individual to a "real" person whose collective affiliations may now become part of the full identity of T. S's disclosures pose for the first time within the curriculum of the course the issue of her own identity as being put in doubt by the conundrum of adoption and the confusion it has brought out.

From the standpoint of traditional postsecondary pedagogy, such announcements by students have happened before and have contributed salutary moments to other classrooms. It is also true that this is in part a writing class, where such things are known to happen. Also, because of the age of the students, eighteen, one cannot predict now what effect these events, including the class' spontaneous collective revision of the curriculum through their new essays, will have. On the other hand, the essay by S and T depicts a desire to "come out" (not in the sexual orientation sense) as much as to disclose experiences that, from their perspective, must be included in the curriculum. They were changing the curriculum in such ways that the instructors became uncertain as to how to treat the development. We have seen, however, that the instructors did not need to "know in advance" how to treat it, since the other students took guidance from it to contribute in similar ways, thus changing the curriculum in response to a contingency.

The classroom experiences unsettled most members of this class. The work kept coming and the afterclass conversations became less casual. The subject matters of this course became living issues, issues that could not be pigeonholed back into the books from which the students learned about them. The knowledge they got could not be tested. Only a conversation with any student in this class might inform an observer what had been accomplished, and that conversation could only take place in the contexts of conversations with other students and the observer's careful reading of the students' yearlong portfolios.

No one student's accomplishment can be understood independently of what happened in the course, of the other students, of the teachers. Although the teachers often felt separated from one another, they did not think of their effort apart from the course, they reported to me. The classroom experience had gotten inside them, inside all of us (even though I was an outside advisor the second semester). The most respectful assessment of this work involves learning the documents, stories, and readings contributed by each student, which made up this course. Also, one can describe but cannot measure what the students are now "prepared" for, what other courses, what other challenges. Some of them are pursuing independent studies. Many are looking for new combinations of subjects and are beginning to get ideas along unorthodox lines.

Because of the course's having been linked, because of the multiple faculty perspectives on the material the students had for the year, because of the suspension of traditional grading practices, and because of the ability of the nine students to learn to respect one another's individual traits and styles, the relationships among them have continued, including chain letters and periodic reunions. Professional and personal interests have become part of the same connection, providing a social basis for their work in school most students do not achieve.

The majority of writing teachers do not have the luxury of working with nine students for one year. Most classes that pay attention to writing and language use are limited by time and by rules handed down by administrators. Yet, I claim and am trying to show in this book, that the kinds of experience represented by S and T, as well as by the other students cited earlier, are potentially available to all students in writing classes, even the larger ones. Each of the principles, perspectives, and procedures that have already been discussed can take place to one degree or another in classrooms of any size. Institutionally, there is one main obstacle to creating this availability: the system and traditions of testing, grading, evaluation by ranking and other quantitative measures. The next two chapters consider this obstacle and what can be done about it.

Chapter Seven

Military, Corporate, and Bureaucratic Interests in Testing and Grading

Evaluation and the Pedagogical Scene of Writing

Richard Ohmann[1] describes the entering student's sense of college:

> She is . . . to assume responsibility for her education and to trust the college's plan for it; to build her competence and to follow a myriad of rules and instructions; to see herself as an autonomous individual and to be incessantly judged.
>
> The writing class heightens these tensions. Writing. The word whispers of creativity and freedom; yet there is usage, there are assignments and deadlines, there is the model of The Theme, there are grades. (252)

The structure of postsecondary education revokes the promises made by its ideals to students. The writing class, one of the immediate sources of promise, begins the process of disabusing students of their ideals. The writing course delivers the effects of bureaucracy, incessant judgment, and grades. Because, as Ohmann observes, these antagonists take over, students are erroneously taught that it is either/or. Creativity or judgment; errors to learn or downgrading for poor performance; generous attention from faculty and administrators or surveillance for slackers. They should be taught that the

---

[1] Richard Ohmann, *Politics of Letters* (Middletown, CT: Wesleyan University Press, 1987).

processes of being judged and judging others, of making errors during work, and of taking time off from focused attention are part of the work habits of accomplished people. Genre, disclosure, and membership try to create an identity for the subject of writing and language use that keeps its promises and teaches discipline.[2] College students should be able to expect an atmosphere of creativity, generosity, and understanding while investigating, focusing, taking positions, and sitting still for a long time exchanging thoughts with each other, with teachers, with the public.

Testing and grading comprise one of the oldest institutions of education, and it is also one of the most troublesome and complained about. This institution is where the bureaucratic values of school administration and political desires to control society meet classroom practice. Through testing and grading—judgment of students' work by both external standardized tests and by in-class tests and grades—schools establish that students have done the work needed for certification. But also, as many have observed, claimed, written about, and objected to, testing and grading add up to unacceptable limits to learning, especially to collective, cooperative, and collaborative learning. Testing and grading depend on the continued public acceptance of individualism as the standard set of values to be taught in and through school.

The ideas and practices of genre, disclosure, and membership will likely not grow, much less flourish, if testing and grading continue to govern the teaching and learning of writing and language use. Collective styles of classroom practice are needed to permit these ideas space. Individual work will always be part of schoolwork, but it requires the space provided by cooperative pedagogies; it requires the exchange of perspectives with groups and clusters of inquirers. This chapter considers the issues of how testing and grading have come to exist in society and in school; how they enact military, corporate, and bureaucratic values; and what practical problems they cause. It also suggests that the subject of writing and language use needs to be taught without tests and grades in order for it to serve its constituencies.

The Mass Test: Its History and Purposes

To many, evaluation through testing and grading seems to be ingrained in the "DNA" of society: there are an indefinite number of

---

[2] More detail on the teaching of discipline in writing and language use is given in Chapter 8, in connection with the discipline of working with others.

contexts and situations for testing, grading, and ranking.[3] The earliest form of didactic evaluation is the mass test. F. Allan Hanson[4] traces mass testing back about three thousand years to the Chou dynasty in imperial China, where it was a means for "identifying the talented among the common people" (186). If his reading is correct, the purpose of testing is unchanged between yesterday's and today's "imperial" societies, especially because the structures of political rulership, even in "democratic" societies, are not that different today.[5] Hanson's discussion of subsequent dynasties shows a similar situation:

> The class holding power, wealth, and prestige was composed mainly of administrators and bureaucrats in the emperor's civil service. Membership in this class depended more on passing the civil service examination than on parentage. . . . For nearly a thousand years, beneath the overall control of an emperor, China was governed by a meritocratic elite. (187)

Whether or not the ruling class was "truly" meritocratic, it held power, wealth, and prestige. One purpose of the test was to control the distribution of power and wealth. The Chinese tests functioned in ways consistent with what Hanson wants to show about today's tests, namely, that "they are mechanisms for defining or producing the concept of the person in contemporary society and that they maintain the

---

[3] I dispute the attitude toward grading proposed by Lad Tobin in *Writing Relationships: What Really Happens in the Composition Class* (Portsmouth, NH: Boynton/Cook 1991), 69: "Making the messiness of grading public is almost always healthy in a writing class. There is never a danger that grades will lose all meaning, because they are so deeply embedded in our culture and consciousness, but we can make them a little less threatening—to our students and ourselves—by exposing the process."

I doubt this approach. I read with disappointment Tobin's remarks about how the deep-rootedness of grading practices inhibits his thinking toward change. Others have already given principled positions about grading that advocate its removal. My discussion of narrative evaluation in Chapter 8 cites sources showing that many benefit and none lose with the elimination of testing and grading. Tobin does not discuss that the "deep-rootedness" derives from social values that are harmful to people who are not exempt from the social screening performed by grades: this is just about everyone but a very few.

[4] F. Allan Hanson, *Testing, Testing: Social Consequences of the Examined Life* (Berkeley: University of California Press, 1993).

[5] In *The Politics of Women's Biology,* (Rutgers, NJ: Rutgers University Press, 1990), Ruth Hubbard observes something similar about the ideology of science: "Science or, rather, scientists—that relatively small group of economically and socially privileged white men with the authority derived from being scientists—have had an important share in defining what we [women] . . . can do and be. . . . It is a fact of practical politics that the ruling group or class not only generates the reigning ideology but also controls the means that make this ideology the dominant or even exclusive 'truth.' This is so irrespective of political form—in democracies, where everyone can say what she or he thinks but is not able to publicize it equally, and in totalitarian states, where the discourse itself is limited" (17).

person under surveillance and domination" (3). Hanson's inquiry takes an inventory of the overwhelming level of civil surveillance and control in Western (industrialized) societies. His discussion covers vocational, drug, authenticity, chastity, loyalty, and other kinds of tests. A large part of his attention is on schools and on the habituation of young people to the permanent status of testing in their lives:

> Tests are found everywhere in the process of education. They punctuate progress through the grades, with quizzes, hourly tests, midterms, and final examinations serving as the staple measure for certifying that courses have been successfully completed (or not) and at what level. Recent legislation requiring that all students be given education appropriate to their ability has ignited an explosion of testing to identify those students who require special education, of either a remedial or enriched variety. Then there are the standardized tests that measure students' psychological profiles, interests, and intelligence levels. These are given in enormous quantities: from 100 million to 200 million . . . in the American school system each year, an average of from two and a half to five standardized tests per pupil per year. These tests are used to evaluate the schools as well as the students. . . . [There is] gathering momentum for states to require further standardized tests to determine if students have attained the minimum competency necessary to be promoted at certain grade levels and to receive a high school diploma. The system of higher education pours out its own alphabet soup of further standardized tests: PSAT, SAT, and ACT for college admissions and scholarship competitions; GRE, LSAT, MCAT, GMAT, and numerous others for admissions to graduate or professional schools. (10)

Testing and grading are normalized to such a degree that only a small minority of students, teachers, and administrators can conceive of any alternative to this system. The practices are the legal tender of school, and removing them seems to many as drastic as converting a money economy to a barter economy: everything would change. The fact that alternatives are not understood as viable is a way of saying that testing and grading are ideological ways of maintaining the social hierarchy.[6]

---

[6] Bill Roorbach, "Mommy, What's a Classroom?" *New York Times Magazine,* February 2, 1997, 30–37. Roorbach describes how John Holt's solution to the problem of "credentialism" and "testing and ranking and sorting" has become home schooling. This sounds like a case of throwing out the baby with the bath water. One undoubted contribution of school is its blending of thinking and socialization. If, as Holt writes, "students don't need to be told" how to learn, the solution is not to place them with their parents but to learn how to use the socialization process toward more creative ways of thinking. Why not get rid of "testing, ranking, and sorting" if they are the problem? Why not bring the care and nurturance of family into school? Why *substitute* the family for school, when one can *mix* the genres of school and family so that both can continue to serve in new ways?

Hanson's study supports the view that testing and grading practices indoctrinate the next generation about the forces that govern society. These forces are related to how general testing proliferated following the intelligence testing that began earlier in this century. Hanson observes,

> Test givers are nearly always organizations while test takers are individuals. Organizations are richer and stronger than individuals, so a power differential is established at the start. The asymmetrical relation of power is further evident from the total control that the test giving agency exercises over the situation. (304)

Modern mass testing took on its characteristic forms from its early uses in the military, which distinguished officers from enlisted men through the use of the first intelligence tests. According to Stephen Jay Gould,[7] the idea of possibly measuring intelligence began in the nineteenth century, under the influence of Darwinian considerations—the struggle for existence, survival of the fittest. But it did not get its real boost into mass usage until the army, with its need for leaders who would win the war, agreed to the mass testing of the Stanford-Binet intelligence test in 1917—the Army Alpha test. In spite of the doubtful results[8] the test produced, Hanson continues, intelligence testing became the standard practice:

> With the development of written, standardized intelligence tests that could be easily administered to unlimited numbers of subjects, the dream of Terman [the psychologist who established and named the Stanford-Binet test] and other American psychometricians was on its way to realization. Now it would be possible to determine everybody's intelligence and to use that information to channel people in directions where they presumably would both find personal satisfaction and make optimal contributions to society commensurate with their abilities.[9] (212)

---

[7] Stephen Jay Gould, *The Mismeasure of Man* (New York: Norton, 1981). This is the best and most interesting historical account of intelligence testing as well as the most compelling argument against it: there has never been any *empirical* reason, Gould shows, for the single-factor theory of intelligence, i. e., that IQ corresponds to something real. The evidence suggests to Gould and others that, more likely, intelligence comes in different modes and is not a single capability.

[8] One ridiculous result coming out of this test-of-the-test was that the "average mental age of white Americans turned out to be 13 (barely above the level of morons)" and the average mental age of blacks was about ten and a half.

[9] This issue came up in Chapter 5 in the account of the instructor who, remembering the objections of African American students to the psychology textbook, tried to "teach" the Herrnstein-Murray IQ book without reference to the history of IQ testing as a means of perpetuating sexism and racism.

As we can see in retrospect, the relation of the announced salutary expectation to the actual effects of such testing was that the "dream" was illusory, concealing the role of intelligence testing in establishing an elite and in perpetuating racism. The ridiculous results just cited were ignored because of the more desirable prospect of having a legitimate technique in the hands of testing organizations that could and did control the choices of large numbers of people. This technique survives in today's intelligence testing and has grown toward other forms of nonmedical mass testing we routinely accept. Neither Gould's discrediting of the single-factor concept of intelligence nor the work of others who have proposed multiple-factor concepts has had a significant effect on such testing thus far.

One reason for this lack of effect is that testing, and especially intelligence testing, is sustained more by taken-for-granted military and corporate values than by ordinary scientific evidence. Douglas D. Noble, writing about how educational practices have been routinely derived from the practices of military training, says that "the influence of military research has been arguably the most historically significant and the least acknowledged influence, both on computer-based education specifically and on the alignment of education with technology more generally."[10] Just as intelligence testing became widespread because it was a tool, an instrument that lent itself to administration on a large scale, so too other forms of technology first developed for the military (and well-funded by government) began to make their way into society through the schools. As a result, people educated in those schools cannot discern the limiting effects of military schemata on teaching and classroom values. The technology itself is not the problem. The problem is that the model of military training is accepted to apply to schools, which, however, need to be run in ways much different from how the military is run.

Standardized tests in ancient China came from the desire to maintain a governing elite; our own testing mores came from the need to discriminate among soldiers. Behavioral objectives and mastery learning came from the need to know how soldiers will behave in war. The leitmotif in military psychology, irrespective of technology, is command and control: social relations are organized in an uncompromised hierarchy. In view of how many people are involved in military planning and production, in the organization of people and their lives and families toward these ends, in support of

---

[10] Douglas D. Noble, *The Classroom Arsenal: Military Research, Information Technology, and Public Education* (Bristol, PA: Taylor and Francis, 1991), 3. Also, Douglas D. Noble, "Mental Materiel," unpublished essay, 1989.

the national budgeting committed to these enterprises, military influence on society is much greater than most of us can see.

Deriving from the values of command and control, and hierarchical social organization, is the need to isolate cognitive from affective thought processes. Cognitive science began in the 1950s, with "artificial intelligence." At that time, before miniaturization, the demands made by the development of complex weapons systems led researchers to conceive of people as "information-processing systems," as one component of a weapons operation that was conceptualized to run automatically. Miniaturization made it seem more and more possible to create a "man/machine system." At first, there was the attempt to simulate human thought processes on the computer. But gradually, as smaller computers became increasingly the object of attention, researchers began thinking of people as if they were like computers but whose principles of functioning were still not understood. Scientists sought to eliminate the distinctions between human and artificial intelligence. The term *cognitive* in *cognitive science* represents intelligence as a certain purity of thought, idealized in logic, that has long been an interest of Western science, a value found in Plato.[11] This concept of a "pure" logical intelligence teamed up with the American psychological ideal of "pure" behaviorism—the principle that human behavior is reducible to quantifiable stimulus and response patterns and capable of being manipulated through behavioral engineering—to produce the characteristic idealism of today's cognitive science.[12]

In *The Classroom Arsenal,* Noble reports that the field of cognitive science introduced terms like *problem solving* and *information processing* to describe people thinking (42–43). The latter term referred to how computers translate one form of information into another. *Problem solving* refers to the practical use of this translation, a use that is necessarily isolated from the larger context in which the

---

[11] In Chapter 2, I discuss the desire for ideal purity as it has appeared in conceptions of language, blocking an accurate perception of just how mixed every language has always been.

Still the best challenge to the fantasy of pure cognition is Hubert L. Dreyfus, *What Computers Can't Do: A Critique of Artificial Reason* (New York: Harper and Row, 1972). The updated version is *What Computers Still Can't Do: A Critique of Artificial Reason* (Cambridge, MA: MIT Press, 1992). Among the many noteworthy aspects of this study is that the critique of artificial intelligence is, with a small adaptation and in a footnote, applied to a critique of Chomskyan linguistics, which shares much of the ideology of science with devotees of artificial intelligence and cognitive science.

[12] In case you are wondering, I wish to imply that this value of purity comes from the same source that promoted the value of a "pure" language, as I discussed in Chapter 2. Chomsky's desire to separate competence from performance (language use) is also a subscription to the idea of a pure or essential core of what language "really is."

problem arises. The human problem solver was (originally) a pilot or a missile operator whose "problem" was the destruction of the enemy. This vocabulary, even in the military context alone, promotes a concept of automatic mechanical human behavior as an improvement over such outdated and inapplicable terms as *bravery* or *daring* to explain, describe, or characterize military success. Machine-gradable exams administered by impersonal organizations also presuppose a mechanical sense of human thought.

There is an unacknowledged axiom in the program of cognitive science that intellectual work must be separate from feelings and passions, must be autonomous relative to its human and social contexts. Studying cognition means discovering a pure essence of thought that is performance in an automated system whose larger purposes and functions are still humanly directed, but "efficiently," by those few who have military and scientific authority. Noble tries to show that schools and universities are also describable in these terms, which deemphasize the interpersonal, collective, collaborative elements in learning and do not teach the socially helpful reasons for scientific work.

Bureaucratic Values

The increasing influence of corporate psychology has continued the influence of the military since the waning of the Cold War. Especially, the university has become a much more mercantile institution. Market vocabulary, while different from military and cognitive vocabulary, similarly depends on a mechanization of the educational process and the related need for a mechanical style of testing that separates cognition from everything else:

> If students are reduced to customers and faculty to employees, it follows that education is a "product" and those who produce it are expected to exhibit "productivity." Productivity, of course, is most conveniently measured quantitatively. Hence, higher and higher student-teacher ratios, though they can become an embarrassment when the institution is rated by accreditation organizations and prospective students, can be presented to some constituencies (especially political ones) as evidence of institutional "efficiency." There are always studies which purport to show that students learn as much in a course enrolling 150 as 15, but in these cases, "learning" is typically defined in quantitative terms.[13]

---

[13] Richard Rollin, "There's No Business Like Education," *Academe* 75 (January-February 1989): 15. I think that the only real solution (mentioned again in More Forethoughts) to the slow pace of educational development is the doubling of teachers in schools for the purpose of halving class size. This means higher school taxes and a happier society.

Corporate values, concerned with "the bottom line," pressure universities to think of themselves not as schools but as players in a competitive market. This pressure leads to the demand for quantitative measurement of teaching as well as of "learning" through the use of machine-gradable exams for students and other measures of activity susceptible of "information processing." The fact is, as Richard Levinson observes,[14] that universities "are becoming complex bureaucracies governed from the top down by administrative elites" (23). Similarly, as Adrienne Rich writes,[15]

> The university is above all a hierarchy. At the top is a small cluster of highly paid and prestigious persons, chiefly men, whose careers entail the services of a very large base of ill-paid or unpaid persons, chiefly women. (136)

Bureaucracies don't respond well to changes in society, but they respond very well to orders given from above. It is hard for them to change if change is taking place among the majority. Social change is a potential threat to order, and the bureaucracy becomes one way to slow or stop change. Bureaucracies are especially useful to the privileged, whose way of life always needs to be conserved, while the rest of society always needs to improve its lot.

The conventional responses to testing and grading are similar to responses to bureaucracies: both cause trouble and complicate simple aspects of social functioning, but few believe they can be changed. Many managers who have these responses cannot try to demechanize their bureaucracies without endangering their jobs. They are pulled in opposite directions by practical and moral values. There is reason to understand civil and academic bureaucracies as behaving according to

---

[14] Richard Levinson, "The Faculty and Institutional Isomorphism," *Academe* 75 (January-February 1989), 23–27. These elites, as Sheila Kaplan and Adrian Tinsley show in their contribution, "The Unfinished Agenda: Women in Higher Education Administration," *Academe* 75 (January-February 1989), 18–22, are composed overwhelmingly of men. Only 10 percent of the nation's three thousand higher education institutions are led by women. Of the seven most powerful figures in any one academic pyramid, only one is female.

[15] Adrienne Rich, *On Lies, Secrets, and Silence: Selected Prose, 1966–1978* (New York: Norton, 1979). Rich calls our attention to the attachments of both class and religion to the academic work of men. "The hidden assumptions on which the university is built comprise more than simply a class system. In a curious and insidious way, the 'work' of a few men—especially in the more scholarly and prestigious institutions—becomes a sacred value in whose name emotional and economic exploitation of women is taken for granted. . . . The justification for all this service [by women of men] is the almost religious concept of 'his work.'" Rich is at pains to disclose the scope of academic androcentrism and perhaps to say how bizarre it must be to men as well as to women. The reduction and derogation of academic teaching falls into this larger picture: administrators' jobs are to maintain this feel in the university.

the same social psychology, as discussed by Kathy E. Ferguson.[16] She characterizes bureaucracies as dispensable or at least changeable: neither testing and grading nor bureaucracies, in isolation, can be blamed for injuring society. Rather, bureaucratic apparatuses have emerged historically from men's institutions in society. Testing and grading being principal bureaucratic functions in the academy, they may well be suspected to support, in their status as the predominant machinery of certification, androcentric self-perpetuation: devices for a few people (usually men) to sort, control, and order the total student body. The testing and grading system is in effect in the vast majority of schools.

Here is Ferguson's description of what a bureaucracy is:

> Following [Max] Weber, the modern bureaucracy is usually described as an organization having the following traits: a complex rational division of labor, with fixed duties and jurisdictions; stable, rule-governed authority channels and universally applied performance guidelines; a horizontal division of graded authority, or hierarchy, entailing supervision from above; a complex system of written record-keeping, based on scientific procedures that standardize communications and increase control; objective recruitment based on impersonal standards of expertise; predictable, standardized management procedures following general rule; and a tendency to require total loyalty from its members toward the way of life the organization requires. (7)

Ferguson claims that contemporary mass society is more saturated by bureaucratic functioning than ever before in history, even allowing for the thousands of years of its existence, a claim consistent with Hanson's regarding the contemporary proliferation of testing. The foregoing description suggests that postsecondary schools function according to bureaucratic rather than scholarly or pedagogical principles. Classrooms vary, however. Some teachers run their classes in bureaucratic style, but many do not: when the door is closed, the bureaucracy stops in many cases.

Except for this: even teachers who "close the door" must open it again for the grades to rejoin the bureaucracy.

Here is how Ferguson's description of bureaucracies applies to universities and postsecondary academic institutions.

- *Rational division of labor, with fixed duties and jurisdictions.* There are departments, courses, and curricula, administered by groups of experts who are careful not to step out of their discipline or subject matter. They teach their subjects autonomously, as they see fit.

---

[16] Kathy E. Ferguson, *The Feminist Case Against Bureaucracy* (Philadelphia: Temple University Press, 1984).

- *Rule-governed authority channels and universally applied performance guidelines.* Teachers are supervised by chairs; chairs by deans; deans by provosts, and so on. Teachers must teach and evaluate their students, reporting their performance to chairs and deans on grade sheets. Universal performance guidelines appear in the traditional grading system for students and, recently, in the students' "course opinion questionnaire" that is the same for every course and virtually the same from school to school.

- *Horizontal division of graded authority.* All departments look similar to one another; all schools have a similar hierarchy of faculty and deans; tenure is determined more or less the same way in most schools—deans following faculty committees' advice with veto power residing in provosts and presidents. Hierarchy and supervision from above was mentioned in the previous item.

- *Complex record keeping, with standardized communications and increased control.* Most teachers' grade books are black with small marks showing absences, grades for in-class work, grades for out-of-class work, for class participation, lateness, or any other factor declared to be germane to a final evaluation. Most classroom policies are given by the percentage contribution of any one activity to the final grade, e.g., "the final exam counts 30 percent of your final grade." This is the most common gesture toward "scientific procedures" in most classrooms. For the evaluation of faculty, a similar situation exists, except most of a faculty member's records are confidential or secret.[17]

- *Objective recruitment and impersonal standards.* I have served on several hiring committees. The illusion of objective recruitment is created in part by practices such as weighted votes by, say, five committee members, so that the candidate with the highest score gets the offer. This candidate can be the second choice of every committee member, but he/she will still get the first offer. Few challenge this result. It is considered to be fair that the system is "impersonal." The hard work of molding a

---

[17] We all know how regularly formal procedures are discarded, as teachers grade on how the actual classroom relationships progressed during the semester. The "scientific" policy announcements are meant as hedges against possible lawsuits from disgruntled students and their families who spent many thousands of dollars on college. Faculty reports of their own work and progress are also not used, as recently announced at a faculty meeting by a department chair I know. There is little connection between the announced formula for faculty evaluation and the actual formula, which is usually kept secret.

consensus based on principle, on departmental needs, on interpersonal considerations is eschewed in favor of the imaginary
scientific justice achieved through the weighted vote.[18]

- *Predictable, standardized management procedures.* This means
  that bureaucratically recognized classes of people are assumed
  to be composed of like individuals—teachers, students, seniors,
  untenured assistants, and so on. Even though each person
  departs in important ways from anyone's conception of the standard or norm, this fact is ignored as "personnel cases" emerge.
  A certain number of absences results in failure. An insufficient
  number of publications results in tenure denial. And so on. In
  schools teachers and administrators fear erring on the side of
  generosity toward students and untenured faculty members
  because bureaucratic ideology is the accepted perspective.

The bureaucratic style runs schools because it is a feature of the
society in which, lately, the corporate frame of mind is increasing its
influence. Bureaucratic functioning is growing into bureaucratic domination, as suggested in the recent economic study by David Gordon
opposing the current corporate practice of "downsizing."[19] This book
suggests how and why bureaucrats are instruments of the authoritarian policies of corporations. Well paid by corporate directorates,
bureaucrats serve the needs of power centers rather than of the populations that the power centers are supposed to be serving. While this
is neither always nor necessarily the case, the shifts of public power
into fewer hands renders the bureaucracies more powerful, creating
an independent class of bureaucrats, or as they are more usually
known, managers. Gordon explains why downsizing—reducing the
labor force in corporations—has widened the gap between rich and
poor while increasing the fear and anxiety in those holding nonexecu-
tive jobs. The increased financial health of corporations was achieved
at the expense of job loss and job anxiety in the salaried workforce in
general. Gordon considers why there aren't other secure, appealing
jobs created in other parts of the economy if there has been a general
improvement in corporate profitability. The answer is that wealth has
been redistributed within corporations: taken from the salaried workforce and given to executives and to the larger bureaucracies needed

---

[18] The precedence of rules over human needs is discussed at length in Carol Gilligan's
In a Different Voice (Cambridge, MA: Harvard University Press, 1982) as being
characteristic of men's carrying out ethical principles.

[19] David M. Gordon, *Fat and Mean: The Corporate Squeeze of Working Americans and
the Myth of Managerial "Downsizing"* (New York: Free Press, 1996).

for surveillance and domination of their own workers.[20] It is a simple situation: wealth has been transferred from those who are barely making ends meet to those already having more than enough. To enforce this policy of corporate government by fear, more "police" are needed, and these are called by Gordon a corporation's "bureaucratic burden." Gordon describes this movement as the "stick strategy" as contrasted with the "carrot strategy" he endorses and whose practical forms he outlines in the last chapter of his book.[21]

Gordon's use of the term "bureaucratic burden" puts a contemporary twist on this old idea: the same constituencies that complained about the excessive regulations of "big government" are now using the bureaucratic principle to redistribute the wealth among ever fewer people. The gain in weight in corporate bureaucracies has been matched by the increasing emulation of corporations by universities,[22] and the resulting license to demand "standards," "grade deflation," and "quality products"—students who will fit into the bureaucracies. Furthermore, downsizing in universities is directly related to the attacks on tenure, a "union-busting" activity. This means more part-timers and adjuncts, fewer permanent committed faculty members, greater teaching loads, and ultimately a kind of militarization of postsecondary education.

Testing and grading make such changes possible in universities. They teach people how to be bureaucrats, managers, in the sense described by Ferguson and Gordon. They also teach that some get

---

[20] "Stagnant or falling wages create the need for intensive managerial supervision of frontline employees. If workers do not share in the fruits of the enterprise, if they are not provided a promise of job security and steady wage growth, what incentive do they have to work as hard as their bosses would like? So the corporations need to monitor the workers' effort and be able to threaten credibly to punish them if they do not perform. The corporations must wield the Stick. Eventually the Stick requires millions of Stick-wielders." (5)

[21] I and others thinking about teaching will want to reject the reduction of choices to the carrot and the stick. This formulation can describe the psychology of grading, a practice I contest. With regard to both Gordon's and my discussions, however, it is essential to emphasize that whatever the carrot may mean, the meaning of the stick is much less ambiguous: it is related to the use of force to intimidate those who don't have or use sticks. It also may be thought of in its football meaning, "good stick" (a decisive tackle), and as a verb, to "stick it to" someone. Sometimes the intimidation is used to steal and hoard resources; other times it is used to teach others that the stick is the prevailing way of life in the rest of society.

[22] Increasing numbers of reports in the *Chronicle of Higher Education* tell of trustee interference in the running of universities, especially with regard to limiting or eliminating tenure. These trustees, who are all members of corporate boards, are attempting to micromanage universities and limit even further the room faculty members have to manage educational policy.

through the sieve of evaluative barriers to move into higher social/ economic classes, but that most don't. The bureaucratic ideal slows and stops change. As mentioned at the beginning of this chapter, the recent history of grading shows that many think it is inevitable. However, the fact that changing approaches to grades are connected with wider social changes implies that there is no reason to assume the inevitability of grading: rather than grades being necessary for teaching and learning, they are necessary to preserve social and economic hierarchies.

To sum up the features of the traditional mass testing/grading genre: Messages are sent only one way. The bases of these messages are tests created and evaluated by those responsible to judge, usually organizations or institutions. The relationship of judge to student is hierarchical, and reciprocal only in a minor sense. In classrooms each individual is judged by one teacher or, in some cases, one committee; students are not judged on collective effort. The evaluation message given can be placed on a linear scale that represents comparatively the performance of those in that group. The relationship among the students in a grading group is necessarily competitive. Cooperative relationships among students can often be treated as cheating. The sum of a student's grades compiled during a degree program helps to determine the attractiveness of that student as a job candidate. Systems of letter grades, with few exceptions, are summed up by these features.[23]

---

[23] The film *Casablanca* provides a metaphor, and it reveals an element we don't always see easily: its androcentrism. Rick Blaine has two letters of transit that will permit two people to escape the Nazis in Casablanca. We are given to believe at first that Rick is saving these letters to use for himself and his beloved Ilse so that they may escape to America and "live happily ever after." It seems clear that this is what Ilse also wants to do, as she realizes she can no longer deny how much she loves Rick. However, she becomes confused, as she is already married to Laszlo, and asks Rick to "do the thinking for both of us," expecting that he will find a way to get them out without harming Laszlo. Rick, also holding this ideal of happiness, decides that Laszlo and Ilse will use the letters to escape, while he and Captain Renault will be able to find a way to escape without the letters. Ilse is disappointed, as she had said that she would not be able to "leave him again," as she did once before because of the necessities of war. She respects and admires, but does not love, Laszlo. However her feelings are sacrificed by Rick, who gives the letters of transit to the married couple, and they escape. Thus in this relationship between a man and a woman, the man "does the thinking for both of us" and distributes the letters of transit as he decides.

In school, grades are letters of transit. Sometimes the letter of transit is an actual letter of recommendation for the student. At other times, it is comments on papers or an oral text—things told by teachers to students. But these letters, in whatever genre they appear, count to such a degree that most students fear their effects: their power to prevent the students from "escaping," from moving on with their lives.

Practical Problems with Testing and Grading

People have observed for generations that there are serious problems with an educational style that requires this testing and grading. One British study of interest is Henry Latham's *On the Action of Examinations Considered as a Means of Selection,* published in 1877.[24] As he describes testing and grading of over a century ago, they seem similar to what they are today. "Cramming" was the accepted way to prepare for examinations, and the British faculty faced this fact readily by hiring special teachers called "crammers" to press the knowledge into the students' heads. While in the one instance competitive examinations and cramming were simply assumed, Latham's discussion shows awareness of the inefficacy of this technique with regard to certifying a job candidate's potential motivation:

> Competitive Examinations leave us most in the dark about those qualities which find their sphere in active life, but they also fail us in one important point when we want to select men[25] to fill posts intended for the "endowment of research." It is most important to know whether persons have a taste for their study, and about this Examinations hardly tell us anything. We meet with cases of hard-headed men who obtain high degrees in a course which they select as offering them the most favourable field, but who never care to open a book in their branch of study afterwards. . . .
>
> It must be remarked that if we get wrong results by trusting to Examinations it is usually because we use them to the exclusion of all other modes of judging. . . . We have all the means of forming an opinion that we had before Examinations were introduced, and if these were used with care and method we might get near the truth about some of the moral and personal qualities of candidates. (302, 303)

Latham says that tests don't do two very important things related to providing an accurate credential: they don't tell what a person will do on the job as a result of the test performance, and they don't say what "taste" a person may have for the subject in which the test is given. These two factors are related, perhaps inseparable, in each person: taste for a subject—liking it—motivates work in it, in the "active" life, and it is the most certain motivation for success. Latham also says that

---

[24] Henry Latham, *On the Action of Examinations Considered as a Means of Selection* (Cambridge and London: George Bell and Sons, 1877).

[25] Throughout his study Latham refers only to men as university students and test takers. On the one hand, it seems somewhat surprising to see this assumption used so fluently; but on the other, it is just as clear that the complaints about the exams will apply just as well to women as to men. Today's take on this situation could be that men are more willing than women are to pay the price outlined in this passage.

discerning these salient factors is subjective—"the means of forming an opinion"—that is, not reducible to the formalities of testing and grading. Teachers and employers observe students and applicants as people and form opinions and judgments as we do in everyday life, based on a wide variety of factors not always obvious to us making the judgments. Values such as "care and method" actually do "bring us nearer to the truth" about a person's abilities and motivation.

Judges of students admit that subjective judgments produce performance assessments. Those who give grades and who rely on grading systems acknowledge how even the grades themselves are subjective but that deciding *whether* to give them is not consistent with keeping one's job. Latham's formulations represent the traditional approach to the issue of grading: denial that the actual or accurate bases of judgment can be implemented as a regular part of teaching. These bases are holistic views about how a person functions in the real world as emerging from the person's taste for the knowledge developed in school.

Mary Lovett Smallwood's *An Historical Study of Examinations and Grading Systems in Early American Universities*[26] discusses developments in five major universities from their founding in the eighteenth century to the beginning of the twentieth. Smallwood's information comes from a period before Latham's. Based on five different American universities, it is more comprehensive, and it suggests the ubiquity of the conventional approach to grades. Along the way, her work discloses materials that show, as Latham's do, the patterns trying to deny the harm done by grading.

Smallwood reviews the history of grading in the United States by noting how at the end of the eighteenth century at Yale the four (Latin) categories of best, good, inferior, and bad were used to classify both students and their work. In various contexts after that, attempts were made to reduce the subjectivity of these judgments by introducing more detailed scaling,[27] often given on a scale of 65 to 100. Smallwood observes,

> All these attempts to estimate the student as an individual as well as only one of a group, had desirable results but accomplished almost nothing in obviating the teacher's subjective bias along various lines, particularly in the weighting of various sorts of exercises and subjects on the basis of his view of their value to the student. (109)

---

[26] Mary Lovett Smallwood, *An Historical Study of Examinations and Grading Systems in Early American Universities* (Cambridge, MA: Harvard University Press, 1935).

[27] These moves are repeated commonly in today's universities by faculty councils, which declare plusses and minuses mandatory in grading. I discuss this matter in *The Double Perspective* (New York: Oxford University Press, 1988), ch. 6.

The term *bias* suggests that the teacher's judgment pejoratively off-sets the effects of the detailed scalar ratings. The more schools tried to eliminate such bias through numerical grading, the more it "involve[d] the faculty in further difficulties" (110). Different scales were introduced, gradually developing into a Byzantine set of quantitative evaluative procedures, each with its own significance, but none, either individually or in concert with other measures, overcame the effects of the teachers' subjective judgments. In the early university periods in the United States, therefore, there is evidence of awareness of the strong effects of teachers' personal judgments but also of persistent but failed attempts to eliminate this subjectivity—the same situation that exists today.

Another way in which this ambivalence has emerged historically (in this case in the late nineteenth century) is in the contrast between the ways Harvard and Michigan treated the separation of "passed" from "not passed" when they each experimented with the abolition of the marking system:

> At the University of Michigan a student simply "passed," but if he failed there were different degrees of failure, such as "conditioned" and "incomplete." At Harvard the reverse was true, variations were on the side of passing: if he failed, his failure was unmodified. . . . Harvard was always more interested in encouraging and rewarding the good student; Michigan felt that emphasis on the superior attainments and merits of one student over another was neither desirable nor democratic. (83)

As Smallwood presents it, there is an either-or connotation as Harvard and Michigan are compared. Both want to find ways to reinsert distinctions among students, as it must have remained obvious that each student is different from every other, and in order to help all students, their situations should be recognized both individually and categorically. Both the students who passed and those who failed do need to be understood as having done their work in some identifiable qualitative way. And so new categories emerge on either side of the pass/fail line. Conversely, both the Harvard and Michigan nineteenth-century pass/fail systems succeed in solving some problems brought about by scalar grading. The Harvard system transforms a good grade into a living accomplishment; the Michigan system teaches that qualitative differences in performance are not to be measured against one another, not to compete with one another, and that the categorical distinctions among groups of students do not reflect the relative merit of individuals' inner beings.

Because students need to be recognized in terms of their actual accomplishments, and because abolishing hierarchical evaluation makes such recognition possible, the implied choice of "either

Harvard or Michigan" expresses ambivalence about grades without solving the problem. The best solution would be "both Harvard and Michigan": no grading system *and* recognition of each student's accomplishment (or lack thereof) in a qualitative way. However, now, as then, this solution rarely exists.

In the 1960s, almost a century after the foregoing experiments, university grading once again came under scrutiny, and changes were proposed. From this period we have the small percentage of elective courses that students may take pass/fail and the now ubiquitous student course evaluation forms, where students "grade" the course and the teacher as part of a policy of recognizing student "input." Since their introduction, however, these practices have contributed little to the humanization of grading and, in most cases, have been harmful to the process of evaluation of students and teachers. In pass/fail electives, the teacher is not told that the student has chosen this path. An element of deception has been institutionalized in order to give the appearance of students' control of their performance standards. As a result, the relationship between teacher and student in these cases is not founded on trust and honesty: the teacher's contributions are treated as a tap that can be turned on and off rather than as elements in a living relationship. Teaching has been diluted and trivialized rather than enriched and intensified. Because the pass/fail choice is worked into a traditional grading psychology, learning in new subjects has been converted to GPA enhancement. If pass/fail were the rule in all three zones of college work—the major, the distribution requirements, and the electives—it would then have had its desired effect of substituting attention to the material for attention to the GPA.

Practical Problems with Student Evaluations

This situation may be demonstrated with reference to a document entitled "Evaluation of Teaching Handbook" put out by the Dean of Faculties Office at Indiana University, Bloomington, in 1986. Whether or not it is official and in a handbook, most postsecondary institutions will not go further than this in their attitude and policy regarding the improvement of teaching.

Here is how the policy is presented:

> There are two important reasons for evaluating teaching: to aid in administrative decisions (tenure, promotion in rank, salary increases); and to diagnose areas for improvement. The measures employed to serve each of these purposes will be somewhat differ-

ent. For personnel decisions, faculty members need information that measure overall teaching effectiveness. For improving teaching, faculty members want information that can help identify strengths and problems. Distinguishing the purpose is critical. It influences sources and kinds of information collected, criteria focused on, how information is analyzed and reported, and to whom findings go. (5)

In this paragraph, we find the premises for the Dean's initiative in sponsoring this publication: to help administrators and to get the faculty to teach better. From the perspective of the administration there is really only one premise—to provide a quantitative, documented (that is, "scientific") basis for administrators to make personnel decisions. This premise implies that administrators are the most important and powerful members of an academic community. Some of us who think about and compare the intellectual orientation of universities would say this is not the case, but rather that the tenured and tenure-track faculty members create a university's public identity. Still others might say that the university is identified by its student body—the regularly changing group of the young public getting their degrees from the university. Very few people would identify the support staff (secretaries, accountants, and so on), drawn from the local population, as contributing to the university's identity. And fewer still would say that it is the special *combination* of populations and their historical, social locations that creates the university's public identity.

University administrators have one point in common with scholars and researchers in most academic fields. As Susan Miller has observed,[28] these fields wish "to remove [their] members from the defining activity of any sort of academic practitioner—teaching" (193). If students were considered as determining the university's identity, they too could be involved in determining how subjects can be studied and taught. But except behind the closed doors of the classroom (that is, subversively), neither the teachers nor the students can change the style, classroom structures, social relations, and accreditation for achievement in the university. And as the Dean's handbook suggests, administrators wish no such changes. The regulation of teaching by testing and grading is rigid and is tied to the traditional university structure of the course, the grade, the professor.

Some have observed that the practice of using student evaluations as contributions to the study of teaching is a step in the direction of taking university teaching seriously. The use of such

---

[28] Susan Miller, *Textual Carnivals: The Politics of Composition* (Carbondale: Southern Illinois University Press, 1991).

evaluations began in the 1960s, along with elective-only optional pass/fail grading. This latter choice remains marginal and relatively unimportant in most universities today, but these same universities seem to think student evaluations have a bearing on teaching. The Dean's handbook cites studies to show that, along with chairperson's evaluations, "systematic student ratings" are "the most common sources to assess teaching."

However, the Dean's handbook continues, because student comments "pose problems when trying to sample, analyze, and summarize for personnel decisions" (8, 9), a machine-readable rating system is the most commonly used instrument. Furthermore, the most reliable portion of the often complex evaluation form is the summary statement section, in which the student rates, overall, the instructor, the course, the exams, the lectures, the class discussions, and perhaps the instruction, whatever that may be. Almost all forms ask students to judge the teacher's ability to explain material, preparation, availability, enthusiasm, ability to make the subject interesting. Anonymity for the students is considered essential, and the statistical analysis is considered as authoritative a reading as one can get.

The serious attention paid by the administration to these ungainly forms already takes them out of students' hands. Because they are standardized and systematized, and given without regard to which subjects the courses teach, they are only an instrument of judgment— indeed, a grade given by students in the same way that a grade is given by the instructor. Instead of opening up teaching and learning to discursive attention, they add judgmental attention to the teaching/ learning relationship. If, for example, the availability and personal contact of the teachers are important, how authentic will they be if teachers feel they are going to be graded on them? The coercive psychology that characterizes grading systems for students now is applied to teachers. A university administration that uses this system, however, cannot assimilate the view that machine-readable teacher evaluation is an extension of the problem it is trying to solve. Teaching does not really count, not only because it cannot be measured but also because if it were taken seriously, teachers would have more influence than administrators on how the university is run. At least, teachers and administrators would share equally the task of running the university.

There is reason to think that student evaluations are being used as part of plans to undermine faculty. Professor Victoria Moessner[29] from the University of Alaska at Fairbanks presented

---

[29] Victoria Moessner, presentation, Modern Language Association (Inter)National Convention, Toronto, Ontario, December 1993.

several instances of the abuse of students' teacher evaluation forms at her university. One such instance, referring to the machine-graded statistical evaluation form filled out by all students in all courses:

> Students fill out these forms believing that the terms "Excellent, Very Good, etc." have the generally accepted meaning found in any dictionary. They usually do not know that the statistics from the evaluation forms can produce the following kinds of statements: "Using evaluations for . . . the committee figured the average score for questions #1–4 for the years . . . that number is 3.68, which is in the Good to Very Good range, two-thirds of the way to Very Good. The average decile for these years . . . is 3.4 University-wide and 3.0 within the College of Liberal Arts. The Department Head . . . says that scores are low for that particular department." This person's teaching was deemed not good enough for promotion.

While on average, students considered this teacher to be near "very good," the department head's opinion that the score was "low for that particular department" supervened on *the meaning of the terms to the students* in such a way as to cause the promotion to be denied.

Moessner offered other examples of the manipulation of statistics, suggesting that, as many believe, statistics ensure understanding of very little for those on the low end of the hierarchical structure of authority. She concludes that the *use* of statistics in the practice of evaluation actually amounts to the *abuse* of them:

> Very Good is possibly not Good enough.
>   The only recourse an individual faculty member has is to hire a lawyer and file grievances. This costs the instructor thousands of dollars and possibly years of long drawn out litigation.

These instances show that regardless of what technique is used, as long as evaluation proceeds in one direction, it necessarily involves giving a false picture of teaching that almost always jeopardizes teachers and fails to reflect what the students actually experienced in that class.

In the use of student evaluations of teachers and courses, no attempt is made to acknowledge that courses in different subject matters need to be evaluated differently. Even though courses in drawing, writing, anthropology, math, and biology each require different bases for judgment, it is steadfastly maintained in the interests of administrative expediency that the same questionnaire is equally appropriate for all courses. The questionnaire remains what it has always been: an anonymous and potentially damaging survey on the students' sense of the instructor's *ethical*

stance.[30] Student opinion remains an administrative tool and
does not become, in substantive senses, a factor in how courses
are conceived, designed, required, or conducted.

Grades and the Ideological Constraint of Students

If you are one of those who has objected to grades and tests in
schools, the most common response is, Why, you are being graded
and tested all the time! How can you object? This is true, as Hanson
has described. Grading and testing have an ideological authority,
and they have such great inertia in society because they are one of
the pedagogical means by which an unfairly structured society is
perpetuated. To propose any alternative to testing and grading is not
simply to oppose a practice that happens to be widespread; it is to
oppose a practice that perpetuates conditions favorable to the few
who govern society. It is to take a political position that will cause
trouble to those who benefit from training the "best" into bureaucratic categories.

Some of those who benefit from the grading system were cited
earlier in this chapter. The broadest class that benefits may be further
disclosed by considering why grades are important at the times they
are, namely, from about the third grade to graduation from college,
between ages eight and twenty-one. In the early grades, the relation
between students and teachers is still considered (in Western androcentric societies) a relation between mothers and dependent children. Teachers in elementary schools are mostly women. As the
child becomes literate in the third grade, and thus potentially autonomous in the finding of information and understanding, a more hierarchical pedagogical style becomes prominent in our school systems,
so that by the seventh grade, subjects and students are highly segre-
gated from one another according to a variety of criteria. While more
equal numbers of men and women are teachers in the seventh grade
and after, the pedagogical style is increasingly androcentric; and
finally, school system administrators are mostly men. Through
school systems, the values of an already gender-unbalanced society

---

[30] That is, students can say if the instructor is late or if he or she spends time re-
explaining things. But are students in a position to say how an instructor knows the
material? They can say what they learned, but how can an evaluation form say how
they learned? And so on.

are promulgated through the compartmentalization of subjects and the tracking of students according to their ability to serve a hierarchically organized, bureaucratically heavy society.

For this reason, grading and more comprehensive judging of students can only take place in one direction. Most people cannot imagine a system in which there is mutual judging in ways that help all parties but do not endanger their status as students and teachers. As things are now, regardless of what technique is used, judging proceeds in one direction. The grading system teaches, at the level of ideology or of "presuppositions of society," how to develop and keep a bureaucratic mentality. The way a student experiences school—starting with the standardized tests of literacy and numeracy in the early grades, their annual use, the use of tests and grades in individual classrooms—is governed by bureaucratic values, hierarchy, and competition, leading to the production of "the good student." This figure gets good grades and is tracked "high." This is the same student who knows how to do well on tests, who can discern the special psychology of the test question—what it "wants," so to speak—who can master "reading comprehension" exercises, word analogy exercises, and similar specialized tasks characteristic only of standardized tests and of no other zone in society. The narrowness of these skills, while definitely a problem, does not by itself represent the problem of the "good student." Rather, all the skills a student needs to acquire to do well on examinations are skills of compliance and adaptability. They are not skills of creativity, imagination, and resourcefulness in the service of society. The latter abilities are not usually to be used or practiced in short time periods; they appear in a more measured or leisurely way in the ordinary experiences of daily life. Sometimes "quick" thinking is needed, and it can be useful to be able to parry situations with the speed of thought required by examinations, standardized or local. Yet in teaching for the long run, for how to think in the great variety of contexts of different time lengths and locations, bureaucratic ability is not particularly useful.

If the majority of students emerge from the school years with mainly bureaucratic ability, and if a minority of students who don't have this ability but have a variety of other talents and skills are tracked in "lower" groups, this means that existing pedagogical processes and styles are, in an affirmative way, creating a managerial or bureaucratic majority: those who are ready to serve the power centers of society. If grade-oriented pedagogies diminish in value, influence, status, and power, those people who have something other than bureaucratic ways of thinking enter society and pose a challenge to bureaucratic values.

The Political Identity of Writing and Language Use

We are back to Richard Ohmann's juxtaposition of an entering student's hopes to the realities of college functioning with which this chapter started. The contradictory experiences of students need not take place. They are there because of the ideology of academic life: its individualistic and, usually, androcentric style. The subject of writing and language use has become, under these circumstances, a discipline that teaches that because any use of language must take place in public—with one or more people expected to hear or read it—that use must also have a political function: there is no longer a ground for claiming that the use of language is objective and value-free.[31] Because this subject, like others, has many potential political vectors, those who believe in value-free disciplines might well consider writing and language use as playing oppositional roles, given the present structures of society. The concepts and practices suggested by disclosure, genre, and membership acknowledge the political potential and urge us not to try to deny it or lie about it. This acknowledgment welcomes political consideration of any subject and considers the writing of different disciplines to be one of the paths through which we recognize their political potentials.

The subject matter of writing and language use, conceived in social purpose, is limited by the practices of testing and grading. In many writing programs, the scope of grading has been substantially reduced, and in others, grading is limited to portfolios, a collection of work by students showing in aggregate their accomplishments over a semester or longer. The ideals of creativity, imagination, and generosity are more in evidence in the teaching of writing than they have been in the past, but they are still not playing a large role because they are limited by bureaucratic controls.

In the next chapter, a discussion of possible genres of mutual and self-evaluation considers how the teaching of discipline in writing and the use of language is consistent with judgment and evaluation of one writer/user of language by another, and that teaching this subject requires mutual and multiple judgments, given frequently, continuously, but without formalization or bureaucratic finality. If the teaching of discipline is assimilated to the more generous ideals of genre, disclosure, and membership, the subject of writing and language use can contribute to the lives of all people the way it has contributed, historically, to the lucky and the privileged.

---

[31] There are so many books that have announced or assumed this principle that it would be redundant to cite them. This discussion takes for granted that objectivities are local and are governed by the contexts of inquiry, however small or large they are.

Chapter Eight

Genres of Evaluation and Teaching Discipline

Acquiring Discipline in Writing and Language Use

Many students feel they cannot acquire discipline without the external pressure created by a competitive grading system and its periodic accounting. In some cases, the prospect of graded examinations is effective in teaching discipline. Within grading systems many students with less than the highest GPA go to professional schools or succeed in other ways. The question I raise, however, is, What are the collective effects in society of individuals' becoming acculturated in a grading system, of not facing these effects for the rest of our lives, and of not being alert to the harm that is done?

A grade-governed pedagogy is particularly burdensome in learning to write and use our language. Discipline in writing and language use grows, accumulates, evolves into existence over time. Individual effort and practice in combination with ranked evaluation do not teach discipline either. Rather, we develop our discipline within the flourishing of our imaginations and by sharing thoughts with others. To do this we need to be surrounded by other people who are writing, responding, and growing with us. Like the speech acquired by infants, subsequent abilities with language demand the constant responses of other writers and speakers. People cannot "exercise" the use of language if other speakers and writers don't respond to them. To provide the best conditions in school for one's language to mature into interesting and useful forms means working in as full a social scene as possible—with others in the classroom as interested parties and colleagues. Gradually, if we become motivated, discipline comes to us in writing and language use as we learn to perceive how we speak and write in as many parts of our social existence as possible. When the processes of mutual and self-observation during our social interactions are undertaken, the different genres we use become apparent as a function of our memberships. We are then in a position to work on these genres, as individuals and in collaboration with others engaged in the same study.

The discipline that emerges from this form of study cultivates the ability to exchange views and thoughts with others as well as the ability to write any one kind of text; the oral and informal exchange of language is part of the process of writing texts. To judge an individual text apart from its social context of production is inappropriate because the judgment communicates to the writer the false implication of his/her sole responsibility for the text. Repeated judging of work in isolation teaches the writer to exaggerate his or her sense of responsibility to the point of inhibition; often this is what brings on writer's block. On the other hand, the continuous and collective responsive context for writing and language use, while not free of inhibitory factors, encourages growth, thought, motivation, and self-discipline.

There are instances where "writing for the teacher" has motivated students. The teacher is one good audience who often behaves as a partner in writing. However, both the single-person audience and the combination of the collegial audience with the official judge in the person of the teacher limits the teacher's ability to teach. As a judge, the teacher is working for the institution, for a bureaucratic entity greater than the class. Although we don't often think of it this way, there is a conflict of interest for teachers if they are working for the student and for the institution at once. ("If I don't grade a certain way, my job is jeopardized.")[1] While many teachers escape this sense of conflict, there is no need for it to exist to begin with. Teachers, like other readers of our work, should be able to provide both response and judgment without there being a conflict of interest.

Discipline, teacherly judgments, and certification of individuals can take place if classrooms are cooperative and if a pass/no-credit, or a credit/no-record form of certification is used. However, the self-conscious pedagogical pursuit of collective, collaborative, and cooperative scenes of writing is not possible if a set of individual grades

---

[1] For documentation of this claim see Chapters 2 and 3 in Libby Allison, Lizbeth Bryant, and Maureen Hourigan, eds. *Grading in the Post-Process Classroom* (Portsmouth, NH: Heinemann-Boyton/Cook, 1997).

are the established means to certify students' accomplishments. Grades based on a ranking system do not permit collective work to count on the record.[2] There is no "genre" of grade that recognizes collective work as part of students' acquisition of a disciplined ability to write and use the language. Even when classrooms practice group work and urge the frequent exchange of comments and views, the "final texts" themselves are up for judgment. The bureaucratic system overtakes the practice of developing discipline and writing; the bureaucracy "disciplines" students in the more pejorative sense of the term. The letter of transit remains the only way out of Casablanca, and there is only one Rick Blaine to hand it out after having "done the thinking for both of us."

In this chapter, I first review an experiment done in Israel demonstrating the effects of collective styles of teaching, and discuss further how collective work teaches discipline in writing and language use. I then consider different genres of evaluation that can play a greater role in writing and language use pedagogy: portfolio evaluation, discursive evaluation, mutual interactive evaluation, self-evaluation. Each of these practices uses new genres of evaluative writing, given in the service of building discipline, care, and dedication in writing and language use. These genres, part of a contingent curriculum, are used as needed, depending on the membership of the class and its interests. If discursive genres of evaluation play an on-the-record role, the use of the "letter of transit" is not necessary: students would know, in qualitative and specific senses, how accomplished and sophisticated their work has become; teachers would be able to hear from students candid views on the conduct of class. Under conditions of regular mutual and self-evaluation, only in rare instances do students contest a teacher's sense that they have not yet achieved certification-level competence; under those same conditions, teachers can make allowances and change their approaches to those whom they have not motivated. Class members have gained confidence from not having to compete with others or conceal their own accomplishment because of the race for grades or the need to rank people.

An approach to writing and language use that highlights disclosure, genre, and membership treats evaluation practices as genres of writing. This treatment integrates evaluation and assessment

---

[2] Many classrooms compromise by doing collective work but then "collecting" individual portfolios. This step is welcome, as I will discuss, but there is still no space for the collective work to count as collective work, that is, without dividing it up and giving the individuals fair credit for their contributions.

into the subject matter. Students learn to read and write genres of evaluation of their own and others' work; they learn to write and to evaluate at once. There is then no need for "checking up" interventions by teachers or more distant supervisory figures. Students are learning to recognize and produce different genres, to evaluate in collective contexts, and to acquire discipline through the use of socialized writing practices.

Cooperative Classrooms and Language Use: An Experiment

Collaboration is neither a method nor an ideal; it is a work practice that has recently become part of many writing pedagogies. But it is also the condition under which language is acquired and learned from the beginning. A sense of why one can have confidence in the project of converting classrooms toward cooperative work styles is given in the report of an experiment by Hanna Shachar and Shlomo Sharan.[3] The term they use is *cooperative* rather than *collaborative* to describe the collective accent of the classroom style they are investigating. In English, their term conveys something more of the feeling of mutual giving than *collaborative* does. Of course, this is not about vocabulary, and therefore the terms themselves will become multiple if the classroom as an institution accommodates new forms. Yet we also find in this experiment how essential the students' uses of language are to their ability to function as students. The uses that emerge to show their successes are also those that we can incorporate into several in-class evaluative discourses to replace the judgment-from-without style of certification.

Shachar and Sharan conducted an experiment in Israel over a period of six months in a junior high school.[4] About three hundred fifty students were involved. The important feature of this population

[3] Hanna Shachar and Shlomo Sharan, "Talking, Relating, and Achieving: Effects of Cooperative Learning and Whole-Class Instruction," *Cognition and Instruction* 12 (1994): 313–353.

[4] There are differences between racial discord in Israel and racial discord between whites and African Americans in the United States. For one thing, the student population in this study is all Jewish. No such common ground exists between blacks and whites in America. A better comparison might be made if a combined Arab and Jewish population were studied. Nevertheless, if these considerations are borne in mind, there may be enough in common in American culture for blacks and whites in the cooperative classrooms to achieve comparable integration. Another possible common factor, not discussed by Shachar and Sharan, is that their situation, as well as the situation in American schools, requires *mutual teaching and learning*.

was that it was of mixed background: about half the students were from European Jewish backgrounds, and half were from Middle Eastern Jewish backgrounds. In Israel, the latter group are "second-class citizens," different in appearance (darker skin, usually) and economic standards from the children of European parents. Often, there is animosity between the two groups because of these class, culture, and appearance differences. The purpose of the experiment was to study the difference between how students learn in two different classroom situations: cooperative learning versus whole-class instruction. A few more than half the total of students participated in the six cooperative learning, or "group investigation," classes, while a few less than half participated in four classes taught with the whole-class method (313). The data came from videotapes of classes and small group discussions. The results came from the analyses of these tapes.

The subject matters of the classes were geography and history. All the classes were integrated by ethnic group, as were the small groups that were studied. Two techniques were used to document difference in the students' performance: before and after achievement tests on knowledge of the subject matters, and *language use in class and in small-group discussions.* The former measure is traditional. The latter is unorthodox and revealed a great deal about the performance differences as well as about the social psychology of the classroom, two zones of inquiry highlighted by Pauly's discussion of the importance of the classroom. While the more significant finding in the study relates to what the language use parameters showed, the achievement tests gave the following result:

> Students in the Group Investigation classes registered much larger gains on the achievement test in history than the students in the Whole-Class method. . . . That the pretest mean scores of students in the two ethnic groups were similar in both instructional methods highlights the reliability of this finding. . . . Other experiments with cooperative learning have resulted in reports of improved academic achievement for lower class or minority group pupils, without claims of having eliminated the academic gap between different social groups. (349)

Not surprisingly, given a chance for greater activity and participation, students who were not expected to do well did much better than expected, confirming results of other experiments (cited in the Shachar-Sharan essay) and those of Uri Treisman[5] in California, working with cooperative learning for African American students studying mathematics.

---

[5] See May Garland, "The Mathematics Workshop Model: An Interview with Uri Treisman," *Journal of Developmental Education* 16 (Spring 1993), 14–16, 18, 20, 22.

The language use and social interaction data (considered the same by Shachar and Sharan) have nine language moves that were studied and compared as used by those in the different ethnic groups and those in the different classrooms. The moves are explanation with evidence, unstructured idea, repetitions, generalization, concrete examples, takes a stand, suggests an idea or hypothesis, organizes ideas, repetition with expansion (333). The experimenters went through their transcripts and identified such moves in each class, then counted them and subjected them to statistical analysis. Just a review of the categories of speech acts suggests that they are all desirable. If students feel they can speak in class in most or all of these categories, it is a sign that they are more, rather than less, engaged, and are likely, therefore, to be more confident in the class. The comparisons of gains in these parameters showed the marked differences in performance, first, overall between the group investigation classes and the whole-class classes, and second, the much better participation of the Middle Eastern students in the group investigation than in the whole-class situation. The authors connected the improved achievement test performance by the Middle Eastern students to the overall increase in self-confidence and self-possession in the cooperative classrooms.

The authors divided the language categories into cooperative and noncooperative interaction, a distinction that can only be documented with reference to the videotape or long explanation not needed here. Using this distinction, here is an example of results—germane to classroom populations in the United States—obtained in the experiment (335, 345). Middle Eastern students got more attention from their Western colleagues under conditions of cooperative learning. Then we find that there was more cooperation *among* Middle Eastern students in the cooperative situation than there was in the traditional classroom. Along with these is the fact that Western students addressed themselves cooperatively more to Middle Eastern students than the latter students addressed each other. This last result is not surprising because, in general, the social and school self-confidence of the Western students is greater than those of the students coming from less privileged status groups. This latter result could mean that in conditions of cooperative learning there could be more spontaneous interaction between members of dominant-class and under-class students: conditions in the classroom could contribute to the wider social program by growing toward integration through regular classroom practices.

We also learn that the number of cooperative statements by Middle Eastern students among themselves is doubled (even though it is still not as great as those given in the interaction with the Western students) in the cooperative learning situations. The increased interaction among Middle Eastern students is also an effect that bodes well for what happens in society later on: it means that the cooperative classroom can provide the opportunities for under-class members to achieve both individual and class autonomy much faster than they would in the whole-class system of teaching. In addition, Shachar and Sharan observe, "the Middle Eastern students from the cooperative classes expressed many more cooperative statements to the entire group, without distinguishing between groupmates from one or the other ethnic group, than their ethnic peers from the Whole-Class method" (345). This suggests yet another effect if projected into the social future: cooperative learning situations foster contribution to one's own group interests as well as to society at large. Cooperative learning situations do seem to encourage the formation of multiple perspectives (as does bilingualism, for example) that can spontaneously cope with the multiple perspectives students will find in society later on. Also, the ability to address the general audience is usually associated with members of the dominant group, as if they were the standard. Evidence of members of the under group learning to address the general group is therefore also evidence of acquiring the status of the dominant group as well.

Related to these accomplishments is the following observation, also taken from the language use data. The Middle Eastern students (in the cooperative situation as compared with those in the whole-class situation)

> displayed greater use of the strategy of providing explanation with evidence, which is not only highly valued by teachers in academic settings, but also reflects the students' focus on and involvement in the subject of the discussion. At the same time, this strategy demonstrates the students' ability to detach themselves from the immediate situation of the discussion and relate to the words as representing objective events in the past or future that they are trying to explain. These students also demonstrated more frequent use, compared with Middle Eastern students from the Whole-Class method, of *taking a stand,* which demonstrates their relatively high level of self-confidence, as well as their involvement in the subject compared with students who are less prepared or able to take a personal stand regarding a particular subject. . . . In the traditional classroom, it is primarily the teacher who employs this strategy, not the students. Hence we can conclude that the Middle Eastern students from the Group Investigation classes demonstrated greater control over verbal discourse through the use of a more differentiated repertoire of thinking strategies. (344)

Explanation with evidence and taking a stand. One does not need the academic demand for evidence to validate giving evidence when explaining things. To give evidence of anything during an explanation is a form of help to others. It is also a form of providing a foundation for one's own opinion, but in an interactive situation backing up one's opinion simultaneously provides help for others and demonstrates respect for their intelligence. Then, as the authors mention, taking a stand is a reserved category in school. This is not to say that students don't pretend to take a stand in the many hypothetical situations in which they are asked to write or give opinions (in whole-class circumstances). They develop the forms of taking a stand, a practice some may endorse, but which is questionable if only forms are involved. In the cooperative scenes, however, taking a stand cannot be just formal or hypothetical (unless it is assigned as such). The locus of attention is small: the students are discussing details, say, looking at a map, and to take a stand may only mean to insist on a certain way of reading the map. It is such language uses that Shachar and Sharan placed in the category of taking a stand.

Putting the two traits of giving evidence and taking a stand together adds up to the mutual feeding of the classroom social relations and the processes of mental[6] development. While finding the evidence may be more analytical, taking a stand represents committing oneself in some way. Both moves are urged, required, and evaluated by one's partners in the group. The condition of relatedness to others becomes, under cooperative circumstances, associated with thinking processes as well as with the disclosure of our thinking. The local disclosures involved in taking a stand are the beginnings of the ability to announce facts and viewpoints in the processes of self-disclosure that participate in evaluative genres, autoethnographies, reports of knowledge and experience, and other oral and written genres. In cooperative circumstances, reasoning, disclosure, study, and commitment are learned in the contexts in which they occur outside of school—alongside others engaged in similar work and who will receive our work and assess it.

A related finding is also of interest, as it pertains to the reduction of individualistic statements on the part of Western students:

> The number of individualistic statements made by Western students from the cooperative classes was also significantly smaller than the number for Western students from the Whole-Class method. (346)

---

[6] In their essay, Shachar and Sharan use the term *cognitive* for what I am calling *mental*. I avoid the former term because it suggests that thinking goes on without being anchored in feelings and social relations.

While this distribution is also true for the Middle Eastern students, this result is an ideological effect, discernible in students' language, of the cooperative classroom. Students can be habituated to ways of functioning that will not perpetuate the more extreme forms of individualism. Students, not just Western or white students, need to learn nonindividualist terms, perhaps to counter what is going on in other parts of society, but perhaps merely to have more helpful perspectives as they enter these parts.

Shachar and Sharan make the following claim for cooperative learning that is consistent with the writing and language use pedagogy discussed in this book:

> Classroom organization for cooperative learning in small groups, as well as the variables of group discourse and social interaction assessed in this study, constitute the most crucial means available to the educational enterprise for fostering students' academic, intellectual, and social development. It is becoming increasingly clear that educational settings do not take maximum advantage of these means for designing the process of learning, because they are largely focused on teaching (i.e., delivery of quantities of prescribed academic material to the students by the teacher) instead of expending their main efforts on assisting students to learn though inquiry, discourse, and cooperative interaction. (350)

These terms are similar to Pauly's. The administrative sense of the term *teaching* is the "delivery of . . . prescribed . . . material to students." To get beyond this practice "the most crucial means available" are classrooms that take advantage of their hitherto unrecognized phenomenology. In socially alert classrooms there are different groupings of students and teachers, close by, engaged in similar work, with knowledges and perspectives that will enhance everyone else's work. This is not just a process of getting students to help each other: it is getting students to learn to contribute to each other, to receive other students' contributions to their work, and to contribute to the work and thinking of supervisory figures like teachers and administrators. The classroom necessitates the recognition that any of its members can be resources for any other members.

There are specific forms of discursive evaluation that can become processes of mutual contribution that teach discipline in writing and language use. Before considering them, the following situation should be noted: teaching without grading has been done already, usually showing that there are virtually no ill effects and many good ones. But there remains much resistance to such changes. In the next section, I review some of the initiatives and the resistance to get a sense of the context in which the genres of evaluation would enter.

Doing Without and Resistance to Change

In spite of the historical momentum of testing and grading, these practices have been susceptible to change. In 1976, Sidney B. Simon and James A. Bellanca edited a comprehensive essay collection that appeared during the academic agitation of the late 1960s and early 1970s, when people were thinking about grades more than they are now.[7] This book reviews a wide range of factors affecting grading and many alternatives to grading. It indicates which schools have tried other forms of response to student work and accomplishment. It presents instances in which narrative/discursive evaluation or other forms of nongraded faculty reporting resulted in no reduction in the quality of the students' work, or in the frequency of their admission to colleges and professional schools. As the editors observe, the elimination of the grading culture is something everyone wants but "few initiate" (63). Here are instances of their findings.

In 1973 the few schools that did initiate such changes formed the National Consortium of Experimenting High Schools, which "surveyed 2600 two- and four-year colleges in the United States." As Richard Curwin reports,[8] here is the result:

> Ninety-seven percent replied to the questionnaire with results that surprised even the survey committee. Less than 5 percent indicated that grades or rank in class were an absolute necessity; 18 percent responded that the admissions office had no policy and could not promise fair review; 77 percent indicated that students whose transcripts provided other designated information would receive "fair and equal review." Written evaluation, computer-printed descriptions, and test scores topped the lists of needed information for four-year colleges. The vast majority of public two-year schools needed only a diploma, or a birth certificate showing the applicant to be at least 18 years old. Individual college responses are catalogued in the *College Guide for Experimenting High Schools*. (144–145)

Even though this survey is informal, the only feature of the responses that says tests are important is the reported use of standardized tests for admission to college. Putting that fact aside for a moment, the survey shows that grades and rank in class are not essential to most colleges, and that other faculty notations of a dis-

---

[7] Sidney B. Simon and James A. Bellanca, eds., *Degrading the Grading Myths: A Primer of Alternatives to Grades and Marks* (Washington, DC: Association for Supervision and Curriculum Development, 1976).

[8] Richard Curwin, "In Conclusion: Dispelling the Grading Myths," in *Degrading the Grading Myth*, ed. Sidney B. Simon and James A. Bellanca.

cursive sort are (or would be) more important to determine if an applicant is to be admitted. This fact suggests that if, in 1973, grading and class ranking had stopped in grades K–12, but the SAT had continued, by today colleges might be admitting a whole generation of students that had gone through school mainly under discursive evaluation practices. Colleges would have functioned just as well with only one test, as opposed to a whole school career record based on tests. As we know, secondary school testing, grading, and record keeping continued as usual.

Yet people are still thinking about how to solve the problems raised by testing and grading. A recent proposal by Karl Schilling and Karen Schilling to solve some of the problems of grading shows a local problem solved but replaced by one not much different, suggesting the proposers' implicit belief that testing and grading cannot be eliminated.[9] Like Henry Latham in England in 1877, Karl and Karen Schilling start with the problem of "cramming" in university courses. Students cram in order to demonstrate competence at the end of the course. The Schillings remind us how easily students forget the material of courses for which they have crammed, and how fully oriented they are to the use of the course's end to "prove" something to the faculty—and probably to other students—and then forget most of the experience. Here is the Schillings' solution:

> How might we signal students that education occurs in a continuum? Giving exams to students as they enter courses could serve this purpose, by providing an assessment of—and emphasis on—students' learning in previous courses. Indeed, one might imagine an "entrance-exam week" in which students would show that they had mastered the material necessary to enroll in subsequent courses. (A52)

What has changed? Will students *not* cram for these new exams that are supposed to show mastery in just the same sense as the current final exams are? In some subjects, like English and math, entrance exams are given now; students do not cram, but test givers say that both entrance and exit exams are needed for a true assessment. With the entrance exams, the final exams have been moved up to the next course. And what if there is no next course? For the majority of those trying to solve the grading problem, tinkering with the exam structure is the prevailing option, and there is no shortage of experiments by teachers in the giving of exams, including the very popular

---

[9] Karl L. Schilling and Karen Maitland Schilling, "Final Exams Discourage True Learning," *Chronicle of Higher Education*, February 2, 1994, A52.

take-home exam. All such tinkering retains the existing psychology of one-way learning: individual performance, judged by faculty and formally recorded by the administration, remains the legal tender of classroom pedagogy. This is still the main technique of motivating students to develop discipline.

Portfolio Evaluation

Portfolio evaluation, which was introduced in the teaching of writing in the 1970s, was intended to provide an evaluation practice that taught discipline without grading every piece of work by each student. We may briefly characterize portfolio evaluation as the attempt to understand students' (or faculty members', when they are reviewed) work in aggregate over the period of the course in which they are enrolled. The reviewer or committee of reviewers attempts to see a picture of development rather than judging individual pieces of work. The reviewer tries to discern patterns, styles, and the extent to which the student's "writerly" identity, as it gradually developed (as shown in the portfolio), relates to the student's classroom identity. In some cases, the portfolio is deliberately compiled by students at the end of the semester, including only the "best" work. This is often done if a grade is anticipated. If no grade is expected, the portfolio may be larger, in which case it provides a wider basis for a narrative or discursive evaluation, which is available to students in some schools. Since the use of portfolio evaluation started, there has been dispute over whether the individual teacher should grade the portfolio, or whether a committee of teachers unfamiliar with the writer should reach a consensus grade.

The use of portfolios began at the same time (more or less) as the process writing movement and the use of peer response in writing classes. The process writing approach took the emphasis off single grade judgments of a single text. It opened writing pedagogy in time and space, so to speak, providing a chance for cooperative classrooms to work in the teaching of writing. Attention to the process of writing demonstrated the collective character of writing and language use, and made it easier to include the results of collective effort in each student's portfolio. Practices of portfolio evaluation in schools and colleges nationally have shown how traditional grading and plenary (whole-class) teaching are part of the same teaching philosophy. If you teach the whole class all the time, you have to evaluate individuals; if you have different groups and collective work efforts, the emphasis may be more easily placed on the distinctiveness of the work each group produces; people's portfolios can contain work by coworkers in order to place the individual's work in an accurate context. Teachers' judging students' work takes place in local contexts, using standards of "local knowledge," and is related to needs, values, and purposes of local school and university situations as well as to the requirements of different disciplines.

To get a sense of how portfolio evaluation relates to the other prospective changes in the writing classrooms that have been mentioned, and also to see how portfolio approaches are being resisted, here are citations from two of Wendy Bishop's graduate students.[10] First, Steve:

> The portfolio system is not designed to check up on the TA's, it is designed to promote the concept of the TA as coach, not evaluator.[11] The place where this concept falls apart is that I grade all my papers, as do, I think, all or most of the other TA's. So the concept of TA as coach and peer can only go so far. And in any case, the TA has to give the final class grade.
>
> I cannot see any alternative to grading each particular paper. My students would go ape-s--- without grades. I will also admit that I would have trouble keeping track of how each student was doing in terms of final grade[s] without some sort of paper to paper grading system. (215)

Steve welcomes the relief that portfolio evaluation provides for him but feels he cannot meet his responsibility to the system. Here is the comment of another TA, Peg, in the pedagogy seminar described by Bishop:

> I am so pleased. Every one of my students got in his or her portfolio and arrived to class on time. What a wonderful feeling; I was so proud of them. . . .
>
> I read the midterm self-evaluations that they wrote in class yesterday. I'm impressed by the fact that they really do know what grade each of them probably deserves and will probably get. They all seemed very close. Some were a little harder on themselves than I would be. I think they're impressed with the work they've done. Some feel that their portfolio draft is the best paper they've ever written. Many of them were also actually surprised by the difference between the first rough draft and the portfolio draft. . . .
>
> Monday was a very good day. (215–216)

Although Bishop doesn't make this point explicitly, the two responses to portfolio evaluation might be gender-accented. Let me read them in a somewhat unorthodox way so that I can suggest that

---

[10] Wendy Bishop, "Going Up the Creek Without a Canoe: Using Portfolios to Train New Teachers," in *Portfolios: Process and Product,* ed. Pat Belanoff and Marcia Dickson (Portsmouth, NH:Boynton/Cook, 1991), 215–228.

[11] Should we writing teachers worry about Steve's comma splice in this sentence?

gendered values may play a role in the resistance to portfolio evaluation. Steve's comment concerned his sense of himself; Peg's described how the students felt. Steve commented on his responsibility to evaluate each paper. Peg commented on the students' evaluation of one another's essays. Steve reported on where the concept "falls apart" and does not announce his feelings; Peg, on the "wonderful feeling" she had as a result of her students' full participation and involvement. Steve is concerned with "keeping track" of the students; Peg, with the students being too hard on one another. Without trying to claim that anything has been proved, it seems fair to say that values of individualism teach Steve to suspect portfolio evaluation. Cooperative and interpersonal priorities teach Peg to welcome portfolio evaluation.

In an essay in the same volume, Cherryl Armstrong Smith's argument for writing without testing[12] cites three "questions repeatedly . . . asked about portfolios at my university": plagiarism, students' independent performance, and consistent standards. She characterizes these questions as all raising "issues of authority and control. They are not questions about whether or not we are actually measuring writing abilities" (287). The challenge to portfolio evaluation is whether someone is controlling what the students do. Authority and control are needed to enact ideals of the individual pursuit of excellence: in academic work one must succeed without help, covert or overt, from others, and competing with them; excellence is "measured" quantitatively and is determined by a victory of the highest scores over the lower ones. Smith rejects "ranking writing" and advocates the abandonment of exit testing altogether:

> The subtext of the three questions I found most frequently asked about portfolios seems to be that the purpose of exit testing is to provide an external, higher authority to check up on teachers or to check up on students. . . . By using portfolios but abandoning exit tests in writing programs, we would acknowledge that teachers are authorities about the work taking place in their own classrooms, that collaboration encourages the development of writing ability and of effective teaching, and that learning to write is not a matter of passing tests but is a lifelong process. (291)

Smith identifies and explains the point raised by Steve in his journal entry: he understood that the portfolio system was "not designed" to check up on teachers. But he did not write that it is

---

[12] Cherryl Armstrong Smith, "Writing Without Testing," in *Portfolios: Process and Product,* ed. Pat Belanoff and Marcia Dickson (Portsmouth, NH: Boynton/Cook, 1991), 279–292.

meant to function in a philosophy of cooperative writing pedagogy. Steve, in his comments, did not relate the use of portfolios to questions of fundamental pedagogical approaches. In addition, he did not feel that the use of portfolios addressed his own teaching philosophy: it was only a pragmatic issue for him. He reports in the same passage that he cannot see how his own responsibilities would be met without going through the traditional one-to-one grading process, and that he guesses that his students would be completely disoriented if he did not. The use of portfolios as being a part of a different pedagogical paradigm is not visible to Steve and to many others who use it. However, in the present context, I am moving the practice of portfolio evaluation that began in a traditional teaching philosophy into a comprehensively different way of approaching writing and language use as an academic subject and as a discipline that makes use of fundamental changes in postsecondary teaching.

Even though people (myself among them) give grades to total portfolios as a reasonable first step away from constant judging and grading, discursive portfolio evaluation is in a different pedagogical world from that of individual per-essay grading. Steve's disorientation comes from his experience of incommensurability as well as his gender-identity-influenced tendency toward the traditional deployment of classroom authority and control, which he describes as "keeping track" of the work of each student. In fact, Steve felt that regardless of the new space opened up by a portfolio approach, he must finally return to the style of "responsible" teaching in which the teacher has a dyadic relationship with each student and where grades are assigned per student in comparison with one another (de facto competition). In spite of his perception of the lack of checking up, he does *not* accord it enough importance to have it imply that, perhaps, he must *not* finally return to the authoritative giving of the grade. This happens partly because ideology cannot be taught or inculcated directly. Whatever Steve may learn ideologically must be the result of his learning from his own work environment, which may include peers, teachers, students, university rules, everything that reflects ideological identification. Seen otherwise, Steve's political position now prevents him from overtaking, in its philosophical novelty, what Bishop brought to the class. His achievement has been mainly to acknowledge more than one view: "I felt lucky to have instructors/mentors that *do not* have the same views. I figure a good balance can be struck" (Bishop, 224). In a sense, he does not wish to acknowledge that he is the "authority about the work taking place in his own classroom," preferring instead to enact the received standard through the grade.

Peg does not report a divided frame of mind. She expresses support for the portfolio system and for its collective oversight: a team of readers, the TAs and two faculty members, judged each portfolio for pass or not-pass status. Her remarks suggest that she views the changes brought by portfolio evaluation to classroom social relations without a sense of contradiction or underlying pedagogical dissonance. Because of the collective approach to grading, where grades were discussed by three people before being assigned, Peg had no problem leaving the traditional grading style behind. While grading still depends on and leads to ranking the students, the cooperative social relations of the class overrode this factor for her, and she reported achieving complete success in terms of the work being completed by all the students.

Peg's political perspective and position seemed already to have been receptive to process teaching and portfolio evaluation. As suggested earlier, these practices may be gender-affiliated. She is already student-oriented; or perhaps, she already thinks of herself as part of a collective scene, someone responsible not to "keep track" of others, but, in a spirit of socially oriented teaching, for their comfort and sense of accomplishment as students. She felt responsible for the subjective welfare of the students rather than for a complete account of their performance.

Discursive Evaluation

Students who have been rewarded by learning according to one teacher's standard are surprised when their adherence to that standard in another class is criticized or penalized.[13] Regardless of what individual teachers do about grading, students are penalized by a universal grading scale because different teachers necessarily have different standards and priorities for what should be achieved by students. Without the intrusion of ranked grading, different teachers' standards would teach students openly that what counts as achievement is tied to the status of the subject matter and to the reading of that subject matter by individual teachers. Different stan-

---

[13] Students are often set back in college when, as they move from teacher to teacher, each teacher has different scales of evaluation. This happens all the time. It is not faced because one either has to adopt a completely rigid standard or one has to abandon the letter grade system. Since few want either of these alternatives, the system continues to function without trying to help the students who are less adept at "psyching out" the teachers than at learning material independently of the teachers' specific orientations.

dards are already there (students know), but grading obscures the pedagogical value of these differences. Classification of students into achievement tracks uses the identical letter scale in every subject for every teacher in every school. This practice does not give accurate, appropriate credit to a student who does very well in one subject and very poorly in another, for example. The GPA[14] of that student is low compared to that of the "all-purpose" student who has a GPA close to the maximum. Is it the case that in order to be a good student one has to excel in all subjects?

The practice of discursive evaluation has existed as long as grading has, in the genres of the comment, narrative, description, remark, letter, or conversation of recommendation. Alongside scalar grading discursive evaluation usually plays a secondary role, as it does on the report cards of some primary school systems. As students move farther along in school, discursive evaluation plays an increasingly important part. To get into college, recommendations are secondary to standardized test scores and to high school grade averages; but the recommendations can determine a student's fate if the other materials don't yield a clear decision. In high school and in college, discursive evaluation usually appears on all essays students write—sometimes to justify a letter grade, sometimes by itself. Increasingly, portfolios are given discursive evaluations. As e-mail proliferates, it is becoming more frequent for informal discursive evaluations to be passed along by teachers, with the mail situation facilitating students' answers—that is, conversations between students and teachers about the work. In graduate school, some faculty members give students long commentaries on their work. Often these commentaries justify grades. But just as often, since the grades do not vary much, the commentary/evaluation assumes a more important role. In some programs, there are files of faculty comments on students' work. Finally, as graduate students seek employment as faculty members, the salient element (after the students' dissertations) is the dossier file with the students' letters of recommendation. Businesses also use discursive evaluation for their employees and for their own performance; they also often display evaluative notices given by customers—testimonials in order to promote the business. As this brief review suggests, discursive

---

[14] The GPA has a derivation similar to that of IQ testing, Gould's critique of which was mentioned in Chapter 7. It is a single factor that falsely fixes a student's capability in the eyes of others and often in the student's own eyes. While sometimes other measures (like the GRE examination) offset the GPA, the latter number always has to be explained and justified. A narrative provides comment that is neither explanation nor justification.

evaluation has always been considered an important part of the teaching, certification, and public accountability processes, and offering such evaluations is not new or revolutionary.

Discursive evaluation is a form of disclosure. It is kept in a secondary position *because* it is a form of disclosure. In a sense, discursive evaluation is marginalized as groups of people are—kept in certain places and not permitted to grow. The conflict between grade or quantitative evaluation and discursive evaluation is not unlike the "battle of the sexes": easy to joke about, to become amused about, but underneath reflecting a profound unfairness in society that requires correction. Lately, different kinds of disclosure—the study of previously censored or unread literatures and cultures, for example—have ameliorated other areas of academic work and society.[15] Curricula have come to include political critiques of science, intellectual life, and society. One of the bases of these changes has been the steady, scholarly disclosure of facts previously censored, such as the extent of the history of slavery; the routine use of sadistic violence and local terror; the domination of women and children; the roles of luck, guessing, and power in the practice of science; the domination of nontechnological societies by those with wealth and material, and so on.

Discursive evaluation is a way of telling more of the stories about teaching and learning, more of what happens in classrooms, more of what students think and hope for, than the present systems of mutual grading. To admit discursive evaluation to the contexts of mutual judgment is to transform judgment into conversational styles, to transform binding judgments into opinions that can be answered, to transform categories such as passing and failing into ground for negotiation and change, and especially into a means of getting more people working toward fulfilling lives. Many discursive evaluations are part of teaching because they provide information and opinion in statements that ground the opinion and contextualize the information. The result is the removal of fear from the context of evaluation: one can reason with it, so to speak. Fear is and has been an internalized representation of the power held by society over its young and unprivileged majorities.[16] Historically,

---

[15] Though one can easily believe that society could change back to its old ways quite easily.

[16] Judith Fetterley, in the preface to *The Resisting Reader* (Bloomington: Indiana University Press, 1978), notes that "*fear* and *fear* and *fear*" has kept women from knowing enough to take political initiatives.

fear of more powerful elements of society has kept the less powerful from enhancing their lives. Because such fears are felt in school, to advocate discursive evaluation is to teach ourselves not to fear ourselves and to inform accurately and early what needs to be feared in school and society. Tests and grades in school function as instruments of control, exclusion, and suppression. They are means to substitute a "last word" from above for negotiation, judgment for discussion, inertia for change.

The grading discussions of the 1960s[17] had a political foundation: the opposition to the war in Vietnam, which was considered to be a resurgence of imperial ruthlessness. There were daily visual reminders that this was the case: bombings, massacres, and the corruption of our own soldiers. The objections to power that then surfaced on campuses were rooted in the objections to the exercise of military power. The destructiveness of our own military power was disclosed to a generation that had previously understood this power in acceptable senses—its victories over Germany and Japan. On campus, it was understood that universities collaborated with government and military institutions.[18] The students' lives were jeopardized by the prospect of being drafted to fight an unjust war. "Student power" was directed toward preserving their lives and restoring America's good name. The 1960s critique of grading appeared in the foregoing circumstances. The advocacy of discursive evaluation at that time had an immediate purpose as well as a traditional purpose.

Because of the political content of the 1960s critiques, Max Marshall's *Teaching Without Grades* (1968)[19] is conspicuous in that it does not mention that context. Also interesting is that Marshall taught biology rather than English or another humanities subject. That this book should appear without reference to its political context suggests that there was a temporary breach in the traditional

---

[17] Earlier in this century, John Dewey and other advocates of progressive education discussed similar ideals that, in spite of their wide dissemination, had little effect on how most students were being schooled in the United States.

[18] In the 1960s, I was at Indiana University and was surprised to learn that faculty members were on the payroll of the Central Intelligence Agency.

[19] Max Marshall, *Teaching Without Grades* (Corvallis: Oregon State University Press, 1968). Many who have studied grades conducted complex surveys and showed many tables and details. The upshot of these studies has been, consistently, that college admissions, professional school admissions, and most other situations do not need the grade point average for each student: discursive documentation makes the case helpfully.

school ideology and that Marshall could be credible to argue formally a perspective he had been enacting behind the closed doors of his classrooms for many years. His book, however, is rarely cited in other studies of grades.[20] Here are his main proposals:

> The principles established are substantially two. First, the grading system, including most suggested substitutes because they also use symbols or words which rank students relative to one another can be replaced only by attaining a clean break, a genuine nongrading concept. Second, it is possible during most days with classes to ignore relative appraisal altogether, and when called upon to do so, to replace it with the pertinent description based on salient or outstanding features. (132–133)

This statement identifies fundamental aspects of the grading issue: a "genuine nongrading concept" can be accepted if, on a daily basis in classrooms, the habits of hierarchical evaluation (ranking) are abandoned and the habits of description are used. Marshall observes, "Description is subjective. Grades are more so" (142). The advantage of description over grades is that description identifies biases and perspectives as well as items in both students' and teachers' work. Description can disclose elements that are censored in a grading system, and its use encourages mutuality in the relationships between teachers and students. It is harder than grading, but it is a part of teaching and not of administration.

Description as a feature of responses to teaching and learning leads, toward the end of the classroom relationships, to comprehensive summaries of students' work after a course, a year, or other period, as discussed by James Battersby,[21] who proposes:

> an evaluation system based on written reports for each student in each class. These reports would form the substance of the students' academic records and would be the principal resource of reviewers responsible for making probability judgments. (35)

Battersby's report system is accompanied by a credit/no-record choice for each course taken. In large lectures, the reports are written by the teaching assistants who have contact with the stu-

---

[20] It has a similar status to Edward Pauly's *The Classroom Crucible* (1990) today: it speaks from the practical experience of teaching, announcing facts about classrooms and schools that, if taken seriously, would demonstrate the uncomprehending treatment of schools by federal and state agencies.

[21] James Battersby, *Typical Folly: Evaluating Student Performance in Higher Education,* (Urbana, IL: National Council of Teachers of English, 1973).

dents rather than by lecturers who don't. Battersby is an English teacher, but his proposals are identical to Marshall's, as are his justifications:

> Although written reports do not guarantee the emergence of valid types [of performance by students], they at least make real confusion accessible and provide information infinitely more valuable than grades, national test scores, letters of recommendation, and so forth, since they disclose what criteria of evaluation are being applied to what material. Rejuvenated interest in academic subjects, emotional problems, financial shortages, new insights, etc., can all subvert established and characteristic tendencies and instigate the development of new performance possibilities, but the detailed accounts of realized academic achievement, for all their inherent shortcomings, are best equipped to handle the complex problems involved in the process of evaluation. (39–40)

Every teacher knows the variety of reasons that account for students' achievements in school. Part of the continuing frustration with grading is teachers' feelings that the truth about students cannot be recorded: students cannot be recognized accurately by their records, nor can the next teachers they get discern what help students may need. The fact remains that discursive evaluation, per assignment or per course, or per yearlong performance, of students, of teachers, and of administrators has a chance of contributing to the growth processes of teaching and learning in schools. The processes of competitive grading perpetuate prescriptive control of teaching by administrations, school systems, boards of trustees.

Mutual and Self-Evaluation

The problems with grading are created by the institutionalized separation of evaluation from teaching. This separation creates the teachers' conflict of interest—teachers serving two constituencies who don't have the same interests. Teaching language use, writing, and discipline without conflict for teachers or unwelcome oversight for students depends on our being able to install the social processes and genres of self- and mutual evaluation into the curriculum. Some have taken the genre of reflective writing, a common form in autobiography and memoir writing, to contribute to this goal. Self-analytical reflective writing has been urged for the cover letters of portfolios, where it becomes a student's self-disclosing guide to a teacher's review of the student's collection of writings.

Laurel Black[22] observes that reflective writing poses a problem within the grading system:

> In honest reflection, I may come to some conclusions about my writing—the effort I'm willing to put in under the circumstances, my abilities or experience, or even the honesty of my work (perhaps I bent the truth a little to make a piece funnier or more poignant). But if my audience is my teacher and my teacher is grading my work, how honestly and deeply will I be willing to reflect? (15)

As Black explains this problem, students can "suck up" to the teacher or be more candid and fail to "make us feel good about ourselves," thus creating for students "the danger of being disliked." Black wonders "if it is possible for a student to write reflectively for a portfolio developed in a classroom context and not in some way evaluate me and/or the class as whole" (16).

Black wants to integrate evaluation into involved, responsive pedagogy. If the grading system changed, the consequences of disliking students and of being disliked can become part of the curriculum, and not a danger that is out of the teachers' and students' control. Perhaps Michael Prince's proposal in relation to the use of genre, discussed at the end of Chapter 2, is in a similar predicament: the progressive proposal takes place in an administrative, bureaucratic structure that discredits it. To forestall administrative oversight, reflection, cover letters, and other genres that presuppose the exchange of views between students and teachers can be shared with other students; similarly teachers can share their responses to one student with other students. This practice can reduce or eliminate the dangers Black describes. It would be hard to "suck up" to the teacher if other students were reading the reflection. Similarly, it would be hard to be irresponsibly critical if other students were reading. The collective audience for reflective writing disciplines the writer to solve the several political problems that that genre poses. But it still requires a change in administrative policy for it to "count."

If there were no grades, classrooms could be enhanced by reflective writing becoming part of the course evaluation. It would be desirable, wouldn't it, for evaluations to be shared and for self-evaluation also to become course evaluations? These new genres, like others in the course, can be taken up by students and teachers as part of a contingent curriculum. We would like to involve the col-

---

[22] Laurel Black, "Some Thoughts on Writing and Reading Reflectively: Benefits, Problems, Suggestions," unpublished manuscript, May 1997.

lective circumstance of classrooms to discipline the writing, to provide evaluative comment for teachers and students, and to utilize this genre to replace the process of hierarchical grading and ranking.

Many cooperative classrooms provide instances that show how classes proceed when reflective writing "opens up" the genres under study, by mixing in reflection with more declarative, expository genres. Introducing more supple genres of mutual and self-evaluation permits students to share the custody of their courses. Conversely, sharing custody of courses encourages the integration of the evaluative processes into the curriculum. This style of teaching is more time-consuming than others.[23] A practical structure for students' custody has to be brought into classes for such an approach to take root, to establish itself as a visible choice for post-secondary teaching.

Students' custody of courses can take several forms, some of which are familiar to us from when they spontaneously overtake discussion and lead it toward unexpected thoughts. Less frequent are occasions where students can plan essays, reports, and collective approaches to a subject or a writing project that they defined or have gotten from other students. However, teachers can anticipate and cultivate students' motivation to take the initiative by establishing courses that are oriented toward the principle of pursuing the issues that follow from one's interests. Several instances of such attempts are reported by Alison Warriner in a recent essay,[24] whose purposes were both to describe how student-run classes worked and to report that success was achieved despite her own and the students' doubts that discipline would be maintained under such circumstances. Warriner observes that discipline and involvement were enhanced as compared to conventional courses:

> My impression is that students had better classroom experiences because of the following: they consistently *did* all the reading . . . they read more carefully because they *wanted* to be included in the discussions; they wrote more than other students I have taught . . . attendance was the best I've seen. . . . Their enjoyment is linked less to my influence than to their discoveries of their own knowledge and ability. (338)

---

[23] I defer to "More Forethoughts" the discussion of what that implies: among other things, that tenure has to be possible on the basis of this enhanced teaching technique. This issue involves considering the degree to which school is training for something else and the degree to which it is the place to find firm roots in self-discipline for vocational commitment, for finding a calling rather than only a job.

[24] Alison Warriner, "'I Didn't Think They Had It in Them,' Students Learning from Students," *Journal of Advanced Composition* 16 (no. 2, 1996), 325–340.

From reflection on situations such as Warriner's, even if the statistical n is small and the context narrow, it is plausible to claim that discipline in writing and language use can be taught more reliably by integrating the responsibility for the substance and quality of the course into the curriculum. This means that evaluations of work are necessarily self- and mutual evaluations.[25]

The following are examples of evaluative interchanges that could replace the ritualized judgments and letters of transit we now use. Following Warriner's example, Mary R. Boland taught a writing seminar called "Stories from the Law," in which the students became self-evaluators.[26] The self- and course evaluation were combined in the portfolio cover letter and labeled "final assignment." Here is the prompt:

> I'd like for you to evaluate your own work in this class. . . . The way I see it, you have certain insights into this that I don't have. . . . You could include:
>
> - a discussion of your group work and presentation preparation. What type of experience was that? For those who collaborated and led class for more than one day, what type of post-class analysis did you do to prepare for the next class? . . .
> - a discussion of your writing during this semester. Looking over everything you've written, what do you notice about your own writing? Has anything changed in terms of either how you write or how you feel about writing since the beginning of the semester? Did you try anything new or experimental? . . .
>
> Another possibility might be to consider whether this class has helped you to experience language use any differently or more consciously than before. Given that our goal wasn't simply to argue

---

[25] In Warriner's courses, the grading was negotiated. Students and teacher both graded the students, while a negotiation process worked out differences of judgment. This is one possible solution to the grading burden. But it is still not my solution, as it continues to teach students evaluation through a hierarchical scale, which is the value that teaches competition, rather than cooperation, in the matter of learning things. Obviously, this feature of Warriner's courses reflects her working conditions, as does Mary Boland's grading policy, discussed shortly. Those of us who work in schools that have no grading latitude cannot refuse to grade without endangering the very situation that permits us to try out and establish new initiatives. For us to refuse would be to risk leaving the search for realistic forms of postsecondary evaluation. I am going against my own values, letting students feel competitive, when I use the A/B grading system for undergraduate courses.

[26] This course took place in a traditional grading system, but used the A/B system: B for doing all the work and attending class conscientiously; A for some form of achievement as noted in advance by the teacher. No individual work was graded; only the final portfolios were the basis for the students' final grades, given by Boland. Self-evaluation was a kind of writing included in the final portfolio, which Boland alone evaluated.

issues but to see how they are built in the language that we use, do you feel like your understanding of an issue has changed or deepened? Can you identify any particular classes that your peers ran that seemed to promote this for you? What about those discussions triggered a response from you? (If you don't think that your sensitivity to language changed in any way, that might be something to explore also . . .) . . .

I'd also appreciate it if you'd take the time to evaluate this course and give me some feedback. Again, I'm interested in hearing anything you'd like to say. I'm offering this course again this summer, so I'd especially like to consider your thoughts in relation to preparing for that class.

The cover letter requires a prompt because portfolio contents vary with the individual class.

In the foregoing text, several items should be noted: (1) the teacher's usual assumption that she directs the class; (2) its presentation in the subjunctive mood; (3) its interrogative component; (4) its expectation that the teacher will learn something new from what the students report; (5) the teacher's self-inscription in the cover letter situation.

1. "I'd like for you to" is to be understood partly in its literal sense and partly in its directive sense—"this is what I think should be done." The students may decide to decline this opportunity. The veracity of the teacher's "I'd like" also depends on how previously in the class the teacher used this phrase or similar ones. Because the class started with a genuine division of responsibility,[27] the students had a wide range of choice where what the teacher "would like" was not understood as an implied requirement. The character of leadership is changed in the course structure by reducing the scope of teachers' direct responsibility. The absolute control of the individualistic, graded class is a more contingent and shared form of control with regard to evaluation. If a grade must be assigned in this situation, only the teacher can do it;[28] but if a grade does not have to be assigned, the students' discursive opinions can be presented alongside the teacher's. Third parties can see both.

---

[27] Following Warriner, Boland stipulated the topic, "Stories from the Law," and then offered several subtopics that could be explored. Student groups each picked topics for their exploration and gave the rest of the class assignments for those topics. Thus, a series of student groups ran the course, while the teacher helped out by providing readings and suggestions.

[28] This is the case in this course, but on the A/B system: the teacher gave only A or B once, at the end of the course, and only she was the responsible party.

2. The subjunctive mood: "could include." This grammatical usage, if taken literally, transfers the responsibility of what to say in an evaluation to the students. Teachers often list as possibilities items that are actually expected to appear. In this case, while Boland is teaching the students what kinds of things might appear in a cover letter of evaluation, she also teaches that thoughts she does not anticipate belong in the evaluation too. Related subjunctive usages include "what would you do differently" and "another possibility might be." In a more traditionally structured class, the subjunctive is diplomatic; but here, where there has been a history of choice, the subjunctive can behave more literally and thus provide the additional security of guidance without coercion.

3. The interrogative. Both the mood and the questions themselves are open-ended. These are true (as opposed to rhetorical) questions, for example, "What do you notice about your own writing?" The interrogatives continue the style of investigative interrogation used in the course already: what do you notice about this or that usage of legal language or language in legal situations? Much of the teaching is done here in the interrogative, but with the same proviso: the teacher does not already have the answer. This teacher's skill is to ask the question that will prompt the desire to know as opposed to the desire to please. There is no guarantee that that will happen on any one occasion, but unless it is started, it will never happen. To pose such questions, rather than to create tense Socratic exchanges that are covertly authoritarian, is a change in direction for academic teaching philosophy.

4. The teacher's expectation to learn: "certain insights . . . that I don't have." This statement gets its credibility from what has already taken place in the course—the students' exercise of an independent perspective. By placing the evaluation process into the same inquiry style of the rest of the course, the teacher validates the previously given claims that students' experiences are going to change what everyone learns in the course. The students' perspectives on themselves, one another, and the teacher already contributed to everyone else's acquisition of knowledge about the substance of the course—language use and writing and how to evaluate it. The evaluation forum continues the styles of exchange already established.

5. The teacher's self-inscription: "I'm interested in hearing" (because I want advice for next time). This too is authenticated by previous self-inscriptions in the course. The teacher has persuaded the students that she wants to hear their thoughts in a

sense different from hearing that they are performing well as students. This posture is perhaps the most challenging to traditional discourse styles in postsecondary classrooms. It requires teachers to develop new bases for listening to the students from the beginning of the course. With class members' habits of disclosure of membership and experience, teachers can believe that students teach on the same basis as do teachers: they have perspectives and experiences that the teachers don't have. Disclosure inserts these perspectives into classroom exchanges and builds up their authority as the course progresses.

The ideal of mutuality in teaching applies to the substance of courses in writing and language use. For this sense to stick—for these courses to teach the mutuality of writing and language use—it cannot be revoked by the prospect of closure judgment or by the supervention of the students' motive to "get an A," a respectable motive in a grading system, as one student put it in her cover letter:

> I would like to say and truly believe that grades are meaningless to me. What one makes of life is not found in a letter grade. However, grades are important to me. I like to know how I am doing. I will not lie to you or myself.

As with this course, an "important" grade appears in every other course, and the student is thrown back on herself and her own ideals for achievement, continuing the separation of mutual teaching/learning from individual achievement. Mutuality is part of the subject matter of writing and language use, and can easily be part of the process of evaluation, as it takes place among students in groups and through continuing exchanges between teachers and students. Mutuality within a nongraded course system leads to self-evaluations that are not marked by the quiet desire to please, but by an overt desire to hear from someone experienced and interested.

Cooperative work and mutual evaluation lead to self-evaluations such as this, which appeared in Ms. Boland's course:

> Considering my writing . . . I notice various items. First, I have gotten looser in my interpretation of assignments. I was always pretty rigid in following directions, but the class offered me the chance to open up and explore a bit more, which I really enjoyed. Also, I found that my interpretation of an assignment often differed from the norm, which was not only interesting but informative. I found that I enjoy writing about unique events, or even writing uniquely about everyday events. I like finding a twist to the assignment or adding one of my own. This made writing some of my papers very interesting this semester. I don't think I accomplished very much in terms of the complexity of my writing. We were given such free rein, that I didn't feel that everlasting need to use description to the

max, or to follow every point through to the end. It was, in fact, fun to just write what came to me. One point I'd like to stress is that I never wrote a paper with a certain length in mind . . . without these limits, I can explore the subject a bit more.

This statement describes Ms. L's responses to the latitude of the assignments. One of her keynotes is enjoyment and the unexpected developments that come from comparison of her own readings of the assignments, which were given by each group to the class as a whole, with "the norm." In a noncooperative class, such comparisons are not made; in this class, the comparisons themselves were the common feature. Ms. L's enjoyment was occasioned by the removal of strict constraints, which encouraged her to understand better the relation of her work and thinking to that of others.

Ms. L says that she did not "accomplish very much" in developing the complexity of her writing because of the "free rein." But she attributes her relief at this situation to the removal of the "everlasting need to use description to the max." The course reduced the sense of extremism that usually characterizes the pressure undergraduates feel to excel—"to follow every point through to the end." This upper-level student has stepped out of the grade-motivated pressure into the more relaxed situation in which comparisons between one's own work and that of other students are not competitive. The salutary results in this course that studies language use are also described in her cover letter, as she continues:

I am definitely more aware of language, although probably not in the manner you would expect. I am a lot more aware of people's sensitivities regarding touchy subjects. For example, today Mr. B talked about the "apathy, the laziness and unwillingness to learn" he witnessed in black people in his high school, but then added a little disclaimer about how he really had no idea of how the inner city high schools are. I found this to be a veiled insult. What he said made many people in the class angry. Even the usually placid Ms. R shot a glare in Mr. B's direction. I found that the "disclaimer" may not have been intentional. From Mr. B's language, he just sounded naive and ignorant. However, he also sounded very insensitive, and did not seem to realize the impact his language had on people. When I make statements in this class, I try very hard to show where my point of view is coming from, and I never generalize. I learned this the hard way; in fact, I learned from my self-humiliation that first day when I made a rash judgment about you. God, what a stupid thing to say. In terms of language, however, I feel that I have a better grasp of how the law incorporates language into its documents. I like the document that Mr. J wrote up, because we were able to tear it apart. That is not to insult Mr. J;

rather it is meant as a compliment to the class. While the paper Mr.
J wrote had been relatively well thought-out, we were able to pick
his language apart and look more objectively at the issue of homosexual discrimination.

A salient aspect of this paragraph is Ms. L's placing her own "insensitive" statement with her discussion of her observation of it in Mr.
B. What was given as a first response to her perception of the teacher
now looks like a disclosure of a learning process. In this cover letter,
Ms. L's writing is a discourse of self-inclusion, which encourages the
back-and-forth between her perspective and her judgments of what
others are writing. While I did not cite what Mr. J wrote, Ms. L's
"self-humiliation" helps us to read sympathetically her reports of
the class' "picking apart" Mr. J's language: she presents as one who
had something to learn from the collective analysis. In addition her
sense of deficit with regard to perceiving the teacher may also be
juxtaposed with her confidence regarding perceiving students. Her
picture is many-sided. She is confident but not smug. Because of her
disclosures, she is helping to define a more supple genre for students
to use in writing about their own experience and, continuously, in
writing evaluations of self and others.

Her last paragraph also makes these points:

> In general,[29] I genuinely enjoyed this course. It was such a breath
> of fresh air compared to the stale lectures given by fat, pompous,
> uncaring men in front of a lecture hall of two hundred students. I
> truly admire your ability to let the students take over—I think
> that's a good way to bring out our true personalities (wasn't it hard
> getting to know me? :)) I also liked the comments received on every
> paper. It not only gave us the impression that you truly cared about
> our writing, but it gave us the necessary feedback needed to better
> our writing. I think the presentations were a good idea—communi-
> cation of any form can always use some work. Lastly, I think it's
> really nice of you to offer breakfast on the last day of class. I feel
> like I really got to know some of the people in this class well, and
> this homey touch is really appreciated.

Ms. L places this course in the context of others she has taken as an
undergraduate: "stale lectures," "fat, pompous, uncaring men."
These comments apply to what is happening in the university community, but also to the wider context in society in which this course

---

[29] Remember: "I never generalize." But, "A foolish consistency is the hobgoblin of
little minds." It seems clear that there is a reason only to note Ms. L's distinction
between the two kinds of generalization, something that might be mentioned for
further reflection.

appears: gender inequity. This topic appeared repeatedly in this
course, whose "stories from the law" were about injustice along
these and related lines. Ms. L, in this genre of evaluation, estab-
lishes a circle connecting this course's atmosphere, the college experience, and its having been skewed by the inequities in society
studied in this course. Ms. L emphasizes the contrast between the
personal involvement of this teacher with the self-absorption of
male teachers whose teaching was one-way conversation—lectures.
A realistic touch is offered by the adjective *fat* in her description of
the men, a term whose political incorrectness in this case helps to
authenticate the heartbeat in the cover letter as a whole.[30] Ms. L is a
partisan of the issues of this course, which permitted the appropriate disclosure of this membership and provided space for the development of genres of language use (oral presentations included) that
would render this feature of her identity a topic of interest for other
class members.

Genres of Discipline

When evaluation genres are part of the curriculum, discipline is cul-
tivated by the processes of reflection. Boland's prompt and Ms. L's
cover letter might be construed as the relaxation of discipline, when
in each case they express an access of it. Boland presents the discipline of self-restraint that comes from deciding that the students
will be heard from. Deciding. Because a decision has to be taken, it
is an act of discipline. The "default case" in teaching is for the
teacher to talk, the students to listen, and the teacher to check to see
if they listened. In Warriner's and Boland's classes this is no longer
the default case, and it took some doing, including a great deal of
extra time, to exercise the discipline of establishing viable techniques for listening to the students. Because this took place during
the semester, the scene of evaluation looks relaxed and uncoerced,
which is greatly to be desired.

The discipline modeled by Ms. L is her decision to move back
and forth between self and colleagues, between errors and achievements, between other courses and this one, between other teachers
and this one. Again this must be a decision and not a default statement. To exercise discipline in writing is to stop pretending that the

---

[30] It is not mentioned in this letter, but this looks like an allusion to society's
permitting men to be overweight as contrasted with society's "slim" standard for
women.

audience is "impersonal." The course helped this discipline along by stipulating that groups of students would assign, read, and discuss other students' work. Class members began using multiple perspectives to read the work of others as a consequence of the cooperative basis for work. Gradually, as suggested by Ms. L's cover letter, perspectives of others are taken into account in substantive ways rather than cited as sources or as parallel efforts. Readers and writers are influenced by the action of cohort groups (who, in this case, gave assignments to the class), by the teacher, and by some of the movements of the plenary class discussions. Students developed habits of speaking and writing as if real people, with stakes in what is said and written, are going to respond. The discipline developed in this and in similar courses derives from an enactment of the materiality of language. Finally, by integrating and adapting the genres of evaluation to the curriculum, the class has made a decisive use of the materiality of language to achieve custody of the course and has begun to benefit from it.

More Forethoughts

Materiality, Motivation, Mothering, and Money

Materiality

There is a movement of reference, made by Mary Boland's course and reflected in Ms. L's and other students' portfolio cover letters (see Chapter 8), circulating through personal experience, the community of the course, the action of the teacher, the style of university functioning, and the conditions in society. This course, Ms. L's letter suggests, was addressed to the constituencies served by most writing programs, as outlined in the Forethoughts section of this book.

Like Linda Brodkey's new readings of the classrooms she observed, my review of Ms. L's letter helps to change the address of the letter and thereby its genre. I have enlarged the social scene of the letter from Boland's class to include the readers of this work. But I also include, in principle, other students, graduate students, university communities, and the public. The principle of the materiality of language means that because uses of language are parts of a social scene, the teaching of writing and language use has to reflect awareness of the scene's subcontexts. The discussions in this book speak to this point. The constituencies I identified are also scenes of the teaching of writing and language use; focusing on one scene asks us to understand it by remembering how others play a role in it. In the same sense that the principle of materiality joins evaluation with pedagogy, it reminds us that the constituencies interested in the pedagogy of writing and language use are connected to one another.

Motivation

The practice of GWSI (Generalized Writing Skills Instruction) supplies students with motives for learning: the need to master technical competence and all-purpose fluency. The effort of this book has been to replace these supplied motives with a pedagogical policy that considers the motivation for writing before the curriculum is fixed.

Included in the projected motives of GWSI are measurable technical competences achieved through training or exercise: proper use of documentation, proper use of rhetorical formulas, prudent consultation of reference works such as handbooks, dictionaries, thesauruses, and so on. These competences can be separated from interactive teaching, fixed, defined bureaucratically, tested, and recorded mechanically. They are susceptible, often, of "relentless drill" (see Chapter 2), the advocates of which view these competences to be the foundation of postsecondary writing courses. These skills were said to be the ingredients of the "product" of writing, the competently prepared text or essay. The last century of writing pedagogy was "product" oriented; it then changed in the 1960s toward "rhetoric" and "process" orientation, and then toward recognizing the political and contingent features of language use and writing. Because of the military, technological, and corporate ideals of fast results and favorable "bottom lines," however, the "product" mores of GWSI have not substantially changed; they are tied to the foregoing stronger nonpedagogical values and ideologies that are governing society. One result of this inertia is the repeated searches for the right formula that will solve the conundrum of writing pedagogy and turn out "good writers" fast.[1]

The teaching of writing and language use as I have discussed it is addressed toward motivations of students of the subject. I am not using the term *motivation* in an exclusively psychological sense. It refers as much to interests in the collective sense as it does to individual ideals and desires. The term also refers to individual and collective needs: in teaching through disclosure, genre, and membership, we consciously try to conceptualize what people want and need to know (including what may be expected by other teachers) as derived from the situation they bring to class. We understand language use and writing to be "in effect" in their and our lives at every moment. The first pedagogical task is to discern where we as teachers will begin to address the issues that appear to us through the classrooms'

---

[1] When I was in graduate school, the formula was "voice and tone"; later it was "expository writing"; now it is "argument."

changing populations. We consider what "living" matters should be used at this moment to create our contingent curricula. To orient ourselves around motivation is to try to discern what is "on the minds" of those in our classrooms and to conceive courses, write assignments, contribute writing in the service of what matters to students and to us. When "products"—texts, presentations, speeches, and other material language entities—appear, they then are read in their living form as aspects of subjective and intersubjective motivation.

Mothering

How should teachers view students in order to make it appealing to share and explore motivations? How shall teachers find out what students want to know; and how will teachers learn to coordinate their own motivation with the students' interests and with the curriculum? These questions are similar to ones that ask how "mothers" (caregivers) know what children or other cared-for people may need. Parents do not "just know" what children need. They learn by interacting with them from early in the children's lives. Most parents do learn how to nurture, serve, get along with, and cultivate their children. Similarly, teachers can learn about students' motivation from tradition, from local factors, from early exercise in which information is exchanged and discussed. The issue is that teachers need to *know* to learn about students' motivation, and then they need to decide to orient themselves as teachers around the needs of the students. This is one reason I use the term *mothering* to describe potential teaching postures.

Teaching as I knew it from high school on was more like "fathering," which I thought was "telling the students what they need to know." Although this posture also has a role in parenting and teaching, it has been, in the university, the only way of teaching. It is patriarchal in the less pejorative but still dominating sense: education as a process through which young people acquire enlightenment or knowledge from older, authoritative people. In my school experience, teachers were considered replacements for parents: female teachers teach young children, male teachers older children.

This style of gender polarization in teaching is modern, as Madeleine Grumet has described. Teaching became feminized through the control of institutions by men, who at the same time maintained their own tradition of keeping custody of knowledge, truth, and power. For students such as Warriner's and Boland's to take custody of their curricula has this historical overtone: counteracting men's custody of education. Grumet[2] provides a historical background for the feminization of preuniversity teaching, while noting additionally that the subordinate status of teaching is found as far back as the classical period (29). Her historical and psychosocial discussion helps to account for the conflicting voices in the Boyer report (see Chapter 1): for example, the voice calling for the improvement of teaching through assessment as against the voice calling for teaching having status coequal with research. Grumet's discussion of teaching and gender suggests how competition became so prominent in schools. She reviews some of the nineteenth-century history of school development in America. After detailing how men held the vast majority of administrative jobs in education through the nineteenth century, she offers the following thought about Horace Mann, who was perhaps reacting against "the hard Calvinism of his boyhood." . . .

> theorists like Mann sought the reclamation of mother love by promoting women as teachers of the young. Overwhelmed by the presence of their mothers, women entered teaching in order to gain access to the power and prerogatives of their fathers. (54)

This analysis of Mann's bringing female teachers into the schools suggests two pertinent thoughts. First, while male educators' gender psychology was not hopelessly narcissistic, it was nevertheless a psychology with some connections to today's ego-bound identities. Second, at least some distinct positive value was placed by men and women on the female-identified characteristics of nurturance. This value served both men and women, historically and personally. Grumet implies that men found Calvinist severity burdensome, much as, probably unconsciously, they find military, corporate, and athletic psychology burdensome; they therefore might support making school more responsive to juvenile social psychology. Certainly today many would like to find ways to cultivate in school the home-derived values of relaxation, decency, courtesy, and affection. Most would want school to be the site of enjoyment, feeling, and the celebration of learning. At the same time, women who became teachers (wanting, as Grumet describes, to identify with their fathers) sought recognition for their ability and desire to teach in a "nurturance" mode. To hold the job was itself a partial accession to the authority of the men who hired them. Grumet thus describes this historical development as a kind of psychosocial trade with advantages for each gender as then culturally identified.

---

[2] Madeleine Grumet, *Bitter Milk: Women and Teaching* (Amherst: University of Massachusetts Press, 1988). Her Chapter 2 is entitled "Pedagogy for Patriarchy: The Feminization of Teaching."

But there continues to exist a social hierarchy. Because of this continuing structure, gender inequality was perpetuated in schools, as Grumet describes:

> So male educators invited women into the schools expecting to reclaim their mothers, and the women accepted the invitation and came so that they might identify with their fathers. Accordingly, female teachers complied with the rationalization and the bureaucratization that pervaded the common schools as the industrial culture saturated the urban areas. . . . they acquiesced to the graded schools—to working with one age group for one year at a time. . . . they agreed to large group instruction where the power of the peer collective was at least as powerful as the mother/child bond. . . . normalites accepted the curriculum as bestowed, and deviations from it remained in the privacy of the classroom and were not presented to principals or committees of visitors. (55)

As described here, it was not finally a fair exchange. Because female styles and standards were already considered secondary and inferior, they were suppressed and not themselves permitted growth, expression, and authority. Grumet says that the features of school we consider commonplace and "normal" were culturally coerced by the condition of gender inequality during the period of industrialization. She implies that, under more egalitarian conditions, we could be seeing students of different ages in a single classroom; a variable (contingent) curriculum, perhaps geared to the differing student populations; continuing, carried-over relationships between students and teachers over long periods of time; the presence and use of the peer collective (cooperative classrooms) but not its hegemony of style and demand; and finally, a free exchange of ideas and response between teachers and school administrators, or schools run by teachers.[3] These latter values need not be gender-identified. But as Grumet recounts this phase of the history of education in the United States, that has been their fate. And because of this identification, they have been suppressed, to the detriment of society.

Grumet describes the fragmenting of women's interests and the further consolidation of control over education by established masculine-identified interests:

> Instead of being allies, mothers and teachers distrust each other. Bearing credentials of a profession that claimed the colors of motherhood and then systematically delivered the children over to the

---

[3] Such as Deborah Meier's Central Park East, discussed in Deborah Meier, *The Power of Their Ideas: Lessons for America from a Small School in Harlem* (Boston: Beacon Press, 1995).

language, rules, and relations of the patriarchy, teachers understandably feel uneasy, mothers suspicious. Their estrangement leaves a gap in school governance that the professional administrators, the state, and textbook publishers rush in to fill. Until teachers and mothers acknowledge the ways in which schools perpetuate the asymmetry in class privilege and gender that is present in both the home and the workplace, they will not interrupt the patterns of their own complicity. (56)

Parents and teachers are, in part, adversarially related to one another. While Grumet is emphasizing this opposition in earlier schooling, where both mothers and female teachers are more in the picture, teaching remains "feminized," relative to research, in the university. Masculine cultural psychology being in strong evidence in the academy, teaching and learning are depersonalized and diminished in value as well as distanced from parents, who participate in university life mainly through the payment of tuition. Faculty members have a voice in determining the curriculum, but it becomes depersonalized because a faculty member's research agenda is usually distant from the subject matter of his or her courses. If there is a gap between faculty/research and students/teaching, it is related to the void in governance: neither parents nor faculty members actually govern a university. This gap is not filled but widened by administrators, by the state, by the boards of trustees (on which there are representatives of corporations), and by textbook publishers, who are often seen in university halls and professional conventions persuading faculty to order their wares. All of these interests, insofar as they are not primarily offered as enhancements of teaching and student welfare, represent detached values and styles as well as the ideology of competition and hierarchy. Teachers in the university are "feminized" in the sense described by Grumet. Had the Boyer report (see Chapter 1) conceived the problem in university teaching as being implicated in gender ideology, it might have relied less prominently on appeals to the search for excellence and on the redoubled call for assessments of teaching.

Grumet offers an interesting statement of self-implication in academic teaching, her language use choices contributing to the argument:

We, the women who teach, must claim our reproductive labor as a process of civilization as well as procreation. We can continue to escort the children from home to the marketplace as did the *paidagogos*, the Greek slave whose title and function survive in pedagogy, or we can refuse the oppositions and limits that define each place and our love and work within them. The task is daunting. . . . These words, for all their intensity, have been sifted through the

sieves of academic discourse. The very institutions that I repudiate
for their perpetuation of patriarchal privilege are the ones within
which I have found the voice that tries to sing the tune of two
worlds. This writing has been interrupted and informed by driving
the kids to the pool and to soccer practice, by the laundering of
sweaty sports socks and mildewed beach towels, by the heat of the
summer sun and the soft summons of the night air. (29)

How do we respond to this passage as a function of our gender identity? What do we think and feel as Grumet becomes lyrical by
including the quality of domestic and subjective experience that
supported the writing of her book? How do we respond to terms
such as *reproductive labor* with its deliberate, forceful affirmation
that this form of "labor" may be used to describe teaching? What
might we think of changing our concept of teaching from the transmission of knowledge to others to "helping to reproduce and nurture new cultural generations"? How willing are we to accept the
connotation of teacher as slave and to let our anger mobilize our
commitment to changing the social relations of schools and classrooms? How capable are we, finally, of overtaking the ideological
constraints of academic discourse—advocated by the devotees of
"relentless drill"—that we seem forced to use and making it speak
in new registers, new voices? Grumet has combined familiar registers but has changed the academic genre into a new one where
becoming lyrical contributes to the point, gives it feeling and commitment it may not otherwise communicate.

We are thinking about the "we" who are responding with questions to Grumet's call to "women who teach." We ought to be honoring the subjective and intersubjective experience of the teaching of
language and literature, and of other subjects as well. We ought not
to have to conceal this experience or use it subversively. Susan
Miller,[4] in rejecting the need for "male-coded fortitude" (186) in
political causes, urges that our collective recognizing, using, and
exploring classroom experience, indigenous to the class of students,
teachers, and scholars, is the political step that can give postsecondary education a better role to play. This step cannot be taken without
new attention to graduate pedagogy.

---

[4] Susan Miller, *Textual Carnivals: the Politics of Composition* (Carbondale: Southern
Illinois University Press, 1992).

Mothering and Motivating Graduate Students

It is very interesting how long this profession has functioned without attention to graduate pedagogy, to the details and principles of our own training, to how we reproduce ourselves, our lives, our jobs, our values. Thinking about teaching as "reproductive labor" changes our customary inattention to how we are preparing future postsecondary teachers. Regardless of how distant teaching is from biological procreation, it is nevertheless involved in society's processes of reproduction. Grumet's project arises, on the one hand, as a response to the historic androcentric separation of reproductive labor from the rest of the work done in society, and on the other, as an approach to reducing the frustrations of teaching in large, industrialized societies. Here is a citation suggesting how Grumet pursues this enlargement:

> To be a gendered human being is to participate in the reproductive commitments of this society, for reproduction is present as a theme in human consciousness without providing a norm for human behavior. Male or female, heterosexual, homosexual, bisexual, monogamous, chaste, or multipartnered, we each experience our sexuality as attachments within a set of conditions that contain the possibility of procreation. (6)

Modern social organizations have isolated women's experiences of reproduction, cordoned off its associated feelings and possibilities from other social fundamentals. Grumet attempts not to attach reproduction to teaching—it has always been there in some ways—but to recognize its authority and potential. She tries to make its heretofore predominantly female locus a general locus, one, in a social sense, decisively alternative to androcentric, patriarchal styles of teaching that have gradually eroded the ability of universities to serve all the population, not just a privileged few.

The graduate students in my seminar hoping to become academic teachers of English, writing, and language use are eager for the responsibility of teaching, of having their own classrooms, of using their professional subject matters to explore with the first-year undergraduates the different kinds, styles, and registers of language. They want their students to become competent and confident about how and what they write. However, the graduate students face these issues burdened with the need to accommodate to the traditional academy. This need is so great that Grumet's last-quoted paragraph appears in their commentaries on her book as an act of falsification of the rest of her book instead of as a direct formulation of her ideal. The graduate students do notice what

Grumet says she is aiming for in her treatise, but then cite other parts of the treatise as evidence of her "real" purpose: essentializing reproduction. One student, Ms. X, wrote,

> In effect, Grumet's teaching paradigm reflects the paternalistic and overprotective attitudes that we have today regarding children (and college students for that matter). The nurturing of students not only presupposes dependency and, to a great extent, innate stupidity on the part of the student, but it also presupposes the substitution of a male hegemonic paradigm for a female one. I find Grumet's feminism more harming than helpful. By describing women as nurturers, she is placing us again in the locus of oppressive masculinist discourse, at the same time that she is essentializing both manhood and womanhood.

Ms. X is further disturbed by Grumet's claim that women work in public institutions in ways that "contradicted our own experiences of nurturance" (45). Ms. X sees this statement as a false perception on Grumet's part that women's child-rearing work has been "counter-hegemonic." Ms. X does not see Grumet's statement as a stand against being forced to live in a state of self-denial.

Here is another comment, by Ms. Y. Just after citing Grumet's "To be a gendered human being" passage, Ms. Y writes,

> A previous reader has scribbled in the margin beside this passage, "Strictly speaking, not me." Yes [Ms. Y continues], who exactly falls into her paradigms of compulsory maternity? Who can nod yes and place a hurried checkmark in identification with the processes of "conception, pregnancy, parturition, and lactation"(10)? Actively hetero-/homosexual men? Celibate people of both sexes? Infertile, childess-by-choice or childless-by-economic-necessity women? Grumet's interpolation of her audience throughout the book as "we women" does not merely mobilize a rhetoric of exclusion, it reifies the biological fallacy that all women must-be or want-to-be or always-already-are maternal vessels.

I think these two readings of Grumet by X and Y are mistaken: they did not register Grumet's caveat that reproduction is a theme but not a behavioral norm in consciousness and society. They read Grumet as if *her* perspectives on reproduction were unexamined; they projected their newly learned cautions about essentialism on a scholar who wants them to rethink what they have been cautious about, because, one might want to say, the baby—a pedagogy of caring involved interaction—should not be thrown out with the obsolete academic bath water.

I think that X and Y fear caring about their prospective students as living growing people, as "children" or "offspring" or "young ones" whose school lives, like the lives of their teachers, require a self-conscious blend of knowledge, response, and "fussing" that could be described as nurturing. On the one hand they fear, reasonably, being reduced to mere vessels and caregivers. On the other they want to reject the low status of nurturing by rejecting the connection between nurturing and mothering. They want to be *sure* to teach as intellectuals, scholars, researchers, those who have authorized insight into how things are. This is, after all, the prevailing sense of teaching in the academy in which most of us have been educated. In the anticipation of serious teaching, I am guessing, these two intense, intellectually conscientious students felt they had to get tough when a scholarly work on teaching urged on them an ideal that inserts women's experiences of reproduction into the possible pictures of academic responsibility.

Distressed at this style of response from graduate students for several years, I asked Professor Ellen Weinauer, a faculty member at another university and at the time about to give birth to her first child, to offer some thoughts that would help me understand how and why students want to teach without allowing nurturing in its parental connotation. She wrote,[5]

> Regarding your students' seeming unawareness of the meaning of corporeal life and the potency and impact of reproduction—it seems to me that suddenly all sorts of things that look OK to me in theory have become increasingly NOT OK as this bodily process takes me over more and more. That is, Butler's notion of the constructedness of sex and even of the body somehow starts to look, well—unlikely in ways it did not before . . . for me . . . the very notion of being free of the body is so powerful that it has taken pregnancy for me to rethink some of my positions. All of a sudden—I see this in my teaching—Lacan and Freud too make more and more sense.

Although Weinauer is referring to her response to the gestation of her child, it is also the case that she has two years of full-time teaching behind her, that she is at a point in life different from those who are near the beginning of their certification process. Viewing her opinion from a "reproductive" perspective may make it easier to take her individual history into account, easier to notice that it is pregnancy as coming after experience in teaching that produced her opinion,

---

[5] On November 1, 1995.

rather than the "essential" experience of pregnancy. As teachers the graduate students, eschewing the discourse of reproduction and not yet having taught, cannot take into account the sense in which their attempt to reproduce themselves and their values in the lives of their students is related to other kinds of reproduction. They are, so to speak, only up to the "sex" of teaching (loving and fearing its powers and risks), and not to the reproductive potentialities of that sex. After a time teaching, even if there is no physical "child," there is still reproduction of one's own being in the lives of others found in the language they may get from us; there is still "issue" as well as issues from and in teaching, still something coming out of it with pain and difficulty, some small thoughts and actions that grow near us and change our lives. And for me, as I teach the graduate students, "my children," there are varying degrees in which these offspring take, like, live by, reject, repudiate, or hate what they got in the "home" that our class had become. After I brought in bagels twice a week for twelve weeks, you should have seen their uncomprehending frustration when I failed to bring them once because my car was down!

Part of the machinery that obscures the prominence of reproduction in teaching for us is that we are first-language teachers. The subject of language use alludes to earliest interpersonal relationships: those in which we acquired language once upon a time. In order for this subject to have status coequal with other subjects such as the sciences, a certain amount of neglecting-the-obvious is done. In the search for academic status the study of language led to thinking of it as "langue"—the abstract collection of locutions everyone uses—an identity for language that considers it an independent object. The study of language, either by transformationalists or by philologists, excludes the consideration that language grows into us from others who are close through our different phases of development. Introducing reproduction as a factor in the study of our first language (mother tongue) reintroduces what Walter Ong described as having been successfully excluded by literacy: the affective and interpersonal ungainliness of language as represented in "orality." If reproduction is admitted as part of the study of the mother tongue, the boundaries of the subject drop away, and there is no telling what other subjects it may begin to include, more orthodox scholars fear.

Kelly Oliver's reading of Julia Kristeva[6] suggests a basis of this traditional misunderstanding about just how far-reaching the subject of language is:

---

[6] Kelly Oliver, *Reading Kristeva: Unravelling the Double-Bind,* (Bloomington, Indiana University Press, 1993).

The mother negates the Symbolic [or what Derrida might call the written] order even while insuring its generation. She realizes that the other is the same, that the gap is not absolute in the face of the symbolic and its transcendental signifier, she says, "just the same, I know." The mother's "just the same" constitutes the social bond through love, not force. This "just the same" threatens to do away with difference and "it can crush everything the other (the child) has that is specifically irreducible" (1983). In other words, it threatens to do away with the Symbolic order. . . . This is why even if the symbolic order denies the existence of the mother she cannot for the sake of her child, deny the existence of the Symbolic. She must wean the child. She must instigate the breakup of their primary symbiosis. . . .

It is the mother's love and her love for her own mother, a narcissistic love from generation to generation, that supports the move into the Symbolic order. It is this love that fills language with meaning. (68)

The love about which Kristeva and Oliver write in a seemingly abstract way was censored by the students' reading of Grumet. The foregoing reflection, especially the thought that the mother's love "fills language with meaning" is particularly awkward to consider as one begins to try to teach the first language in a university system that doesn't mind if women fail. And yet, this account suggests what Grumet suggested, namely, that the mothering figure provides a basis in the "giving" of the first language, the mother tongue, that makes it possible to depatriarchalize the "Symbolic Order"—the authoritative androcentric tongue of academic detachment. In her "oral" style and in her physical attachment to the other body, the "mother negates the Symbolic order even while insuring its generation."

This is a new ground for thinking about language as well as about teaching: there remain categories and themes, but not behavioral norms. Language remains a "symbolic order," but not a detached one ruled by the father or by the supremacy of literacy. Teachers and parents need, eventually, to separate from those we nurture. As many have already described, the process of separation, starting from birth, soon occurs in a purely symbolic way in language. There, each phase of separation is a new language phase, a new genre, perhaps, and a symbolic road back to the old phase. New language ability, new vocabulary, new articulations are fresh connections to the past shown by teachers and parents. Kristeva, Oliver, Weinauer, and Grumet teach that language, teaching, and school are dedicated to the restoration of attachments that have been derogated by strong boundaries, rigid disciplines, hierarchies, and the near military austerity and religious solemnity of academic tradition.

One student in X and Y's seminar answered their remarks. Ms. Z wrote,

> Endless theorizings on social constructions, structures and strictures have yet to produce a coherent and/or relevant tale of biological reproduction and its intimate and continually disavowed relationship to symbolic (re)productions(s). . . .
>
> Grumet seems to be trying to provide us with the narrative so absent from the bulk of academic publications. In so doing, she may be the good (bad?) daughter, the one telling fibs, the one offering us redemption. Like Kristeva, she recounts maternity, labor, birth. Like Kristeva, she chooses to remember, to realize the uncanniness of the dialectic between a woman's pregnancy and her own birth. And like Kristeva, she will be accused of "exclusionism." Sure I don't have kids. Maybe you don't either. Maybe we never will. But to use that as an excuse to refute these women's experiences seems mistaken at best.

As Ms. Z and the rest of us may know, we do not learn how and in what ways we will care about our "kids" until we arrive to meet them. Parents and experienced teachers know that only actual relationships with the students/children determine their meanings and social dimensions. However, if we make up our minds to use some of our academic, professional time to talk about how we are reproducing ourselves, reproduction will begin to seem less like biology on the one hand, less like self-replication on the other, and more like the full process of advancing and sustaining different ways of life. The idea of reproduction can become welcome as a way of thinking about teaching with a heartbeat and a backbone. It can become a way to be parents to the new faculty members in the "wombs" of the *alma mater.*

Money

It has been said that the rich get richer and the poor have children. Those who are better off often find it easier to control reproduction so that both parents and children can prosper. Schools attended by the children of the wealthy have classrooms with a maximum of fifteen students. As most of us have experienced, a small number of students in a class, with an optimum number between eight and eighteen, can reduce the arbitrary effects of the grading system: it is easier for evaluations to include narratives—oral or written—with the grades. It also shows how unnecessary for teaching grades are, since the salient information and opinion are given in the narrative. Small classes permit teachers better relationships with students, which in turn makes it easier to identify salient features of students' work and orientation in school. However, for public schools and many private ones to have such classroom conditions, twice as many teachers in schools as there are now are needed. If all schools were as seriously expected to support society as elite secondary and postsecondary schools, the "luxury" of fewer students would be common, and would not be a luxury at all, but an ordinary feature of school. At the national level, because schooling is narrowly viewed as an instrument for upward social and economic mobility instead of for vocational enfranchisement, few appreciate the harm done by overpopulated classrooms. Some may want to keep schools crowded in the interests of keeping things as they are. This failure of perception (or worse) comes in the refusal to pay higher school taxes; yet it would be surprising if most communities would not continue to prosper if school taxes were doubled. Without such fundamental change in the approach to schools, it will remain difficult to advocate noncompetitive, nonhierarchical styles of teaching and learning.

At research universities, the grading system for undergraduates protects the research time for the faculty. Because teachers get tenure mostly for research, the faculty must use the least time-consuming technique of certifying undergraduates, which is the grading system. Most faculty members would not be ready to commit themselves to tenure-through-teaching unless the system itself were different. At universities where one does win tenure through teaching, faculty members are usually responsible for one hundred or more students per semester, and the semi-annual student plebiscite becomes an important means of evaluating teaching, though research universities would do well to learn from teaching universities just how much is already done to cultivate committed teaching.

In the classes of graduate students whose work I cited, most students want to teach and consider teaching their main occupation. Only a minority of students say, at this stage at least, that scholarship in libraries is their main vocational plan. Most students, regardless of their take on "reproduction," take pleasure in teaching and want to learn its subtleties and fulfillments. But they also know that they probably will not get tenure on teaching, that even if they teach at small liberal arts colleges or comprehensive universities where teaching is a stated priority, publication is still the fastest and most reliable way to get tenure. As a rule, small colleges and large comprehensives have programs that are like research universities; courses last one semester, and sequences of courses are not handled cooperatively by teams of faculty members. Finally, the teaching of writing, which goes on at all institutions in one form or another, is of low enough status to not get the attention of "real" teachers—those relatively popular, often prize-winning older faculty members who are interesting lecturers on currently in-play topics. The money issue for future faculty members is job security and salary. Neither writing nor the teaching of writing will bring high salaries or job security.

In the light of the foregoing considerations, this book is about minority ideas. Materiality is a minority view of language; orientation toward students' motivation is a minority view of pedagogy; mothering still seems fearful even to those who want to teach; and money is not likely to come to those who learn and teach writing and language use. These are not ideals to me, but practical stances to uphold and enact in the face of an academic tradition that does not value them highly.

Index[1]

[1] Many thanks to Jeanne Marie Rose for compiling this index.